A-LEVEL
AND AS-LEVEL

LONGMAN
REVISE
GUIDES

SOCIOLOGY

Stephen R. Harris

Longman

LONGMAN A AND AS–LEVEL REVISE GUIDES

Series editors
Geoff Black and Stuart Wall

Titles available
Art and Design
Biology
Chemistry
Computer Studies
Economics
English
French
Geography
Mathematics
Physics
Sociology

Forthcoming
History

NAMES AND ADDRESSES OF THE EXAM BOARDS

Associated Examining Board (AEB)
Stag Hill House
Guildford
Surrey GU2 5XJ

University of Cambridge Local Examinations Syndicate (UCLES)
Syndicate Buildings
1 Hills Road
Cambridge CB1 1YB

Joint Matriculation Board (JMB)
Devas St
Manchester M15 6EU

University of London Schools Examination Board (ULSEB)
Stewart House
32 Russell Square
London WC1B 5DN

Northern Ireland Schools Examination Council (NISEC)
Beechill House
42 Beechill Road
Belfast BT8 4RS

Oxford and Cambridge Schools Examination Board (OCSEB)
10 Trumpington Street
Cambridge CB2 1QB

Oxford Delegacy of Local Examinations (ODLE)
Ewert Place
Summertown
Oxford OX2 7BX

Scottish Examination Board (SEB)
Ironmills Road
Dalkeith
Midlothian EH22 1BR

Welsh Joint Education Committee (WJEC)
245 Western Avenue
Cardiff CF5 2YX

Longman Group UK Limited,
Longman House, Burnt Mill, Harlow,
Essex CM20 2JE, England
and Associated Companies throughout the world.

© Longman Group UK Limited 1991

First published 1990
Third impression 1991

British Library Cataloguing in Publication Data

Harris, Stephen
  Sociology.
  1. Sociology
  I. Title
  301

  ISBN 0–582–05786–8

Designed by
The Pen and Ink Book Company
Huntingdon, Cambridgeshire
Set in 10/12pt Century Old Style.

Produced by Longman Singapore Publishers Pte Ltd
Printed in Singapore

CONTENTS

	Names and addresses of the examination boards	ii
	Acknowledgements	iii
	Editors' preface	iii
1	The syllabuses and examinations	1
2	Study, examination and assessment techniques	5
3	Stratification	12
4	Race and ethnicity	23
5	Gender	33
6	Power and politics	43
7	Development, urbanisation and community	53
8	The family	62
9	Education	70
10	Work	80
11	Organisations	90
12	Professions	98
13	Religion	106
14	The mass media	115
15	Health	124
16	Deviance	134
17	Suicide and official statistics	142
18	Methods	150
19	Sociological theories	163
20	The nature of sociology	175
	Additional reading	184
	Index	187

EDITORS' PREFACE

Longman A Level Revise Guides, written by experienced examiners and teachers, aim to give you the best possible foundation for success in your course. Each book in the series encourages thorough study and a full understanding of the concepts involved, and is designed as a subject companion and study aid to be used throughout the course.

Many candidates at A Level fail to achieve the grades which their ability deserves, owing to such problems as the lack of a structured revision strategy, or unsound examination technique. This series aims to remedy such deficiencies, by encouraging a realistic and disciplined approach in preparing for and taking exams.

The largely self-contained nature of the chapters gives the book a flexibility which you can use to your advantage. After starting with the background to the A, AS Level and Scottish Higher Courses and details of the syllabus coverage, you can read all other chapters selectively, in any order appropriate to the stage you have reached in your course.

Geoff Black and Stuart Wall

ACKNOWLEDGEMENTS

I am indebted to the following examination boards for permission to reproduce their questions. The answers given are not the only possible answers and are entirely my own responsibility.

Associated Examining Board
University of London School Examinations Board
Welsh Joint Education Committee
University of Cambridge Local Examinations Syndicate
University of Oxford Delegacy of Local Examinations
Joint Matriculation Board Examinations Council
Scottish Examination Board

My thanks go to Geoff Black and Stuart Wall for their encouragement, Alan Ducklin and Hal Westergaard for their critical comments, Patrick Toal for teaching me word processing in ten minutes and the students and ex-students from Redbridge Technical College who allowed me to use their answers.

I also wish to thank Melanie, Sarah, Lily and Prudence for tolerating my neglecting of them during the writing of this book.

THE SYLLABUSES AND EXAMINATIONS

STUDYING SOCIOLOGY

TOPICS AND SYLLABUSES

METHODS OF ASSESSMENT

GETTING STARTED

Who is this book for?

This Revise Guide is intended to be a useful tool for students taking an examination course in Sociology at A-level or AS-level. It also covers aspects of the Scottish Certificate of Education higher grade in Modern Studies. The book offers a systematic review of the major sociological issues covered by the various syllabuses, gives guidance on how to study sociology for examinations and provides a large number of real examination questions. These questions have outline answers or full model answers provided by the author or an answer written by an A-level student accompanied by an examiner's comments and mark.

How should this book be used?

It is intended that the book should be useful throughout your course.

- **In the beginning**
  The Table of Contents indicates the major areas of sociology which are studied. Each chapter identifies the major issues to be considered for a particular topic. This should guide you in your reading from other sources.

- **In the middle**
  Studying sociology is not just a question of memorising lots of facts and theories. It also involves learning how to apply your knowledge to sociological problems and how to evaluate sociological evidence. You should attempt to respond to the questions in outline form or to give a complete answer. Your answers can then be compared with the examiners suggestions. If you are not satisfied, you can then refer to the appropriate material in this book, in a text book or in your own notes.

- **At the end**
  This book has been written very much with examination success in mind. There are suggestions on study skills, including revision. The summaries of sociological approaches and studies in each chapter can help you compile revision notes, and there are over 90 questions to choose from for practise and to assess your progress. You can see what the examiners are looking for in answer to questions, either by reading the outline answers or the full model answers. You can also see how other actual students have attempted past questions, and what an examiner thinks are the strengths and weaknesses of those answers.

ESSENTIAL PRINCIPLES

STUDYING SOCIOLOGY

Sociology has become increasingly popular as an A-level subject, even during a period marked by a fall in the numbers of 16 to 18 year–olds in the population. Many candidates are adults returning to study who find it both interesting and useful as a preparation for higher education or for various kinds of professional training and qualifications. This good news for teachers and Examination boards is matched by the good news for students, namely that the quality of examination answers is improving and so too are the grades awarded to candidates.

General changes in the curriculum have been reflected in the development of sociology. Two boards now offer an Advanced Supplementary (AS) level syllabus and coursework is available as an option for the AEB A-level and is a central part of the ULSEB AS-level syllabus. The success of coursework in GCSE suggests that more boards will offer coursework as part of the examination in the future.

The division of sociology into distinct topics is a fairly arbitrary exercise, so I have been guided by the various syllabuses in producing separate chapters. The chapters are not intended to erect barriers between the topics, as some issues are discussed in more than one chapter. There are themes which run through all the topics, such as theoretical and methodological issues and the various forms of inequality (including class and gender).

TOPICS AND SYLLABUSES

This book covers some or all of the knowledge and skills necessary to study the following syllabuses:

- **A-LEVEL**
  AEB New Syllabus
  AEB New Syllabus with coursework
  Oxford
  London
  Cambridge
  JMB
  WJEC

- **AS-LEVEL**
  AEB
  London

- **SCOTTISH CERTIFICATE OF EDUCATION HIGHER GRADE**
  Modern Studies

Fig. 1.1 Analysis of examination syllabuses by topic and chapter

Topic	Chapter number	AEB A	AEB AS	London A	London* AS	WJEC** A	Cambridge A	Oxford A	JMB† A	Scottish†† Higher
Stratification	3	✓	✓	✓	✓	✓	✓	✓	✓	✓
Race and ethnicity	4	✓	✓	✓	✓	✓	✓	✓	✓	✓
Gender	5	✓	✓	✓	✓	✓	✓	✓	✓	✓
Politics and power	6	✓		✓		✓	✓	✓	✓	✓
Development, urbanisation and community	7	✓	✓	✓		✓	✓	✓	✓	✓
Family	8	✓		✓		✓	✓	✓	✓	✓
Education	9	✓		✓		✓	✓	✓	✓	
Work	10	✓		✓		✓	✓	✓	✓	✓
Organisations	11	✓		✓		✓	✓	✓	✓	
Professions	12	✓		✓		✓		✓	✓	
Religion	13	✓		✓		✓	✓	✓	✓	
Mass Media	14	✓	✓		✓			✓	✓	✓
Health	15	✓	✓	✓	✓	✓	✓	✓	✓	✓
Deviance	16	✓	✓	✓		✓	✓	✓	✓	✓
Suicide and official statistics	17	✓		✓	✓	✓	✓	✓	✓	
Methods	18	✓	✓	✓	✓	✓	✓	✓	✓	
Sociological theories	19	✓	✓	✓	✓	✓	✓	✓	✓	
The nature of sociology	20	✓	✓	✓	✓	✓	✓	✓	✓	

* Can choose any substantive area for coursework
** Welsh options not included
† Emphasis on theoretical issues. Topics used to illustrate arguments
†† International issues not covered.

The table in Fig. 1.1 shows which syllabuses offer which topics and tells you the chapter number where that topic is covered in this book. In addition to variations in *content*, there are differences in the *approach* to sociology preferred by the different boards. The JMB A-level and the ULSEB AS-level are orientated towards *theoretical and methodological issues* whereas the ULSEB A-level requires a *comparative approach*.

METHODS OF ASSESSMENT

The methods of assessment also vary. Boards have different aims and objectives for the syllabuses and use different types of question. Fig. 1.2 analyses the examination syllabuses according to their methods of assessment.

Method of assessment	EXAMINATION SYLLABUS									
	AEB A level	AEB A level with course work	AEB AS	ULSEB A	ULSEB AS	WJEC A	Cambridge A	Oxford A	JMB A	Scottish Higher
Essay	√	√	√	√	√	√	√	√	√	√
Structured and/or data response question	√	√	√	√	√	√	—	—	√	√
Number of examination papers	2	3	2	3	1	2	2	2	2	2
Total length of papers in hours	6	4½	3	9	2¼	6	6	6	6	5
Coursework assessed (% marks available)		√(25%)			√50%					

Fig. 1.2 Analysis of examination syllabuses by methods of assessment

TYPES OF QUESTION

Essays

These are required for all the examinations, although their domination of examinations is now challenged by other methods of assessment.

Structured questions

Here a whole question is broken down into a series of components which test different abilities, e.g. knowledge, application and evaluation. Usually the mark for each component is provided and this indicates the suitable length of an answer.

Stimulus questions and data-response questions

Here candidates are presented with a stimulus in the form of a written passage, graph, table or even a map or cartoon. There then follows a series of questions. In *stimulus* questions the data presented is intended to suggest possible responses. Whereas in a *data response* question, detailed reference to the material is required, e.g. interpretation of statistics.

Coursework

This is currently available for only two of the syllabuses. In both cases a single piece of independent research is required. It is initially marked by your teacher and then moderated by the Board.

MARKING SCHEMES AND OBJECTIVES

The examination boards are becoming increasingly open about the methods of assessment used by their examiners. Some have made sample marking schemes available, particularly where new syllabuses are being introduced. For more information, write to the board or ask your teacher.

The abilities which are rewarded and their relative importance is useful information. In general the list is likely to include:

- **Knowledge** of studies and theories.
- **Understanding** of data.
- **Interpretation** of data.
- **Application** of concepts and theories to actual problems.
- **Analysis** of sociological issues and personal experience.
- **Evaluation** of theories, methods and arguments.

For example, the AEB has published a specimen marking scheme for essays which awards up to 9 marks each for:

1 Knowledge and understanding.
2 Interpretation and application.
3 Evaluation.

With a maximum of 25 marks to be awarded.

Incidentally, to gain maximum marks you need *not* achieve perfection or be as competent as the Chief Examiner. The AEB standard is based on the best that could be achieved by an 18-year-old student who has studied the subject for two years. Therefore, full marks *are* attainable for part or whole questions.

2

STUDY, EXAMINATION AND ASSESSMENT TECHNIQUES

AN INTRODUCTION TO SOCIOLOGY

DEVELOPING SKILLS

REVISING

THE EXAMINATION

COURSEWORK

GETTING STARTED

Doing well in a sociology course involves a great deal more than learning an enormous number of facts and theories. The key abilities which distinguish good students from weaker students are application and evaluation. Your *knowledge* of concepts, theories and studies must be *applied* to meet the demands of questions, whether in class discussion, homework or examination. *Evaluation* of the evidence, methods and theories, is the skill most highly regarded by examiners. Therefore during your course, as well as attempting to acquire a comprehensive knowledge of sociological issues, you must practise these skills of application and evaluation in order to obtain a good pass.

This chapter will provide what is often commonsense advice about the whole study process, from the beginning of the course to the last ten minutes of your final examination. My excuse for repeating some things you may already know is that teachers and examiners continually encounter students who make the same sorts of errors in organising their work and sitting the exam, and thus do not realise their full potential.

AN INTRODUCTION TO SOCIOLOGY

ESSENTIAL PRINCIPLES

Place six sociologists in a room and they will probably give you twelve explanations of what is going on. Disagreement between sociologists is the basis of most questions and can provide a framework for answers.

The reasons for disagreement do not just depend on the whims of the individual sociologist but can be seen as more systematic. Differences in perspectives, approaches, methods and theories can be identified.

- PERSPECTIVES are the different ways sociologists perceive the social world.
- APPROACHES are the different ways sociologists choose to define problems in sociology, decide what to study, and how.
- METHODS are the different ways of gathering and interpreting information.
- THEORIES are explanations; eg why it is that certain patterns of behaviour are observed.

Perspectives

The conventional division of perspectives distinguishes a number of 'types'.

- **ACTION perspectives**
  These see the construction of the social world as being the result of a process whereby individuals attribute meaning to behaviour and situations. Society is therefore seen as being made by individuals. Theories associated with these perspectives include Social Action theory, symbolic interactionism and ethnomethodology.

- **STRUCTURALIST perspectives**
  These see the social world as existing independently of individuals whose behaviour is constrained by external social forces. Society is seen as making the individual. Structuralist perspectives are sub-divided into:

  - CONSENSUS perspectives, which see societies as harmonious with order based on shared values. The dominant theory here is structural-functionalism.
  - CONFLICT perspectives, which see conflict as normal, and order being imposed by the strong on the weak. Theories associated with conflict perspectives include Marxism, Weberian theories and feminism.

Approaches

These are different ways of defining sociological problems and of deciding what should be studied, and how. The major distinction is between positivist and interpretive approaches.

- **POSITIVIST approaches** involve the search for *cause and effect* laws, using methods similar to those employed in the natural sciences.
- **INTERPRETIVE approaches** involve the search for the *subjective meanings* which people give to behaviour. These are also referred to as **phenomenological** approaches.

There are real, but not inevitable, links between perspectives, theories, approaches and methods. Structuralists tend to adopt a positivist approach and those who have an action perspective tend to adopt an interpretive approach. However, although this makes answering questions more straightforward, it is an oversimplification as sociologists do not necessarily see themselves as belonging to distinctive schools which limit their interests or research. These rather difficult issues are discussed in the later chapters dealing with SUICIDE, THEORIES, METHODS, and THE NATURE OF SOCIOLOGY.

DEVELOPING SKILLS

Learning to *organise* your thoughts so that you provide informed, coherent and critical sociological arguments, requires practice. In class you should take every opportunity to ask questions and to take part in discussions. Try to *use* sociological concepts and terminology wherever relevant, and to answer the *specific* question put to you rather than to display all your knowledge on the subject in a rambling account.

Reading can be guided by the topic or issue you are covering in class, and also by previous examination questions. These can help you identify what the examiners see as important *aspects* of the various topic areas. You can then undertake further reading on these aspects to give a well rounded view. Examination essays usually contain less than 1 000 words so it is not necessary to be able to write in detail about a single study, however important or interesting. Many answers on the class structure of modern Britain suffer from epic accounts of the 'Luton Studies' at the expense of competing and often more recent and relevant material.

A useful aid in organising your thoughts might be a *summary chart* on a particular topic or issue. On one or two sides of A4 paper you might write briefly on the following:

- Key terms and definitions.
- Major theoretical arguments and viewpoints.
- Major empirical studies and findings.

You might then look at past questions set on that topic and use your summary material as a basis for writing *outline answers* to those questions. This will help you see how important it is to emphasise different aspects of your knowledge when faced with different questions.

It is also useful to practise writing *full answers* under examination conditions, i.e. without notes and giving yourself the same time as in the exam itself. You can always review your work later, this time with your notes and book open.

Text books

There are some excellent *text books* available for A-level Sociology. Your teacher will usually indicate which texts to use, since some are better suited to particular syllabuses than others. However do try to use various texts on a particular topic in order to get a broader view, rather than to slavishly follow a single book. The following text books are widely used:

- *Human Societies*, G. Hurd et al, (RKP).
- *Introductory Sociology* (2nd edition) Bilton *et al*, (Macmillan).
- *Sociology: Themes and Perspectives* (2nd edition), M. Haralambos with R. M. Heald, (Unwin Hyman).
- *Sociology*, A.Giddens, (Polity Press).
- *A New Introduction to Sociology* (2nd edition), M. O'Donnell, (Nelson).

Topic books

As well as text books which try to cover the whole syllabus there are several series of *topic books* which cover particular areas of the syllabus. These are particularly useful where there are gaps in text books or where the topic book is considerably more modern than the text book. However, the most popular text books have all been revised and updated since their original publication. An example of a series of topic books is:

- *Sociology in Focus*, (Longman). Separate titles cover Crime, Education, Methodology, Religion, Gender, Media, Work and Unemployment, Suicide, Knowledge.

Reading lists

Examination boards provide *reading lists* which may give you guidance on useful sources. The addresses of the Boards are listed at the front of this book. Do however remember that the reading lists are suggestions for teachers as well as students, so that you should consult your teacher about the value and degree of difficulty of any particular book. There may well be some original works included in the list which you would not be expected to read in their entirety.

Readers

There are also *readers*, which contain *extracts* from significant original works. These may provide a useful source of relevant quotations. Often they contain an introduction from the editor, reviewing a series of contributions, which provides a helpful overview of a broad range of material.

Examples of readers include:

- *New Introductory Reader in Sociology* (2nd edition), M. O'Donnell, (Nelson).
- *An Introduction to Sociology: A Reader*, Edited by R. Bocock, P. Hamilton, K. Thompson, A. Watson, (Polity Press).
- *Perspectives on Society*, R. Meighan, I. Shelton and T. Marks eds., (Nelson).

A number of *journals* provide a convenient way of reading around a topic and of getting advice for tackling sociological problems.

- *Social Studies Review*. This is aimed at A-level students of sociology and politics. It is very readable and contains both new material and simplified accounts of older debates.
- *The Social Science Teacher*. Although primarily directed at the teacher, this also contains good reviews of the research on particular topics and shows how it can be taught to, and thus learned by, students.
- *Society Today*. This is a supplement for sociology students found in *New Statesman and Society* (previously *New Society*).
- *Social Trends*. This is published annually by the Central Statistical Office and is available in most town reference libraries. It gives a detailed breakdown of patterns of household wealth, income and expenditure, together with demographic, housing and social trends.

Serious newspapers often publish useful tables or provide accounts of government survey data, thereby updating text book material on sizes of households, illegitimacy, crime, employment, incomes, etc. Do cut-out any such data and file it under a suitable topic heading for later use.

REVISING

In order to revise effectively and efficiently you must be familiar with your syllabus and with past papers. Choosing how much of the syllabus to revise, and in what depth, is a crucial activity. The syllabus may help by indicating that there is a *minimum number of topics* which can be studied and yet still provide you with sufficient questions for examination purposes.

For instance the AEB syllabus states that candidates must study:

1 Theory and methods for both papers.
2 At least *two* from the *paper one* topics; i.e. family, education, stratification and work, and leisure.
3 At least *three* from the *paper two* topics; i.e. deviance, development, mass media, community, organisations, power and politics, religion and health, welfare and poverty.

Restricting your revision to just the minimum is, of course, a dangerous strategy. At best you will have no choice and so will be unable to avoid a difficult or unusual question. At worst you may find that an unpredictable interpretation of the syllabus by the examiners means that you cannot complete the necessary number of questions. One strategy might be to learn the minimum *plus one* topic for each paper fairly thoroughly, and to learn one more topic for each paper in a more superficial manner, for insurance. There are, however, no hard and fast rules. The more able the student, the fewer the number of topics which need be prepared, since revised material can usually be adapted to meet the needs of a range of possible questions. One way to test if you *have* covered sufficient topics is to see if you could answer the appropriate number of questions on the recent exam papers without difficulty. Remember that questions often benefit from the insights you have gained from *more than one* topic area of the syllabus; gender and class for example are issues which provide a basis for discussing aspects of many topic areas.

Having chosen your topics for revision, it may be worth returning to our idea of **summary charts**. You could distil the essence from the major approaches and studies you have encountered, and record the key points on a side of A4 paper say, or on cards. Having the key points listed in this way will be a useful 'memory jogger' to the more detailed expositions in your notes.

You might try organising your notes within a 'perspective framework'. This involves identifying the theories and/or approaches which have been applied to a topic, citing examples of research, and indicating various critiques and criticisms as appropriate.

For example, explaining inequalities in health might follow this plan:

1 Positivist studies.	5 Marxist studies.
2 Criticism.	6 Criticism, including other conflict theories.
3 Interactionist studies.	7 Functionalist studies.
4 Criticism.	8 Criticism.

This kind of structure works well with questions that ask 'How have sociological approaches to the study of . . . changed?' or 'Critically examine sociological explanations of . . .'

It is less appropriate for questions which ask you to 'Compare and contrast . . .' or 'Examine the similarities and differences between . . .' These questions benefit from a *point-by-point* comparison.

This would be true of the following question: 'Compare and contrast the approaches of Marx and Weber to the role of religion in society.' A first sentence might begin: 'Marxists see religious belief as shaped by the economic substructure, whereas Weber saw religious belief influencing the economic organisation of society.' Explain this and then go on and discuss their different views on religion and social change.

> **Revision should be an active process.**

Above all, your revision should be an **active** process. Use the concepts and evidence you have learned to answer questions. Do not just memorise chunks of material without considering how to apply it.

THE EXAMINATION

1 Read the rubric, i.e. the set of instructions at the start of the exam paper. This should be familiar to you, but do make sure you answer the right number of questions and from the appropriate sections.

2 Choose your questions carefully. Read through all the questions before making your selection. Students often fail to 'recognise' questions they could actually answer because they have scanned too quickly through the exam paper.

3 The order in which you attempt the questions is unimportant, as long as your answers are clearly numbered. Some students prefer to start with a straightforward question and not necessarily with the one they could do best in order to complete the first question on schedule. Whatever tactic you adopt, a good start to the exam will give you confidence for the rest of the paper.

4 Calculate the right amount of time to spend on each question and part of a question, and stick closely to your schedule. This depends on the mark allocation. On most papers essay questions carry equal marks. It is bad practice to spend disproportionate amounts of time on different questions, just because you know more about some topics. Once you have written a competent response it gets increasingly difficult to accumulate more marks, whereas the first few marks are relatively easy to acquire. So do make a reasonable attempt at *every* question you need to answer. To miss a question altogether is to throw marks away!

5 Write a *plan* for your answer. You can list the points you wish to make, and then sort them into an appropriate order. Make sure, of course, that your plan answers the question actually set, and not one you wish had been set! Having a plan will help to keep your answer coherent and tightly structured, and will help to stop you from lapsing into irrelevant waffle.

6 Pay close attention to the terms and phrases which are used by the examiners.

Argue   Use theories and evidence to make a case.

Account for   Explain rather than describe a social phenomenon. Answer the question 'why?'

Analyse   Show that you understand a complicated issue by breaking it down into simpler component parts. Identify and explain any relationships which exist between these component parts.

Assess   Examine the strengths and weaknesses of an argument. When assessing a sociological approach the majority of the marks are for criticism rather than for description and illustration.

Compare   Identify similarities. Criticism from the same source is a similarity.

Contrast   Identify differences. Usually paired with 'compare'. Do not write *separate* accounts of two approaches and leave the comparison implicit.

Criticise	Offer arguments for and against. Usually the emphasis is on the limitations of an explanation. This term is often added to another term, such as 'critically examine' or 'critically analyse'.
Discuss	Present at least two views on an issue. Discussion involves criticism.
Evaluate	The same as 'assess'. You must offer a judgement based on evidence.
Examine	Like 'analyse' in that an in-depth view is required of something, say the relationship between two variables.
Explain	To identify the reasons for something or to clarify a situation.
Illustrate	Cite relevant sociological examples.
Outline	Provide a brief description of the essential points. At A-level, this is likely to be combined with another instruction.

GETTING HIGH MARKS

Relevance

Answers must be explicitly relevant to the question. Examiner's reports identify common errors and these include writing everything you know about the topic, answering last year's question or answering the question you would have liked. Examiners are sometimes unable to decide *which* question has been attempted, where the answers have not been numbered accurately or at all. Competent answers should not need to be identified by numbers!

Organisation

Produce a logical and coherent argument. If a question asks you to 'Critically assess the interactionist approach to deviance' then you should not begin with an epic account of positivist approaches. Rather, start with the interactionist view and then use other approaches to criticise it. Some recent questions on suicide have asked about the significance of 'coroner's decisions'. This is a warning *not* to run through the whole of Durkheim's 'Suicide' but instead to begin with the studies that treat suicide verdicts as problematic. Careful planning is the key to well organised and balanced answers.

Content

Introductions, if used at all, should be brief. They should indicate how you intend to interpret the question and to organise your answer. For essay-type answers you can organise your main points in separate paragraphs. A conclusion can review your findings in the light of the original question. On occasions the Chief Examiners have amended mark schemes to deal with a novel interpretation that they had not anticipated. Even though the questions should be clear and unambiguous, so that you know what is required, remember that in sociology there is never a 'right answer'. There is, however, a 'right approach'. The main body of an answer should include:

- THEORETICAL AND METHODOLOGICAL ISSUES.
- EVIDENCE FROM RESEARCH STUDIES.
- CRITICISM.

You will often benefit from using comparative material, from linking material with other topics, and from introducing broader debates on theoretical and methodological issues.

> Remember women.

Answers which ignore the existence of women, e.g. on deviance or work may irritate some examiners. Much pre-feminist sociology is guilty of this omission.

Style, grammar, punctuation, spelling and clarity of writing are not usually assessed separately. (SCE and JMB do warn students that such deficiencies can be penalised.) However all contribute to the clarity of your responses and to the force of your arguments, and in this sense are positively rewarded.

Conclusions, like introductions should be brief. There is no point in repeating material without good reason. If asked to evaluate or assess arguments, then a conclusion based on the evidence you have presented is necessary. Conclusions should certainly not contradict the rest of the answer. If you have written a powerful critique of Marxist approaches to education, with little positive comment, do not undermine your answer by giving a balanced conclusion. I have read powerful feminist indictments of family life followed by functionalist sounding conclusions about the beneficial effects of the family on all concerned. Such contradictions suggest that you do not realise the implications of what it is you have written.

COURSEWORK

This section refers to formal coursework which is assessed and contributes to the final examination mark. London has examined coursework at AS-level since 1990 and the AEB has introduced coursework at A-level for the 1991 summer examination, which means that students on two-year courses may have started this option in 1989. It is likely that other Boards will introduce coursework at A- and AS-levels in the future.

It is the success of coursework at GCSE which has encouraged its development at higher levels. Although it remains an option for AEB students it should be an attractive one as it provides the opportunity to *do* sociology rather than to just read about it. This should enliven the whole course and allow students to gain a substantial proportion of the final marks before the traditional examinations. This means that work can be spread more evenly throughout the year and other kinds of abilities can be tested and rewarded. Students must however learn to manage their time and to work independently.

There are certain key questions which need considering before starting coursework. The answers can usually be found by consulting your teachers and by referring to the syllabus, and to any coursework guidance notes that accompany it.

1 What marks are available for coursework?
2 How are these marks allocated to the assessment of different abilities? For example is the emphasis on knowledge, evaluation, presentation, etc?
3 What subjects may be chosen and do they need teacher and/or Board approval?
4 What methods may be chosen and do they need approval?
5 What is the timetable for selection, planning, gaining approval and completion? Teachers will have a deadline for submitting their marks to the Board.
6 Is there a required or recommended format for the presentation of work?

The answers to most of these questions can be found in the syllabuses and regulations of the Examination Board concerned. Your research must, of course, employ an accepted method and be on an obviously sociological topic. Here is some further information on the respective Boards.

- AEB A-level allocates 25% of total marks to coursework; London AS allocates 50%.

- Teachers mark the coursework, which is then checked and moderated by the Boards.

- AEB only requires teacher approval of a proposed project; London requires approval by the Examination Board.

- A normal proposal will include:
  a) the working title
  b) the area of investigation
  c) research methods and sources of data.

- Both AEB and London stipulate a 5 000 word maximum for a project.

- In terms of presentation there are a number of requirements.
  - The AEB requires:
    1 Rationale: reason for choosing subject, hypothesis, aims etc.
    2 Context: theoretical context of study.
    3 Methodology: statement of methodology and critical assesment.
    4 Content: the research evidence and arguments.
    5 Evaluation: evaluation of evidence and conclusions.
    6 Sources: list.
  - London requires:
    1 A title page.
    2 Table of contents.
    3 Division of work into appropriate sections.
    4 A bibliography.
    5 A research diary as an appendix containing a critical record of the research process.

- Teachers can provide guidance, supervision and advice. The actual study must be your own independent work.

The above material summarises the respective syllabuses and mark schemes, but you should of course obtain your own copy, where appropriate.

3

STRATIFICATION

MARX

WEBER

THE FUNCTIONALIST THEORIES

SOCIAL MOBILITY

THEORETICAL AND EMPIRICAL STUDIES

GETTING STARTED

STRATIFICATION refers to the division of society into layers. These layers are distinguished by unequal rewards and life chances. Most sociologists see stratification as involving a classification not only of the groups, but also of the relationships which exist between them.

Class is the kind of stratification found in Industrial (Capitalist) societies. Other forms of stratification found in pre-industrial societies include **caste** and the **feudal system**.

The issue of social inequality is immensely important to sociologists and crops up throughout sociology. It is of course often seen as a social problem as well as a sociological one. This chapter is called Stratification rather than Social Inequality in order to restrict our discussion to this particular form of inequality. Other forms of inequality, such as gender, ethnicity and age, are discussed elsewhere.

Since 'inequality' as a concept is at the heart of much of our discussion, it is worth noting that it can be used in at least three contexts:

1 The unequal distribution of opportunities to reach rewarded positions (sometimes called life chances).
2 The unequal distribution of socially valued rewards as between those positions.
3 The subjective feelings of superiority and inferiority, and feelings of class consciousness.

Class is a major variable in considering topics such as health and education. Topics such as poverty, the distribution of power, work, professions and development are frequently analysed as forms of inequality and of course Marxists reduce the explanation of all social phenomena to a discussion of economic inequality.

The major themes involved in questions on this topic are:

1 **Critical evaluation and comparison of major theories of inequality offered by Marx, Weber and the functionalists.**
2 **Analysis of changes in the class structure and in class consciousness in modern industrial societies.**
3 **Critical evaluation of major studies of social mobility.**
4 **Critical evaluation of major studies of poverty.**

ESSENTIAL PRINCIPLES

There are a number of major theories which seek to explain social inequality.

MARX

Economic production is the foundation upon which other social institutions and ideas are built. Classes, which exist in all pre-communist societies, are defined in terms of their relationship to the means of production. The *Ruling Class* own the means of production and dominate and exploit the subject class. The *Subject Class*, who do not own the means of production, are forced to sell their labour to the employers in order to live. They are not paid the full value of their work. This 'Surplus Value' provides profit and rent, and allows the accumulation of capital. In Capitalist society the two classes are:

- The **Bourgeoisie** who own the means of production, such as factories and railways. This ownership can either be directly, as sole proprietors, partners or shareholders, or indirectly, e.g. as bankers.
- The **Proletariat** who are the class of wage labourers working in factories and generally living in towns.

CRITICS OF MARX

Theoretical criticism comes from Weber and his followers and from the functionalists (see below). In addition, some modern Marxists now question certain aspects of his work in the light of subsequent developments. *Empirical criticism* comes from analysing the class structure of modern industrial societies (see below).

Critics challenge the following aspects of Marx's analysis and predictions:

1 Class is based on ownership of the means of production.
2 There are only two significant classes.
3 The relationship between classes is based on exploitation and oppression.
4 The working class (Proletariat) is subjugated by both physical and ideological control.
5 Economic laws will lead to the development of class conflict. Marx predicts:

- **Monopolisation** of capital.
- **Homogenisation** of the working class.
- **Pauperisation** of the working class.
- **Polarisation** of the two classes.

6 Class conflict will lead to revolution, the triumph of the working class and the development of a classless communist society.

WEBER

Social inequality is based on differences in *power* held by groups, and not just on differences in class.

The sources of power are:

- **Class**.
- **Status**.
- **Party**.

Class

This is an objective economic category, so people are in a class whether they are conscious of it or not. A class is a group who share the same economic causes as determinants of their life chances, i.e. the opportunities to acquire goods and services. There are three kinds of classes:

- **Property classes** who own more or less wealth (compare this with Marx).
- **Commercial classes** whose market situation varies. This 'market situation' refers to the price they can command for their labour, which in turn depends on their skills, on any control they can exercise over entry, and on other sources of

bargaining power (compare this with the functionalist explanation below and refer to Chapter 12 on The *Professions*).

■ **Social classes** are groups within which mobility is typical and easy.

Status

This is a subjective category based on honour or prestige, which could be influenced by occupation or birth. Status groups share the same lifestyle, they consume the same goods and may have a common education. They may or may not be conscious of their group identity.

Party

This refers to a group who are organised with the objective of gaining power. A party may represent all, or part, of a class or status group. Examples include Trades Unions, Professional Associations, Bureaucratic Organisations and Political parties.

CRITICS OF WEBER

The value of Weber's work, according to A. Giddens, is that it 'provides what is missing in Marx'. Thus both negative and positive criticisms are to be found in the debate with Marx and with modern Marxists. We might consider the following points on the class structure of modern industrial societies.

1   Class does not depend solely on ownership.
2   There are more than two classes.
3   There are middle classes and working classes. (This is a favourite source of questions.) The middle classes are growing.
4   Social change is not necessarily economically determined. (See *Religion* and *Development* chapters.)
5   Class consciousness may or may not develop.

The empirical studies later in this chapter will throw further light on these points.

THE FUNCTIONALIST THEORIES

The dominant writers here are PARSONS and DAVIS and MOORE. These theories offer a critical view of the conflict explanations of inequality provided by followers of both Marx and Weber. Inequality is explained in terms of its *functions* and is, in effect, justified. Parsons claims that stratification systems are based on common values and thus **integrate** rather than divide societies. The ranking of individuals is based on a consensual view of the importance of positions. Thus winners, as well as losers, see inequality as legitimate, since the rules of the game are 'fair'. Power is granted to those in important positions in order to help them organise others, and this interdependence of workers is seen as a further encouragement to social integration. Because goals are shared, and because inequality helps achieve these goals, everyone benefits (compare with Marx). Davis and Moore identify the functions of stratification as **role allocation and performance** rather than integration. Here inequality ensures that the most important positions in society are conscientiously filled by the most able individuals.

CRITICS OF FUNCTIONALIST THEORIES

Conflict theories reject the whole idea that inequality can be based on consensual values and thereby benefits all members of society. Specific criticisms of Davis and Moore come from both Tumin and Buckley. Tumin questions the following propositions which are made by the functionalists (this also serves as a useful check list of Davis and Moore's work):

1   Some positions are functionally more important than others.
2   Only a few have the natural talents required to develop the skills needed to perform these tasks.
3   Developing talents into skills through training, requires sacrifices, such as loss of earnings.
4   Motivation to make these sacrifices comes from an unequal share of rewards in the future.
5   Unequal rewards lead to differences in prestige, which are generally accepted and are the basis of a stratified society.

Buckley offers some important logical criticisms. He claims that Davis and Moore try (and probably fail) to explain *differentiation* rather than stratification. Differentiation refers to the attaching of unequal rewards to particular **positions** at one moment in time. Stratification refers to the unequal **opportunities** individuals and groups have to reach the highly rewarded positions and is seen as more or less permanent. Thus class, race and gender inequality prevent the most able from achieving the most important positions. Thus stratification may be seen as dysfunctional, as it wastes talent, reduces motivation and causes conflict.

SOCIAL MOBILITY

Social mobility refers to the movement up or down the class structure by individuals or groups. Sociologists are most interested in *cross-class mobility*. *Intra-generational mobility* describes the movement within an individual's working life. *Inter-generational mobility* compares the occupations of fathers and sons. *Stratum mobility* is the movement of a whole occupational group within the occupational ranking.

The main sociological issues include:

1 The **causes** of the observed mobility rates. These include changes in the occupational structure, educational reforms which provide increased opportunity, and differential fertility rates between classes.

2 The **effects** or **importance** of social mobility. An open society (with high mobility rates) ensures that the best get to the top and reduces class conflict. According to Giddens, low rates of mobility encourage the development of class consciousness and are a feature of a *structurated* society.

3 The difficulties of classifying occupations and assessing the extent of mobilty.

THEORETICAL AND EMPIRICAL STUDIES

THE WORKING CLASSES

Marx anticipated an impoverished and increasingly homogenised working class who would become class conscious and ultimately revolutionary. The studies below, including those by most of the modern Marxists, accept the decline of the traditional working class.

Rose 1968

In a study of working class conservative voting, Rose found that only 25% of *manual* workers had all five characteristics of his 'ideal type'. These characteristics of the 'ideal' working class type included being a manual worker, a trade union member, a tenant, having a minimum education, and being a self-assigned member of the working class.

Lockwood 1966

Lockwood identified three groups within the working class, their differing values being based on residential and occupational communities. He identified: *Proletarian Traditionalism*, e.g. miners; *Deferential Traditionalism*, e.g. farm workers; and the *Privatised working class*, e.g. car workers. Many subsequent studies have reinforced this division between the traditional and the 'new' working class.

Goldthorpe, Lockwood *et al* 1968

In one of three books based on a study of both manual and non-manual factory workers in Luton in the early 1960s, they tested and refuted the then fashionable *Embourgeoisement* thesis which suggested that affluent workers had become middle class. (see Outline Answers to Question 5, Chapter 6). They argued for the continued existence of a gap between manual and non-manual workers. Nevertheless they did suggest the emergence of a new working class, with instrumental attitudes to work derived from a privatised family life.

Penn 1985

Supports the Goldthorpe *et al* study by seeing a continued divide between manual and non-manual workers and thereby a divided working class. However, rather than a 'new' working class he identifies a privileged group of skilled craft workers whose rare skills and organisation maintain high rewards. (The fate of print workers after the Wapping move perhaps challenges this view.)

Hill 1976

Hill found that the allegedly new instrumental attitudes to work existed in a traditional working class community of dockers.

Parkin 1968

Parkin identified three value systems in modern Britain. A *dominant* value system supporting middle and upper class interests influencing increasing numbers of the working class through education and the media. A *subordinate* value system found in sheltered working class communities. A *Radical* value system found among left-inclined middle class workers.

Rex 1970

Rex used a Weberian approach to identify an ethnically differentiated 'underclass', one which was separate from the white proletariat. He also sees the possibility of an ethnic consciousness cutting across class boundaries. (see Chapter 4 on *Race*.)

Feminist studies (see also Chapter 5 on *Gender*)

Women are seen as particularly disadvantaged in the labour market. Whether or not this demonstrates a division within the working class depends on the extent to which the writer is influenced by orthodox Marxist views. The same applies to studies of racial disadvantage. The concept of a *reserve army of labour* as applied to women, immigrants and minorities, accepts their disadvantage but still locates them *within* a unitary working class.

THE MIDDLE CLASSES

These studies are concerned firstly, with establishing the **existence** of a distinct middle class separated from manual workers by rewards and consciousness, and secondly, with identifying **differences within** the middle classes.

Roberts et al 1972

This study distinguished five groups within the middle classes based on the *image* the group had of the place of the middle class in society. He called these images of society:

- The middle mass.
- The compressed middle class.
- The finely graded occupational ladder.
- The proletarian middle class.
- The new radicals.

Goldthorpe 1978

Goldthorpe suggested that the British middle class was becoming increasingly large and fragmented, and that beneath it there remained the remnants of a traditional working class. By examining the origins of parents, and the likely life chances of children, he identified four major groups within the middle class.

- The *old* middle classes, which were recruited from the higher class parents.
- The *new* middle classes, which were recruited from the lower class parents.
- The *established* middle classes, which have children whose future is secure.
- The *marginal* middle classes, which have children whose future is insecure.

Thus clerks could be described as new and marginal, the service class as new and established, small proprietors as old and marginal, and professionals as old and established.

Lockwood 1958

Although his 'Blackcoated worker' is the earliest study mentioned here, it has been left to the end as it provides the best link with the modern Marxist studies which follow.

Lockwood tested the Marxist hypothesis that clerks were in fact 'falsely conscious' proletarians. He used the Weberian distinction between class and status to show that the clerk remained a superior worker in terms of *market situation, work situation* and *status*. (See Tutor's Answer to Question 3 below). He did, however, predict a diminishing of these advantages and he accepted that clerks were not part of a traditional middle class, but rather part of a new instrumentally collectivist one. (This idea should remind you of the Luton Studies.)

MODERN MARXISTS

These writers attempt to deal with the various criticisms already mentioned and with the changes in modern industrial societies, such as rising incomes for all classes, the growth of non-manual work at the expense of manufacturing, the institutionalisation of class conflict and its diminishing effects.

Mills 1951

Although his work contains both Marxist and Weberian influences, it extended the concept of alienation from the factory to the office and suggested the increasingly popular hypothesis of 'proletarianisation' of the middle classes. His work is not restricted to routine office workers but also covers managers, professionals and salesmen.

Carchedi 1975

Carchedi adds the **feminisation of office work** to the usual list of factors encouraging proletarianisation of clerical workers.

Braverman 1976

Braverman offers a variation from traditional Marxism by accepting that changes take place in the composition of classes as the methods of production change. His writing (which is further discussed in Chapter 10 on *Work*) emphasises the effects of routinisation, bureaucratisation, fragmentation, and the deskilling of work on the composition of classes.

Westergaard and Resler 1976

These two conducted an empirical study of class in modern Britain which used a Marxist perspective. They argued that too many discussions of class ignore the overwhelming importance of **wealth**. Thus they only deal with divisions **within** the working class and fail to consider the crucial division between the *bourgeoisie* and the rest.

Althusser 1972 and Bowles and Gintis 1976

These studies explain the lack of class consciousness among the working class by discussing the development of *ideological controls*. Both studies identify the importance of **schooling** in this process. Althusser adds the **media** to the list of *ideological state apparatuses* which substitute for overt oppression.

Marcuse 1968

Marcuse attempted to deal with the problems which affluence presents to those Marxists who predict impoverishment. He saw the rich working class enslaved by 'chains of gold'. He thought that they were forced to work in order to pursue 'false needs' created by advertising.

SOCIAL MOBILITY

Miller

In a study of Britain in the 1940s and 1950s, Miller showed high rates of upward mobility for manual workers and high rates of downward mobility for non-manual workers.

His 1960 comparative study suggested similar rates of mobility in modern industrial societies, including communist ones. Lipsett and Bendix suggested something similar in the 1940s, although subsequent studies have questioned this view.

Glass

In a major study conducted in 1949, Glass found high levels of short range mobility. He suggested the existence of a *buffer zone* preventing access to the top positions, but a strong possibility of movement up or down for both skilled manual workers and non-manual workers.

Goldthorpe 1972 and 1980

The Oxford mobility study was interested in the effects of post-war economic growth and education reform on mobility. It found a more open society than Glass, e.g. only 25% of the top class had fathers from this class. However the life chances of those at the top remained much better than those at the bottom. The major cause of increased mobility was identified as being the expansion of the service class, owing to technological change, rather than to any increased open competition in order to get to the top.

Goldthorpe and Payne 1986

This update on the earlier study found that the previous trends had continued except that the opportunities for manual workers' **sons** had improved. Downward movement was also reduced, but the arrival of high levels of unemployment had increased the risk of moving down for manual workers themselves.

Criticisms of the empirical studies on social mobility

Evaluation of the major studies is a popular question. Some criticisms are specific to a particular study, others are more general, involving methodological or even ideological concerns.

The positive value of the mobility studies is that they allow us to test hypotheses, such as *Embourgeoisement, Proletarianisation, Structuration, Elite theories* and the success or otherwise of *educational reforms*.

Problems of **measurement** of mobility include:

1   Comparing the father's final position with a possibly temporary one for the son.
2   Relying on possibly unreliable records for fathers' occupations.
3   The ranking of jobs may change.
4   The studies are not strictly comparable, as different categories are often used. For example, Glass used the Registrar General's classification (which in any case has been updated) whereas Goldthorpe used his own scheme.
5   Studying only two generations conceals the possibility of the sons of downwardly mobile fathers **returning** to their original class. This is illustrated by Jackson and Marsden's finding that working class boys in grammar schools often had mothers with middle class origins.
6   The classification of women is problematic and they were excluded from both the Glass and the Goldthorpe studies. HEATH found that women are more often downwardly mobile and are excluded from both skilled manual work and top jobs.
7   Studies tend to neglect both the Bourgeoisie and the unemployed.
8   Mobility studies only consider individual access to jobs, and ignore the fact that the class structure may remain unchanged.

The *Goldthorpe* studies have been specifically criticised:

1   His Service class is so large that it encourages the view of increased mobility.
2   Giddens claims that it ignores the small exclusive elite recruited from the Public schools.
3   Heath used Goldthorpe's data to support the view that there was 'closure' at the top.
4   The Marxists Westergaard and Resler point out that it neglects any consideration of wealth.

EXAMINATION QUESTIONS

1   'Social stratification is beneficial for societies, ensuring that the most important positions are conscientiously filled by the most qualified people.' What arguments would you use (a) to support and (b) to criticise this contention?

(JMB 1988)

2 'We are all middle class now.' Are we?

(Cambridge 1988)

3 Have white-collar workers been 'proletarianised'?

(Oxford 1988)

4 Outline the major studies of social mobility in Britain and examine criticisms of them.

(AEB 1989)

5 To what extent have sociological explanations of poverty helped us to understand poverty in Britain in the 1980s?

(AEB 1989)

6 'The Marxian assumption of two basic antagonistic classes is, in certain important respects, sociologically unsatisfactory' (Anderson and Sharrock eds. Applied Sociological Perspectives). Critically examine this view.

(AEB 1985)

OUTLINE ANSWERS TO SELECTED QUESTIONS

Question 1

This has been a very popular question for a long time, so examiners now expect increasingly sophisticated answers. A summary of Davis and Moore followed by Tumin's critique and nothing more will not score high marks, however detailed it is.

You are asked to **evaluate** the functionalist theory of stratification. The quotation suggests Davis and Moore's emphasis on role allocation rather than Parsons' contention that the main function is integration. Both should be outlined for the first part of the answer.

Criticism should not be restricted to Tumin, but could also include Buckley. Perhaps more importantly it could include modern Marxist and modern Weberian criticism which challenges the view that stratification is based on value consensus. Westergaard and Resler offer a Marxist critique and Parkin can be used to develop Weberian ideas on closure.

Remember to relate this material directly to the question.

Question 2

This question requires more than just a run-through of the 1960s 'embourgeoisement' debate. You should use both Marxist and Weberian theories and studies to discuss some or all of the following issues:

- Whether there is a middle class at all or just two classes.
- Whether the lower (or even higher) levels of non-manual workers are being proletarianised.
- Whether there are divisions within the middle class.
- Whether the boundaries between the middle and working classes are being blurred by embourgeoisement.

Question 4

This is a straightforward question. At least two studies must be considered. Glass and Goldthorpe are the most likely, but others will be rewarded. You are asked to 'examine' criticisms, which means look at them in some detail, but the best answers will **assess** the criticisms as well. You should include positive evaluation of the studies as well as pointing out their shortcomings. At the time of writing, feminist criticism has become as popular as the more traditional consideration of methodological issues. Here is a suggested outline plan:

- The main findings of the Glass study.
- The Goldthorpe study showing how it confirms some aspects of Glass but also suggests different patterns of mobility.

- The methodological problems involved in doing mobility studies.
- The Marxist criticisms denying the significance of an 'open society'.
- The feminist criticism concerning the invisibility of women in such studies.

Question 5

This question requires more than a critical evaluation of explanations of poverty, although this may be the major part of the answer. The other necessary ingredient is the extent to which they can be applied to Britain in the 1980s. A knowledge of the effects of government economic and social policy will be rewarded, as would your mentioning the implications of international economic issues.

a) The extent of poverty can be assessed by looking at the work of Mack and Lansley and by comparing this with relatively recent empirical studies, such as Townsend.
b) Cultural theories applied to Britain in the 1980s. Are the poor different? The various forms of the culture of poverty theories (Lewis and Harrington) could be considered critically. You could revive Matza's Marxist view that the poor are stigmatised to legitimise poverty, by looking at work on the reporting of poverty in the media and the new right attack on the 'nanny state' which has legitimised cuts in some benefits.
c) The effects of social policies. Conventional material on the failure of the Welfare State could be supplemented by right-wing justification of the running down of the 'nanny state'. The influence of market liberals on economic policy is worth noting.
d) The view that poverty is the result of structural inequality. The welfare policies of the government, even if generous rather than mean, cannot remove this inequality. Structuralist-conflict accounts influenced by Marx (Kincaid, Miliband) and Weber (Rex) could be cited and applied to Britain in the 1980s.

TUTOR'S ANSWER

Question 3

Have white-collar workers been 'proletarianised'?

The essence of this question is the dispute between some modern Marxists and critics of Marx concerning the current position and future of the middle classes.

Marx himself saw capitalist society, like all other kinds of pre-communist society, as being divided into two basic antagonistic classes. These classes were defined in terms of the ownership of the means of production. The ruling class of owners he called the Bourgeoisie, and the subject class of wage labourers, the Proletariat. The proletariat were largely factory workers.

Weber rejected both Marx's definition of class and his view of only two classes. Weber saw inequality as based on party and status as well as on class. Weberian writers identify three kinds of classes: firstly property classes, who own more or less wealth; secondly commercial classes, distinguished by their market situation; and thirdly social classes, who are defined as a group within which mobility is likely. Weber observed and predicted the growth of the middle classes prompted by bureaucratisation.

Subsequent critics of Marx have argued for the continued existence, expansion and fragmentation of the middle classes. They also point out the failure of Marx's prediction that class conflict would intensify. The diminishing of apparent conflict is explained by the decomposition of capital, the institutionalisation of conflict through voting and collective bargaining, and the rising of incomes for all classes. Thus it seems that class consciousness is diminishing, not increasing.

This last point is picked up by C. W. Mills who was among the first to argue that it was little more than false consciousness that separated the alleged middle class from the rest of the working class. In 'White Collar' he suggested that office workers had become proletarianised because of changes in their work situation and in their relationship with their employers. Routine clerical workers had become as alienated as factory workers as their jobs became routinised, fragmented and deskilled because of bureaucratisation. Unlike others who argue for proletarianisation, Mills also looks at higher levels of the middle classes, such as salesmen and managers, who are forced to present an alienated self to others, and professionals who have lost their autonomy to the large corporations which now employ them or pay their fees.

In 1958 Lockwood, in 'The Blackcoated Worker', tested the Marxist hypothesis that clerks were falsely conscious proletarians. He used the Weberian concepts of class and status to compare clerks with manual workers. Class was measured by the workers market and work situations. Despite a narrowing of wage differences, the clerk still enjoyed the advantages of job security, pensions and other disguised forms of pay. Although working conditions in factories had improved, clerks still had a superior working environment and worked more closely with managers and employers. All these factors helped perpetuate the superior status of the clerk. Though Lockwood still saw the clerk as a superior worker, he did not see him as part of the traditional middle class but as forming a new instrumentally collectivist middle class. This view is echoed 20 years later by Goldthorpe when writing about the British middle class. He describes clerks as part of an intermediate class comprising both the 'new' and 'marginal' middle class, as well as skilled manual workers. These are distinguished from the 'old' and 'established' middle classes who are part of the Service class.

Lockwood did, however, predict the **diminishing** of the advantages experienced by clerks compared to manual workers. It is this decline which has been documented by modern Marxists in trying to argue for the proletarianisation thesis.

In separate studies, Bowles and Gintis and Braverman comment on the importance of the fragmentation and deskilling of office work. Both studies see the continuation of the capitalist relations of production, with office workers being controlled and exploited by the owners.

Carchedi describes similar developments in Italy. The differences in pay, conditions, status and consciousness between office and factory workers have become blurred, and office workers have become increasingly collectivist and unionised. He also sees the feminisation of office work encouraging the proletarianisation of clerical workers as their pay and status declines.

From a more traditional Marxist view, Westergaard and Resler see the issue of proletarianisation of white collar workers as unimportant, since such workers were always part of the working class. Differences in rewards enjoyed by various ranks of employees are seen as insignificant compared with the gap between the owners of the means of production and the workers.

In conclusion, it is worth considering the implications for the debate above of certain developments in the 1980s, such as high unemployment and changes in the distribution of post-tax income. These may have widened, rather than narrowed, the gap between manual and non-manual workers.

STUDENT ANSWER WITH EXAMINER COMMENTS

Question 6

'The Marxian assumption of two basic antagonistic classes is, in certain important respects, sociologically unsatisfactory.' Critically examine this view.

> Yes, Weber is a suitable critic.

It would be too simplistic to dismiss the Marxist argument of there being two basic antagonistic classes in society. Weber himself did not totally reject the argument but instead highlighted different aspects of the explanation.

> Defines the two classes and mentions hostility.

Marx saw society as having two classes: the Bourgeoisie and the Proletariat. The main factor dividing the classes is that the Bourgeoisie own the means of production and the Proletariat do not. This was evidently the cause of inequality within society which caused hostility between the two classes.

> Yes, Weber did. Should explain commercial classes and develop beyond the supply and demand for labour. Social change is not a central issue.

Weber claimed there were a multitude of classes. He saw classes formed from those with different labour skills. However he did agree with Marx that economic relations were of importance but that ownership was not the prime determinant of class. Other classes, for example, commercial classes existed. Marx suggested that only when the infra-structure altered did the rest of society i.e. norms, values, education system etc. also change. The infra-structure was therefore the main reason for social change. Weber rejected this claiming that ideas could contribute to social change. He also claimed that the supply and demand for labour influenced class not just ownership.

> **Weak explanation of life chances.**

Weber identified three main sources of power: class, status and party. He argued that certain people were more likely to be placed in more powerful positions simply because they had more access to greater life-chances. For example children born into powerful families received better education. Life-chances depended on the occupation of the family.

> **Functionalism should be related to class not power.**

Functionalists dismiss this Weberian argument and conclude that life-chances depend on natural talents. The functionalists reject the Marxist view that ownership of the means of production is the source of power. They claim that those who are most able to make use of power for the good of society are given power. They also see inequality as functional for society. They believe it exists because it is beneficial and necessary for the survival of the whole society.

> **Relevant but not expressed clearly.**

Marx would disagree that inequality in power is justified by value consensus. Instead he would argue that it is based on false consciousness. The proletariat are unaware of the fact that they are being manipulated and exploited. Marx suggested that only when the proletariat realise their exploitation will there be a revolution. This will involve the working class becoming a class for themselves not just a class in themselves.

> **Relevant comparative views on revolution.**

Functionalists do not anticipate a working class revolution. Neither does Weber see revolution as inevitable but does not dismiss the possibility. Marx believes that only after the revolution will there be a classless society and this will be the final stage of economic change.

> **Legitimising inequality conceals antagonism. Integration point is good.**

Marxists believe that the ruling class legitimise their power by transmitting ideology to the working class. These ideologies are channelled through the education system, the media and religion. The ruling class make people believe that those who are in positions of power deserve to be there. Functionalists support the argument that the working class accept inequality as being in the interests of all. They think that stratification can integrate society rather than creating hostility between them as suggested by Marxists.

> **Not adding much.**

Even though the Marxist explanation is criticised by functionalists and Weberians there still remain similarities between the explanations. Weber seems to develop Marxist ideas of class further and adds the question of how do people actually gain power. While Marx relates power solely to ownership of the means of production. Weber rejects this and sees inequality also dependent on the supply and demand of labour. The more a skill is in demand the more the person who possesses it will be rewarded.

Overall comment

Overall this answer would be worthy of a D grade pass, but not a good grade. The question has been understood and the issues of two classes and antagonism have been addressed.

There is a wealth of material written by modern Marxists and the followers of Weber which could have been used to support the arguments, such as the debates about the fragmentation of the class structure and the proletarianisation of office work. Dahrendorf has explicitly discussed the issues in the quotation dealing with antagonism as well as the more obvious consideration of two classes. Good answers always go beyond the juxtaposition of theories.

RACE AND ETHNICITY

MARXIST APPROACHES

THE UNDERCLASS

INTERACTIONIST APPROACHES

FUNCTIONALIST APPROACHES

THEORETICAL AND EMPIRICAL STUDIES

GETTING STARTED

Most sociological studies of race tend to adopt a conflict approach. Race relations are seen either in terms of socially structured inequality or as a social problem.

Some syllabuses treat race and ethnicity as a discrete topic; others treat it as a form of inequality which exists in many aspects of social life, and thus it is considered in different parts of the syllabus. There is generally more interest in ethnic disadvantage than in simple diversity of experience.

The main themes of questions are:

1 **Describing and explaining ethnic disadvantage in the fields of: housing, employment and education.**
2 **Examining racism as a cause and effect of inequality.**
3 **Examining the relationship between ethnicity and class by evaluating Marxist and Weberian theories.**
4 **Examining the causes and effects of media representation of ethnic minorities.**
5 **Comparing the experience of ethnic minorities with other disadvantaged groups such as women.**

DEFINITIONS

- *Race* refers to real or perceived biological differences which are given a social meaning, e.g. skin colour.
- *Ethnicity* refers to a distinctive cultural identity accepted by the group themselves and/or attributed to them by others.
- *Racism* usually refers to a hostile attitude towards, or prejudice against, an ethnic group. Marxists use the term to describe practises and social institutions as well as the ideology of inferiority.
- *Racial discrimination* is behaviour which treats those in ethnic minorities worse than others.
- *Related topics* include all those where there is evidence of disadvantage, such as work, education, media, health and deviance. Race and ethnicity are central issues in the study of development and stratification. Discussions of immigration need to include a consideration of race, and vice versa.

Remember to emphasise the diversity of experience **between** different ethnic groups as well as the differences **within** a single group based on age, gender and class. Many questions benefit from using a comparative approach in the study of ethnic differences.

ESSENTIAL PRINCIPLES

Despite the differences between the following perspectives, they all tend to see the sociology of race as being concerned with conflict and social problems.

MARXIST APPROACHES

Marxists begin with the assumption that there are only **two** classes, and these are based on the ownership of the means of production. The whole working class is exploited by the ruling class, and any apparent differences such as race and ethnicity are objectively irrelevant.

Racism is seen as the ideology of inferiority and is part of the superstructure of capitalist society. Racist ideas, practises and institutions enhance the control of the ruling class over the workers. The effects of racism include:

1 Legitimising slavery, colonialism and continued deprivation in capitalist society.
2 Dividing the working class, thereby helping prevent the development of class consciousness. The segregation of the labour market allows further exploitation.
3 Providing scapegoats for the inevitable tensions and frustrations of capitalism. Unemployment, poverty, crime and bad housing can be blamed on a visible and vulnerable group.

CRITICS

Weberians and others reject the view that there are only two classes based solely on ownership. Ethnic minorities are seen as having a distinct position in the class structure. Other critics see the possibility of racism existing independently of economic exploitation.

THE UNDERCLASS

This is based on a Weberian analysis of inequality, where class exists alongside divisions based on status and party. Racial inequality stems from competition for scarce resources and from the differing ability of groups to exclude others from the rewards available in the labour and other markets. An *underclass* is not just the bottom of a class gradient, but is beneath and indeed distinct from the rest of the working class. An underclass could comprise one or more of the following: racial or ethnic minorities, immigrants or temporary migrant workers.

The poverty and powerlessness of the underclass is maintained by racial discrimination in the labour and other markets, by exclusion from working class organisations and by barriers to upward mobility due to the slowing down of changes in the occupation structure. (This last point can perhaps be criticised on the basis of a predicted shortage of skilled labour in the 1990s.)

Racism is not seen as the cause of the development of the underclass, but as the basis for the allocation of workers to something like a secondary labour market. (See also the Tutor's Answer to Question 2 below and the consideration of dual labour market theory in Chapter 5 on *Gender*.)

CRITICS

Some critics reject the existence of an ethnically distinct underclass on empirical grounds, pointing out the spread of minorities throughout the occupational structure. Or, whilst accepting the low class and status of minorities, some offer a different explanation of exploitation, such as Marxism, or racism based on other criteria.

INTERACTIONIST APPROACHES

Both Marxists and those supporting the underclass theory see racial disadvantage as part of a wider pattern of socially structured inequality. *Interactionists* are mainly concerned with the social construction of racism and with the variety of social meanings attributed to groups which have objective or perceived biological or cultural differences.

Slavery in the USA was facilitated by the distinct skin colour of slaves, but Nazi Germany was able to pursue persecution using bureaucratic means such as identity papers. Apartheid combines both methods of segregation. Interactionists are interested in the role of the media and education in perpetuating racist meanings and in the relationship between the police and offenders. Writers like S. Hall and Pryce provide a Marxist explanation of the negotiation of reality between blacks and the institutions of the dominant white society, such as the media and police.

Some sociologists lean towards social psychology as a basis for explaining racism, using concepts like prejudice. The psychologist Adorno saw racism as explicable in terms of the individual's 'authoritarian personality'. Others see it as being learned, not from direct contact with the object of prejudice but from other prejudiced people.

CRITICS

Some interactionists ignore the systematic nature of racism and its relationship with the class structure. The source of social meanings, such as colonialism, is not always considered.

FUNCTIONALIST APPROACHES

Functionalism tends to offer the most optimistic view of race relations. Immigration is seen as a temporary threat to social order which will be overcome by integration. This integration is aided by the immigrants acceptance of the dominant values (consider Herberg's claim that religion integrates immigrant Americans) and the tolerance of the host society. (See Chapter 13 on Religion).

CRITICS

Parsons offered this functionalist view in the 1960s, when the move towards political rights for blacks was very apparent. The persistence of class inequality now makes him seem unduly optimistic, like his English follower Patterson, who thought that immigration, and not colour, was the source of temporary disharmony. Economic and political gains by minorities are also explicable in Marxist and Weberian terms, where conflict rather than consensus would be emphasised.

THEORETICAL AND EMPIRICAL STUDIES

MARXIST APPROACHES

Westergaard and Resler

These think that academics and politicians are misguidedly preoccupied with race, when the real inequality is based on class exploitation. They see Britain as having a unitary working class, which is not divided by ethnicity or race.

Castles and Kosack

As Marxists, they see a single working class. But they see one that is significantly divided, so that in all Western European societies there is a group of workers distinguished by race, nationality or other characteristics, who tend to do the worst paid and dirtiest jobs. They use the concept of a reserve army of labour to explain the class position of migrant workers in Europe. These tend to be denied citizenship rights, to experience discrimination and to be confined to low paid, insecure work. When not required they can be sent home and thus unemployment can be exported. This explanation of exploitation can easily be linked to the sociology of development.

Miles

Miles has criticised the two views above. He argues that there is a distinct *racialised fraction* at each level of the working class where the minority worker is at a disadvantage. The divisions within the working class predate new commonwealth immigration and immigrants were recruited into various levels, not excluded from them.

WEBERIAN APPROACHES

Glasgow

Glasgow used the concept of an underclass to describe the position of blacks in American society. Unlike subsequent groups of immigrants who did not share the history of slavery, black Americans had not experienced much upward mobility. The racial nature of poverty and unemployment in the USA persists. More recent political struggles, the emergence of a substantial black middle class and the growth of Spanish speaking ethnic minorities, have all weakened the view that blacks form a distinct underclass.

Rex and Moore and Rex and Tomlinson

These introduced the concept of an underclass to describe the position of blacks and Asians in British society. Their studies of Birmingham describe minorities as experiencing disadvantage because of discrimination. They see these groups as having a worse market situation in the markets for education and housing as well as labour. They are seen as having low status, because of old colonial attitudes reinforced by contemporary racism. Finally, looking at the slow development of ethnically based political groups, they note the exclusion of minorities from working class organisations such as the labour party and the trade unions. Their work is particularly useful in documenting and explaining changes in the patterns of housing of ethnic minorities.

STUDIES OF RACIAL DISCRIMINATION

Daniels

Daniels pioneered the study of racial discrimination in Britain and his work has been followed up by a variety of surveys and experiments by the PEP and PSI. Daniels studied discrimination in employment, housing and the provision of services such as banking. He used a variety of methods to produce both objective data (the amount of discrimination) and subjective data (the victims' experience of discrimination and the discriminator's reasons for doing it).

The Swan Report

The Swan Report and separate studies by DRIVER, EGGLESTON and WRIGHT, and COARD, among others, have described and explained differential educational achievement and the role of the 'hidden curriculum'. It is worth noting that the findings on this subject are often contradictory and subject to change. Also the performance of different minorities varies, and class and gender are also relevant variables (see Outline Answer to Question 4 below and Chapter 9 on Education).

Hartman and Husband

These suggested that the media did **not** form or change attitudes but did provide a 'framework for thinking' about race relations by consistently portraying issues in terms of conflict. The hostile portrayal of minorities was the result of the existing culture and the news value of 'bad news'. The Commission for Racial Equality (CRE) backed up this view in 1984 showing how minorities were presented as a threat or a problem.

GOLDSMITH'S MEDIA RESEARCH GROUP linked racism with the fabricated 'loony left' press reports preceding the 1987 election (see Chapter 14 on the *Mass Media*).

'INSIDER' STUDIES

Some studies try to describe race relations from the viewpoint of ethnic minority members.

Pryce

Pryce studied the St. Paul's district of Bristol before the riots. His participant observations revealed a community under considerable strain. The responses to this pressure varied from commitment to religion to 'hustling'.

Chevanne and Reeves

This study also provides participant observers' experience of racism, but more unusually it describes the feelings of a Jamaican nurse towards the white community she has entered.

Cashmore and Dhaya

Cashmore has described and explained the growth of the Rastafarian movement in Britain. Dhaya has written about the diversity existing within the Pakistani community in Britain and how their experiences here have led to a more unifying culture. Both family life and housing are discussed.

EXAMINATION QUESTIONS

1 How have sociologists helped us to understand the experiences of different ethnic minorities in any ONE society?

(AEB 1984)

2 'The theory of an underclass offers an inadequate explanation of the social position of ethnic minorities in Britain.' Discuss.

(AEB 1988)

3 'Racism is the only reason for the disadvantage experienced by ethnic minorities.' Assess the sociological arguments for and against this view.

(AEB 1989)

4 Describe and account for different educational achievement between any TWO ethnic groups in any ONE society.

(Cambridge 1988)

5 Study the following material and answer the questions below.

ITEM A
Adapted from *Black Like Me* by John Howard Griffin (1960)

> This began as a scientific research study of the Negro in the Deep South of the USA, with careful compilation of data for analysis. But I filed the data away, and here publish the journal of my own experience living as a Negro.
>
> How else except by living as a Negro could a white man hope to learn the truth? Though we lived side by side throughout the south, communication between the two races had simply ceased to exist. The Southern Negro will not tell the white man the truth. He long ago learned that if he speaks a truth unpleasing to the white, the white will make life miserable for him.
>
> The only way I could see to bridge the gap between us was to become a Negro. I decided I would do this.
>
> With my decision to become a Negro I realised that I, a specialist in race relations, really knew nothing of the Negro's problem.
>
> After artificially darkening my skin to look like a Negro, I searched for an opening, a way to enter the world of the Negro. My greatest preoccupation was that moment of transition when I would 'pass over'. Where and how would I do it? To get from the white world to the Negro is a complex matter.

ITEM B Adapted from *Racial Disadvantage in Britain* by David J.Smith (1977)

> The importance of the question how many acts of discrimination actually take place can be seen in relation to the work of the Race Relations Board. The Board's report for 1973 states that during that year a total of 150 complaints were received relating to recruitment to employment; decisions that discrimination had occurred were made in 16% of all employment cases – perhaps 20 or 30 cases.
>
> However, tests using actors from different ethnic groups applying for jobs suggest a much higher figure. The tests show that Asians and West Indians will face about 6 000 cases a year of discrimination against job applicants in the non-skilled field alone. This is quite enough to show that the cases of discrimination that come before the Board are only a tiny fraction of all the acts of discrimination that occur.

a) Drawing upon examples from Item A, assess the strengths and the limitations of covert participant observation in the study of race relations   *(8 marks)*

b) Drawing upon examples from Item A and Item B, discuss how both qualitative and quantitative research methods could be used to complement each other in the study of race relations. (*8 marks*)

c) What explanations have sociologists offered for the extent of racial discrimination at work suggested by Smith's research? (See Item B.) (*9 marks*)

(AEB, AS-level, 1989)

OUTLINE ANSWERS TO SELECTED QUESTIONS

Question 3

The question requires an examination of racism and the competing explanations of disadvantage. An answer could be organised around *areas of inequality* (like housing, education and employment) or around the various *perspectives* of inequality and the way in which they deal with racism.

Different definitions of the concept of racism must be considered. Whereas some writers define it as involving attitude rather than behaviour, Hall sees racism as encompassing ideology, practice and institutions, all of which he links together within a Marxist framework.

a) Marxist views share common assumptions about the use of racism in maintaining ruling class hegemony. Racism is not seen as the prime cause of ethnic disadvantage. Class inequality explains exploitation. Racism is seen as false consciousness and divides the working class.

b) The neo-Marxist views of Hall and Pryce attribute rather more importance to racism and extend the meaning of the term. Racism supports the continuation of colonial oppression, both at home and abroad.

c) Underclass theories see racism as only one of a variety of factors which maintain the poor market situation of ethnic minorities. Occupational closure strategies and the absence of political power are other contributory factors.

d) The role of education and the media in creating and maintaining or even challenging racism can be discussed.

Question 4

Do note the requirements of the question. You must identify clearly which **two** groups you wish to consider and refer to others only in order to make critical or comparative points.

Reference to the differential performance of class and gender groups must be tied directly to the question. For example, to explain the poor performance of a group which is disproportionately found in the working class or to point out the internal diversity within an ethnic group.

If a broad category such as 'Asian' is chosen, an awareness of internal diversity is essential.

a) Point out the difficulties of assessing differential achievement. These are because of the contradictory nature of the studies, the changing performances recorded in the last 20 years, the changing social position of minorities, the problem of isolating other variables (such as class), and the diversity of performance within groups. (See Chapter 9, Education)

b) Apply the conventional explanations of differential achievement to your two groups. This could include *out of school factors*, such as material and cultural deprivation (then consider criticism) and *in-school factors*. The latter could include a consideration of labelling, the curriculum, the racism of teachers and pupils, the quality of schools and the difficulty of attracting and retaining teachers in inner city areas.

c) You might refer to Marxist notions of reproduction in order to examine both the curriculum (including the hidden curriculum) and performance of pupils.

Remember that your studies should be up to date. Generally, the performance of all minorities has improved, native born children do better than immigrants and recent studies in London and Bradford show some ethnic minorities doing better than white (particularly working class) children.

Question 5

The marks are divided roughly equally on this question, so equal time should be spent on each part. Read the whole question carefully and decide in which part you want to make particular points. The question is about methods as much as race, and the answers should reflect this.

a) Drawing on examples from Item A, assess the strengths and limitations of covert participant observation (PO) in the study of race relations.

   Methods can be evaluated in three ways looking at:

   i) *Theoretical issues*: does participation produce greater validity as the researcher can share the experience of his subjects? Alternatively, are less subjective and more scientific methods more valid? Mention 'my own experience'.

   ii) *Practical issues*: covert research is one way of gaining access to subjects ('communication . . . had . . . ceased'), although Liebow made a virtue of being different. Daniels and others have subsequently used deception in experiments to uncover racial discrimination. The problems of PO include gaining access, moving freely if undercover, taking notes, etc. Research is not repeatable and therefore unreliable. Williams found that the responses to questions were influenced by the race of the interviewers. (See Chapter 18, Methods)

   iii) *Ethical issues*: the researcher is involved in deceiving his subjects and may find himself involved in shameful or illegal activities. Pryce was involved with deviants as well as with church-goers in St. Paul's. The justification lies in the importance of the subject and the illegal nature of racial discrimination itself.

b) Drawing upon examples from Item A and Item B, discuss how both qualitative and quantitative research methods could be used to complement each other in the study of race relations.

   The essence of this part is to understand the advantages of complementary methods which produce different kinds of data and which can be used to complete, or cross-check, findings.

   Participant observation is a qualitative research method which provides insights into the subjective experience of living as a 'Negro in the Deep South'. It permits an in-depth study of a small social group. This method is often associated with interpretive sociology.

   The experimental testing of racial discrimination using *quantitative* research methods allows an objective picture of the overall extent of the problem, provided the data is representative. It does not provide us with explanations of discrimination, nor does it describe the feelings of victims. Daniel's study used complementary methods. Quantitative data is often more influential in shaping social policy but qualitative data may provoke a greater public reaction.

c) What explanations have sociologists offered for the extent of racial discrimination at work suggested by Smith's research?

   The problem here is in compressing a whole essay into one third of an answer. The response must be carefully planned to ensure at least two explanations are clearly examined and evaluated.

   i) Varieties of Marxist explanation and criticism.
   ii) The underclass theory and critics.
   iii) Daniels' empirical research, where actual discriminators give reasons and rationalisations for their behaviour.

   Other appropriate explanations could include functionalist or dual labour market theories.

TUTOR'S ANSWER

Question 2

'The theory of an underclass offers an inadequate explanation of the social position of ethnic minorities in Britain.' Discuss.

The concept of an underclass has developed from the critical view of Marx's theory of class offered by Weber and those influenced by his analysis of industrial society. Class and other forms of inequality are seen as the result of the struggle in the market place for scarce resources and the tendency of groups to gain advantages by excluding others. This emphasis on 'closure' is repeated by Halsey when describing class in Britain and is developed at some length by Rex and Tomlinson in their study of ethnic minorities in Birmingham. The actual term 'underclass' was used earlier in the USA (in the same context) by Glasgow when describing the social position of black Americans who, unlike the Birmingham ethnic minorities, were not relatively recent immigrants.

The inequality experienced by non-whites in Birmingham was identified as occurring in all the three dimensions of inequality distinguished by Weber. These minorities were disadvantaged in the markets for education, housing, and particularly labour. In addition to class inequality, Rex and Tomlinson also looked at the low status resulting from colonial history and contemporary racism, and the disadvantages in 'party' terms because of their exclusion from trade unions and political parties. Since the publication of this work there has been a gradual increase in the number of black and Asian politicians and trade union leaders.

Unlike the Marxist idea of a two-class society, an underclass is identified as consisting largely of non-white immigrants and their descendants. It is seen as being beneath, and clearly distinct from, the white working class. Their poverty and powerlessness is maintained by racial discrimination in the three markets and by exclusion from working class organisations. Unlike previous immigrants, their upward mobility is further limited by immigration control.

Marxist critics persist in their view of a more or less unitary working class, as argued by Westergaard and Resler who play down the importance of race. Castles and Kosack see the least rewarded members of the working class being the reserve army of migrant labour found throughout Europe. Unlike the women or the black and Asian British workers who allegedly form a reserve army of labour here, European migrant workers frequently lack citizenship or even residence rights. Miles offers an alternative Marxist critique of the underclass theory, emphasising not so much the exclusion of immigrant workers but their deliberate recruitment into a society where racism already existed because of colonial history. Thus there is, he claims, a racialised fraction of relatively disadvantaged workers at all levels of the working class, and not a single, ethnically distinct, underclass.

Apart from the Marxist view there are other critical views which still acknowledge racial inequality but deny the existence of an underclass. Some more or less optimistic research on educational achievement and upward mobility indicates the mistake of seeing ethnic minorities as an homogeneous group. There are differences between and within ethnic groups in patterns of employment. Ethnic minorities are not even predominantly found in the lower working class, let alone in an underclass. Neither, despite the persistence of discrimination, are they segregated from the white work force.

The more ethnographic studies of S. Hall and Pryce, though both influenced by Marx, put more emphasis on racism as a cause of racial disadvantage. Hall sees racism as both ideology and practice and the result of the continuation of the colonial relationship between Britain and Jamaica which affects the black British. Pryce sees the behaviour of blacks in Bristol as also being influenced by colonial attitudes towards them. Their responses to racism vary, from deviance to pentecostal religion.

Dahya concentrates on the internal relationships between Pakistani communities in this country and their continued relationship with Pakistan. He thus offers an explanation of their social position where inequality and disadvantage are **not** identified as major influences. The Rushdie affair perhaps reminds us that Islam may have more influence on attitudes and behaviour than does race relations.

In conclusion, it could be argued that the underclass theory fails to offer an adequate explanation of the social position of ethnic minorities in Britain for two basic reasons: *either* it has not been demonstrated that the class position of ethnic minorities is unambiguously beneath that of the native white working class; *or*, even if such inequality has been demonstrated, there are competing explanations for it.

STUDENT ANSWER WITH EXAMINER COMMENTS

Question 1

'How have sociologists helped us to understand the experiences of different ethnic minorities in any *one* society?'

> **Identifies 3 suitable areas of experience and 2 minorities.**

> **Appropriate evidence introduces gender.**

> **Relevant evidence.**

> **Marxist point is not clear.**

> **Good distinction between ethnic groups.**

> **Challenges conventional view. Gender differences again.**

> **Marxists confused with conventional deprivation material. Good point about prejudice.**

Since immigration began, sociologists have been focussing their attention upon the experiences ethnic minorities face in their host society. Most sociologists have concentrated their research upon ethnic minorities in the education system, housing and employment. This is where the essay will begin highlighting the experiences of predominantly black and Asian immigrants in England.

A study carried out by Rose looked at the occupational distribution of male immigrants in London. He found the occupational distribution was fairly widespread with no overwhelming concentration in a particular job. Rose did discover a high proportion of black workers in transport and engineering work. He found that in the West Midlands the pattern for male immigrants showed little differences between groups but concentration for all of them in particular occupations. Black females were found in nursing as well as engineering and Indian women in clerical and professional jobs. Both black and Pakistani women were under-represented in white collar work. Rose concluded all ethnic groups were under-represented in desirable jobs. This implies discrimination against minorities in the field of employment.

A study by Daniel used three actors: a Hungarian, white Englishman and West Indian. A controlled study gave each similar qualifications and then had them apply for the same jobs in housing, mortgage and insurance. In each case the West Indian was less successful. This phenomenon was demonstrated again in a television programme 'Black and White' in 1988.

A Home Office report also showed higher levels of unemployment and lower wages among West Indians and Asians. This confirms a Marxist view that changes in the infra-structure causing unemployment are reflected by changes in the superstructure.

Research suggests that black children do worse in education than white or Asian children. The CRE in 1985 claimed that black children were four times more likely to be suspended than white or Asian children. The report blamed insensitive teachers. Black children tended to be stereotyped as less hard working but better at sport than white or Asian children – who were perceived as more academic and hard working. These stereotypes were transmitted to the children and thus effected their performance.

Driver challenged the view that black children do worse than others. He studied 2300 school leavers and found the examination results of black children were better than those of white children. He also found that while white boys did better than white girls black girls did better than black boys. He concluded that while black children did worse in primary school and the early stage of secondary school they subsequently improved.

Marxists see the lack of educational achievement as a class problem. They see under achievement linked to deprivation both social and economic. However, Asian children do as well as white children despite deprivation. It has been found that racial prejudice does not have identical effects on every minority group. White attitudes towards different groups varies.

Sociologists also examined ethnic minorities experience in the

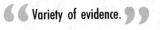

❝ Variety of evidence. ❞

housing market. The 1983 Home Office report found that West Indian
and Asian immigrants were forced to pay higher rents for run-down
accomodation. West Indians had moved from private to council
housing. This suggests they had problems in obtaining mortgages.
In a study of housing in Newcastle it was found that Asians were
more likely to live in privately owned accomodation than council
housing. This suggested both their preference for ownership and a
way of avoiding discrimination. The housing was often run down and
overcrowded.

❝ Hints of possible Marxist
vs. Weberian debate. ❞

   In Rex and Moore's study of Sparkbrook they found immigrants were
concentrated in the poorest and most dilapidated properties. They
were then seen as responsible for the decay of the area. Marxists
have criticised Rex and Moore for seeing the housing market as
independent of the wider class structure.

   As it can be seen there are different ethnic minorities with
different experiences but they all experience discrimination.

Overall comments

Overall a competent Grade D/C answer. Its strengths lie in the use of sociological research to support arguments and in an awareness of the diversity of experience between and within particular ethnic groups.

   The most apparent weakness is the absence of any theoretical context for the evidence. The debate about the existence of an 'underclass' could be brought in.

5

GENDER

GETTING STARTED

Sociological interest in gender is relatively recent. Gender issues were for a long time either ignored altogether or submerged in the sociology of the family. The emphasis was formerly on **difference** rather than on **inequality**, with the rather optimistic suggestion often being advanced of a progressive convergence in roles. The rise of women's movements since 1970 has had a major influence on sociology, and the sociology of gender can be largely seen as the sociology of women.

The main themes of questions involving this topic are:

1 **Women in the labour market.**
2 **The domestic labour debate.**
3 **Sex, gender and sexuality.**

Answering a question based on any one of these themes usually requires reference to the other two areas. Although most text books and examination syllabuses have separate sections dealing with gender, the issue of gender inequality now runs through all of sociology. Other topics where gender must be considered include education, media, health, crime, and, of course, the family.

DEFINITIONS

- *Sex* refers to the biological differences between male and female.
- *Gender* refers to the socially defined differences between men and women.
- *Sexuality* refers to desires, needs and behaviour which are seen as specifically sexual in nature.

WOMEN AT WORK

THE DOMESTIC LABOUR DEBATE

GENDER, SEX AND SEXUALITY

THEORETICAL AND EMPIRICAL STUDIES

WOMEN AT WORK

ESSENTIAL PRINCIPLES

The main concerns are:

- women's earnings. ■ patterns of employment.
- relationships between home and work.

In general, women are concentrated in low paid, low status work. They may be segregated into particular kinds of work which is seen as feminine or located in the lower ranks of those occupations shared with men. Women are frequently found in part-time work.

The main explanations of gender inequality in the labour market include the following.

1 Functionalist

Gender roles are assumed to 'fit' the needs of individuals, the family and the social system. These roles are influenced by biology, are learned through socialisation and emphasise that the woman's primary responsibility is the home.

Critics see such approaches as avoiding a proper consideration of inequalities in the distribution of labour and power, with the consequent exploitation of women in work and at home.

2 Feminist

Emphasis is placed here on the importance of the housewife-mother role in maintaining male advantage in the labour market. Housework is unpaid and housewives are seen as economically inactive. Feminists, in contrast, see it as real productive work. Women's occupations are often extensions of their domestic roles (cooking, caring, cleaning etc.), and are low paid and low status occupations. The primacy given to the housewife-mother role often interferes with women's careers; for instance, women may end up as low paid home-workers, in an attempt to combine economic activity with the housewife-mother role (See Tutor's Answer to Question 2 below).

Critics argue that women are not exploited at home, or that the cause of any exploitation which might exist is capitalism and not men.

3 Marxist

Marxism was the inspiration for many feminists (but today it is the modern Marxists who are often influenced by feminism). Women's confinement to the home is to ensure the reproduction of labour power for capitalism. Women are a *reserve army of labour*, available for low paid insecure work when required but not seen as having a right to work. This view is reinforced by higher rates of female unemployment and by their concentration in part-time work (See Tutor's Answer to Question 2 below).

Critics see this view as underestimating the particular disadvantages of women, and failing to explain gender inequality in socialist societies.

4 Dual Labour Market Theory

The labour market is divided into two sectors. The *primary sector* comprises secure, better paid jobs with career prospects. The *secondary sector* comprises insecure, low paid jobs with few opportunities. Access to the primary sector depends on having and displaying those characteristics preferred by employers who may see women as worse trained, less experienced and less reliable. Like the Marxist approach, this explanation can be applied to ethnic minorities and to immigrant labour.

Critics see this theory as avoiding the issue of class exploitation and denying the special position of women.

Alternative explanations explain female inequality using concepts like *caste* and *underclass* to emphasise their lack of mobility.

THE DOMESTIC LABOUR DEBATE

Currently the debate over the significance of housework has become rather one-sided. Feminists have successfully challenged the traditional views that housework is naturally a woman's responsibility and that there is a tendency towards more equal conjugal roles. (Both these views are argued from the functionalist perspective in Chapter 8 on *The Family*.) Feminists see women as being exploited by men in the home. Marxists explain the development of housework by linking it to the development of the factory system in the early days of capitalism (see Student's Answer to Question 1 below).

GENDER, SEX
AND SEXUALITY

Most sociologists reject natural or biological explanations of gender roles and of women's position in society. Functionalists see gender roles, which are learned through socialisation, as fitting the needs of the social system. Feminists see gender roles as unequal, as well as different, and as being imposed on women by men. Marxists also see gender in terms of socially structured inequality, but only as a part of the more important class division of society.

Apparent differences in masculine and feminine sexuality are seen by feminists and Marxists as ideological rather than natural. Interactionists, while agreeing that sexuality is largely a social construction, would emphasise the way in which behaviour follows negotiation, rather than being determined by structural influences. The wider significance of differences in sexuality is the way they are used to control and oppress women. Rape, fear of rape, and the use of hostile language, can all be seen as limiting the freedom of women and encouraging them to seek the protection of marriage. The role of the media is seen as increasingly important, reinforcing the images of femininity and masculinity which develop in the home and school.

You will be rewarded for considering masculinity and homosexuality as part of the debate on sex and gender.

> **The sociology of gender is not exclusively about women.**

THEORETICAL
AND EMPIRICAL
STUDIES

HOUSEWORK

Bernard

'In truth being a housewife makes you sick.' She distinguished 'his' marriage from 'her' marriage. Married men are more successful in their careers, better paid, healthier and live longer. This is an effect rather than a cause of getting married. The 'duties of a wife' enhance his life. Married women are less healthy and less content with marriage than men. They initiate divorce more often. Single women are the cream of the crop. Single men are the bottom of the barrel. (You can also use this study in Health questions.)

Delphy

Housework is productive domestic labour, e.g. food is processed and clothes are cleaned. She presents a Marxist analysis where men own the means of production (the house, washing machine and oven) and exploit women. There is no symmetrical family. Men own and control the family resources and consume more than their fair share. Men and women control the personal spending of women, who are expected to make sacrifices. Women support their husband's work without pay, e.g. as farm labourers, secretaries and hostesses. They provide unpaid health care for children, men, the old and the disabled. Women are pushed into marriage by economic and ideological pressures. Divorce is no escape, since the responsibility for home and children remains.

Oakley

Housework is seen by many as an exclusively feminine activity, regardless of time or class. It is a woman's main responsibility, and women are mainly involved in undertaking it. Oakley's 40 subjects described their housework in the language of the alienated assembly line worker. They saw it as monotonous and fragmented and lacking in pay, pension, sick-pay or holidays. It is not contractual nor is it observed by adults. Labour-saving devices fail in practice to free women from domestic labour, as standards and expectations rise. Average hours rose from 70, in 1950, to 77 in 1971. The fact that housework is not seen as real work is both the cause and effect of women's low status. The beneficiaries of domestic labour are men, and those employers who have a fit and suitably motivated workforce.

In 1987 Oakley looked again at family life and concluded that the family itself was not the cause of women's problems, but rather a symptom of those problems and a location in which those problems were expressed. The male-female relationship was based on family life and on the class relations of domestic production located in the home. The dual causes of the problems were gender oppression by men and class oppression in a capitalist society. 'The main function of marriage is to keep men and women apart.' This is achieved through women's responsibility for housework and childcare, and paid employment for both men and women outside the home. The family is the *location* for differential gender role socialisation.

Boulton

Boulton noted that men thought that the division of domestic labour had become more equal and should become even more equal. However empirical research contradicted these views. Only 9 of 50 subjects helped 'extensively' in the home. Men enjoyed and participated in childcare but not that which involved the routine messy stuff. It also seemed as if men were only advocating an equal division of labour after office hours.

WOMEN AT WORK

Structuralist views

Structuralist arguments see women's disadvantaged position in the labour market as not resulting from individual cases of discrimination, but as being embedded in socially structured inequality.

BARRON and NORRIS applied the dual labour market theory to women in the UK. They explained how women, like other disadvantaged groups, can be largely excluded from the *primary sector* of the labour market.

BRAVERMAN in the USA and BLAND in Britain applied the Marxist concept of a *reserve army of labour* to women. CARCHEDI, an Italian Marxist, argued that the feminisation of office work was a significant factor in the proletarianisation of white collar work. Feminisation can be seen as both cause and effect of the low pay and status of a job.

Home and family life

This is seen as a major handicap for women in the labour market by many feminist writers. These arguments are not necessarily alternatives to those above, but could be contributory to women's exclusion from good (or indeed any) work.

OAKLEY has described how the primacy of the housewife-mother role impinges on all other aspects of women's lives. Paid work may be the extension of this housewife-mother role. Apart from caring and cleaning, BENNET has added secretarial work, which is described as the business equivalent of housework.

LAND has shown how the inadequacy of proper childcare facilities limits women's choices of work. The projected labour shortage of the 1990s is likely to encourage the expansion of day care for children. In earlier work, she has shown the crucial role women played in maintaining poor families and in keeping families above the poverty line, thus exposing the myth that women worked for 'pin money'.

KLEIN has produced a study on the causes and effects of more married women working in Britain. HUWS has developed previous studies on homeworkers to include those using new technology. The same experience of alienation was noted.

Education and the labour market

The links between education and the labour market are discussed in Chapter 9 on Education. SHARPE, and more recently GRIFFIN, have shown how schooling lowers girls ambitions.

Other occupations

Finally it may be worth considering those women's occupations which are not usually considered to be real work. These include housework, care for the disabled and dependants at home, prostitution and other forms of crime.

GENDER, SEX AND SEXUALITY

MORGAN suggested the following possible relationships between sex and gender:

1 Sex determines gender. Biological differences explain behaviour and the social meaning we give to it.
2 Sex sets rigid limits within which minor cultural variations might exist.
3 Sex has a minimal influence, but culture produces a wide variety of gender behaviour and meanings attached to it.

We could, for example, assess the relative importance of gender, race, age and class in different cultures.

Biological determinism

Biological determinism is rejected by sociologists but is supported by other disciplines.

TIGER and FOX argue that natural selection has encouraged hormonal differences which can explain gender differences in instincts, emotions and behaviour. They claim 'nature intended mother and child to be together.'

WILSON advocated the development of socio-biology where contemporary behaviour is explained by reference to primitive animal instincts. He cites aggression, maternal instincts and male dominance as examples. This approach is echoed by the zoologist, Desmond Morris, who has popularised the reduction of social behaviour to simple animal behaviour.

BOWLBY wrote a *psychological* account of the ill effects of maternal deprivation on children. This has subsequently been misused as an ideological argument to keep women at home.

Functionalist views and critics

Functionalist sociologists argue that the alleged universality of gender roles is explained in terms of their *usefulness*, rather than biology. The sexual division of labour is seen as functional for both individuals and society.

MURDOCK emphasises the importance of motherhood and claims the mother role and the family are universal.

PARSONS emphasises the importance of the functions of the family, particularly as regards the stabilisation of the adult personality and socialisation of children. The expressive female role is compared with the instrumental male role, and they are seen as complementary.

The view that gender is largely socially defined is supported by evidence of cultural and historical variation. Therefore comparative and historical studies are important.

MEAD was able to identify considerable variation in sex and gender roles in simple societies, including the reversal of traditional roles and the virtual absence of role differentiation.

OAKLEY, using Murdock's secondary data, refuted his claim that gender roles were universal. The kibbutz was cited as an example of successful child rearing outside the family. She accepted that sexuality, reproduction and maternal care are influenced by biology, but reminded us of their cultural variations. Norms of sexual behaviour vary (even the incest taboo) and fertility and pregnancy have been medicalised and are socially controlled.

Sexuality

ROWBOTHAM gives a Marxist-feminist history of sexuality. Sexuality is part of the *superstructure* which is produced by the economic *substructure* and helps to maintain it. In the 17th century, women were seen as sexually insatiable and thus threatening. In the 19th century, early capitalism saw a distinction between the brutish sexuality of working class life and the pure non-sexual bourgeois ideal of women. The sexual liberation of the 20th century has seen sex used to sell goods and as a commodity itself. This history is a description of norms rather than of actual behaviour.

DE BEAUVOIR and later MCROBBIE condemn romantic love as a myth to enslave women.

MCINTOSH notes the acceptance of the male need to casual sex and compares it with the surprise expressed that women can be prostitutes.

MILLET sees prostitution as an extreme model of all male-female relations.

SMART notes that women are seen as victims and potential victims of sex-crimes and that this controls their movements. Women, and their male 'protectors', ensure that they take precautions against rape. In other cultures women may be seen as sexual aggressors and men also take precautions to avoid sexual attack. (Men in prison avoid homosexual rape.)

MCROBBIE sees the development of a feminine youth culture based at home, rather than on the streets, as a result of this confinement. Though in later work she sees shopping for clothes as part of a feminine youth culture.

GILLESPIE writes about women shouting sexual insults at men in West African cities where single women have been freed from their subordinate position in extended families.

LEES has described how sexual insults from boys and girls about girls, controls girls behaviour. Girls can deny they are sexually available and reject labels such as slag, slut, slapper, dog, bitch, cow, etc. They do not however reject the right of boys and other girls to judge their reputations. Escape from this language comes with a regular boyfriend or separation from boys. The latter course makes girls vulnerable to other insults, such as 'tight bitch' and frigid. The effects of this social control can be seen in a girl's behaviour, clothes, friendships with boys and girls, and social life.

EXAMINATION QUESTIONS

1   'The issue of housework is of major interest to feminists, especially its historical development and functions for society.' Explain and discuss.

(AEB 1987)

2   Evaluate TWO different sociological explanations for the continued existence of gender inequality.

(ULSEB 1989)

3   Why do women take different jobs from men?   (Oxford 1988)

4   In what ways does women's paid employment affect domestic labour and power relationships within the family?   (AEB 1988)

5   'Certain biological drives may be innate but gender roles and the ways in which men and women express their sexuality are socially constructed and socially controlled.' Discuss.

(AEB 1986)

OUTLINE ANSWERS TO SELECTED QUESTIONS

Question 3

Competing explanations of not just differences, but also inequalities, in the labour market must be evaluated. Evaluation involves positive as well as negative criticism. You might question the notion of choice suggested by the use of the word 'take' in the question.

a)   ■ Feminists discuss the effects of patriarchy on occupational choice and employment patterns.

■ The predominance of the housewife-mother role disadvantages women in the paid labour market.

■ Housework itself can be seen as a woman's job.

■ Sexism in the family, school, media and workplace can be discussed.

b)   Marxists focus on the reproduction of labour power by the family. They see women as part of a reserve army of labour.

c)   The dual-labour market theory offers a critical alternative to Marxist and feminist views.

d)   Functionalist writers concentrate on difference rather than inequality, but do not really focus on paid labour. They do, however, offer an alternative view on socialisation to the previous accounts.

Question 4

This question links gender difference and inequality in the labour market with the sociology of the family. The domestic division of labour and power is discussed in the family chapter. You should examine the effect of the type and levels of women's employment on family roles. Discuss both the division of labour (housework) and power (decisions, violence etc.).

a) Functionalists see family roles as complementary and functional and do not often address the question. GOODE, however, does discuss the influence of women's paid employment on role-bargaining within the family.

b) Marxists see the family as part of the superstructure of capitalist society. The existing relations of production influence the domestic division of labour and power. Early Marxist writing suggested that paid employment would lead to more gender equality and encourage class consciousness in women.

c) Feminists are more concerned with reversing the argument and with looking at the effect of the domestic role on the workplace. Paid employment does not necessarily change domestic responsibility, even in dual-career families. Neither does male unemployment.

d) Discussion of the roles of grandparents and children, distinguishing boys and girls, will be rewarded. For instance, Griffin saw paid work as freeing daughters of school-leaving-age from housework.

Question 5

This is a variation on more straightforward 'nature versus culture' questions as sexuality is specifically mentioned. You must also consider the social control of girls and women.

a) The biological determinist case comes from disciplines outside sociology.

b) The functionalist explanations tend to take some gender differences, like maternal care, for granted. Others are seen as complementary and functional rather than as exploitative. Social control is, of course, easily explicable in functionalist terms.

c) Comparative studies contradict the idea of innate differences. MEAD, and later OAKLEY, used cross-cultural material to demonstrate the social construction of gender roles and sexuality. ROWBOTHAM gives a historical account of changes in the norms of women's sexuality.

d) The social control of sexuality is examined in studies of rape (The Smarts), feminine youth culture (McRobbie), and language (Lees). You can refer to the sociology of deviance and note how male sex crime controls women and how sexual misdemeanours lead to girls and women receiving custodial sentences.

e) References to masculine roles and sexuality, including homosexuality, are asked for and will be rewarded.

TUTOR'S ANSWER

Question 2

Evaluate TWO different sociological explanations for the continued existence of gender inequality.

- The explanations should be sociological, not biological, psychological, or common-sense.

- The evaluation should include both positive and negative criticism. Functionalism which deals with differences rather than inequality should not be chosen.

- Marxism and feminism can be compared and contrasted with some subtlety.

Marxist explanations of gender inequality developed from the work of Engels on the family. He traces the historical development of gender inequality as the mode of production changes. Both the ideology and the institutions which support gender inequality are seen as part of the superstructure reproducing the existing relations of production. Modern Marxist explanations focus on capitalism itself (and not on a patriarchal society) as the source of inequality. This inequality will be resolved by a communist revolution rather than by the separate liberation of women.

Women, apart from those in the ruling class, have always worked, although the rewards and recognition gained are frequently less than for men. Following the early capitalist period when women and children did work in factories, there has been a long period of partial exclusion from paid labour. Women have become part of a reserve army of labour; available for work if required, but not seen as entitled to employment. This reserve army of labour depresses wages and disciplines the workforce, whilst ensuring that labour is available for expansion. Braverman sees women as sharing this disadvantage with others, such as the migrant workers described by Castles and Kosack. It is sexist ideology and social norms which confine women to the home; this view is shared by the feminist writers below. Carchedi observes that the feminisation of occupations such as office work can depress pay and encourage proletarianisation.

The Marxist view of women's domestic role is their part in the reproduction of labour power. This involves both physical and ideological reproduction. Children are reared and subordinated at no cost to employers, and men are returned daily to the workplace, refreshed by their wife's attention and motivated to work to support their dependants. Feminist accounts observe similar processes except, as Ansley notes, that men may take out the frustration of alienating work by ill-treating wives and children.

Parsons, from a functionalist viewpoint, approves of the soothing and supportive role played by wives. More generally, Marxist accounts have been criticised by feminists for disregarding the special disadvantages experienced by women as compared with other groups within the working class. As with some ethnic minorities, the social meaning given to biological differences prevents social mobility. The major disadvantage for women is the pre-eminence of their housewife-mother role. This both commits her to unpaid domestic labour and inhibits her opportunities in the paid labour market.

Studies of women in communist society by Lane and others, suggest that although women have more success in the job market, they remain disadvantaged compared with men. Class exploitation appears not to completely explain gender inequality. However, the Marxist view does allow us to recognise the privileged position of women in the Bourgeoisie and suggests that class inequality is more significant than gender.

This last point is, of course, rejected by feminists. Here patriarchy, not capitalism, is the primary cause of inequality. Oakley and Delphy have borrowed Marxist concepts, like exploitation, subordination and false consciousness, to explain male dominance rather than Bourgeois control.

Sexism and the social construction of sexuality are seen as contributing to the social control of women. Fear of rape and abusive language are seen by Smart and Lees respectively as controlling the movement and behaviour of women.

Critics of the feminist view come from orthodox Marxists. They feel that the gender divisions within societies lack the significance of class inequality, but do contribute to a false consciousness and to the division of the working class.

Weberians, like Parkin, see feminists as underestimating the significance of the husband's occupations on women's lives.

Functionalists concentrate on gender difference rather than inequality. The close relationship between Marxist and feminist approaches must be acknowledged. Modern feminism is largely borrowed from Engels and modern Marxists have been influenced by the contribution of feminism, particularly in analysing the family. Rowbotham sees patriarchy and capitalism as inseparable.

STUDENT ANSWER WITH EXAMINER COMMENTS

Question 1

'The issue of housework is of major interest to feminists especially its historical development and functions for society.' Explain and discuss.

> Housework can be described as labour within a household for the maintenance of its occupants and upkeep of the home and would include such tasks as cleaning, cooking and child care. It is seen very much as a female activity and Oakley estimates that 76% of employed women and 93% of non-employed women are responsible for the housework in their families. These high percentages are not surprising in view of the prevelant assumption in society that housework is women's work. It can be argued that because women do bear a greater load in the division of labour within the home this has a detrimental effect of their status in society notably within the labour market.
>
> Historically, women have played an important part in production

and although the advent of industrialisation did mean that some women were excluded from production, when the home and work place became separated and they became primarily housewives, this was certainly not always the case. Women and indeed children worked alongside men in the mines and factories in the early stages of industrialisation. As Harris argued, industrialisation did not immediately lead to a differentiation of domestic and factory labour based on gender. As technology increased there was less need for labour and partly as a result of this and partly from changing values both women and children were excluded from the work place in many fields. In the early twentieth century it was even a measure of wealth if the wife could stay at home while her husband supported her.

Functionalists such as Talcott Parsons would argue that the family has become a more specialised institution and these developments are a good thing because they enable the family to perform its central responsibilities such as maintenance of members more efficiently. Functionalists tend to see women as a gender group playing an expressive role within the family. Feminists would criticise this approach arguing that functionalists do not discuss how the roles women play can adversely effect them.

Ansley, a Marxist-feminist, suggested in her study that the housewife-mother acts as a buffer between the capitalist system and her exploited husband-worker. So the husband takes on a dominant role and his wife a submissive role where she has to cook and clean for her husband who takes out his frustrations of being exploited on his wife. Evidence in support of this view can be seen in the Dobash and Dobash study that found one of the three main reasons for wife beating is the husbands dissatisfaction with the housework. Housework is then, a means of control, that enables men to be dominant.

It would seem that research conducted by Willmott and Young on the symmetrical family would be evidence against the unequal division of labour. However, they used a very loose criteria for male participation in domestic tasks and the very fact that men are seen as 'helping their wives' shows where the responsibility for housework lies in the end in the eyes of the researchers.

Rapaport and Rapaport in 'Dual career families re-examined' noted that husbands were only tolerant of their wives careers as long as they did not interfere with their own needs. This again emphasises what society, and especially men, see as being primarily important in the role women play. Oakley states that as long as work is seen as being only paid labour then housework will be dismissed as being merely part of the feminine role. This will maintain the low status of women in society.

Marxist-feminists would argue that the low perception of women and maintenance of ideologies which place women in the home make women suitable for the reserve army of labour needed by the capitalist system. So a woman can adopt the role of a housewife if she is not needed in the labour market.

Women are also functional for society in that they provide unpaid care for the young, sick and elderly and in their role being supportive of their husbands. Delphy showed they also act as unpaid secretaries and hostesses. From a series of studies conducted during the 1960s and 1970s in the USA Hartman concluded that the average working wife will have a combined domestic and paid labour total that will be much higher than her husbands. This trend will persist as long as wives and mothers are subject to ideology from sources such as the media which promotes the idea of

---

Margin annotations:

"Description not necessary. Last sentence successfully shows effects of housework on areas outside family."

"Reasonable history; 'changing values' could be seen as ideology."

"Needs tying into question; insert 'see housework as a family role rather than domestic labour.'"

"Relevant studies."

"Better linked to functionalist studies, para.3."

"O.K."

"Good. Deals with outside family again."

"Functional for whom?"

"Total hours, not pay, I presume."

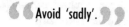

Avoid 'sadly'.

good housewives. Although women have made some progress into traditionally male spheres of employment this has sadly not been matched by equal sharing of domestic labour by men.

Overall comments

Overall a sound answer, worth a C grade. For an A or B grade response, theoretical issues need to be further developed. For example, Delphy's view that men appropriate women's labour could be compared with Ansley's view that the wives help in the exploitation of workers by the ruling class by keeping their husbands quiet. Good selection of studies and a relevant answer.

6

POWER AND POLITICS

VOTING BEHAVIOUR

THEORIES OF POWER

THEORETICAL AND EMPIRICAL STUDIES

GETTING STARTED

Politics is about power relationships of all kinds, from the family to international relations. In this chapter we concentrate on the macro level of the whole society, which generally coincides with the nation state. The issue of power is also discussed in **particular contexts** in the chapters on *The family, Work, Organisations, Deviance* and *Development*. The major debates in this chapter tend to be about the competing claims of consensus and conflict perspectives to explain power relationships, political institutions, political attitudes and political behaviour.

The main themes of questions on this topic are:

1 **Evaluating sociological theories of the nature and distribution of power.**
2 **Evaluating sociological theories of the role of the state.**
3 **Examining the arguments about the existence of a ruling class.**
4 **Examining explanations of voting behaviour and other forms of political behaviour.**

DEFINITIONS

- *Power* is the ability to achieve your will against the will of others.
- *Authority* is legitimate power.
- *Ideology* is a set of ideas, based on values, which serve particular interests.
- *Hegemony* is domination based on the consent of those who accept the ideology of the powerful.
- *The ruling class* is a Marxist term describing those who have political power because they own the means of production.
- *Elites* are groups whose power or influence is based on factors other than ownership. The concept, though generally found in conflict theories, is used to criticise Marxists.
- *Parties* are organisations which seek to govern in order to achieve their common aims.
- *Pressure groups* are organisations which seek to influence government decisions, but not to actually govern.

Related topics include *stratification* and the *mass media*, as well as the topics mentioned above.

VOTING BEHAVIOUR

ESSENTIAL PRINCIPLES

Class and voting

The key issue in the study of voting behaviour has remained the relationship between class and party allegiance. The traditional assumption about British voting being that the middle classes voted Conservative and the working classes voted Labour. Sociological concern focussed on the so-called 'deviant' voters who were seen as explaining Conservative electoral success, despite there being a majority of working class people in the country. In fact as changes in the occupational structure have led to a decline in the number of manual workers, the left has become rather more successful. This is illustrated by Britain in the 1960s and 1970s, Germany in the 1970s, and France in the 1980s. Despite the Conservative parties success in winning elections in Britain it has actually lost votes, while the number of office workers has increased.

However, the link between class and voting has become so tenuous that the concept of deviant voting is no longer useful, and the debate has now broadened to consider a variety of explanations of voting behaviour. The failure of the Labour party in the last three elections and concern for its future prospects have led to new analyses, and to the revival of old theories such as embourgeoisement.

The new explanations of voting behaviour which still see class as significant point out that:

a) Changes in the occupational structure have led to the shrinking of the traditional working class.
b) The fragmentation of the working and middle classes has led to new groups developing within these classes.
c) All classes have become increasingly affluent.

Other correlates

The dissolving of class loyalties, particularly since 1974, has led some writers to suggest that the other divisions in society have become more significant in predicting voting. Some of these divisions are still more apparent in other societies. They include:

a) Cultural divisions such as nationality, language, religion, language and ethnicity; e.g. Scottish and Welsh nationalism.
b) Geographical divisions based on region or housing in urban, sub-urban or rural areas; e.g. the North-South divide in England.
c) Generation and gender.

Issues

Class de-alignment and partisan de-alignment have led some sociologists to adopt a more 'social action' based approach to voting. Instead of seeking structural correlates which are seen as causes of behaviour, they emphasise individual reasons for choice of party. The voter is now seen as a more-or-less rational consumer who considers political issues in terms of individual costs and benefits. This suggests a continued volatility in voting behaviour and in electoral outcomes.

Marxist views

There are three main explanations here of the demise of the Labour party. Firstly, the working class is fragmented by changes in production, such as the decline of manufacturing. Secondly, there are non-class divisions emerging based on gender, ethnicity, region, education, and consumption. Thirdly ideological control has been extended, so that the political agenda is set to the disadvantage of the Labour party.

THEORIES OF POWER

The three major theories of power are:

- The Pluralist model.
- The Elitist model.
- The Marxist model.

As well as the debates **between** these theories there are differences of opinion **within** each model. The three models can provide a framework for answering questions on the nature and distribution of power, the role of the state and the existence of a ruling class. More detailed discussions about political organisations, such as parties and pressure groups, can also be seen as part of the discussion of pluralism.

THE PLURALIST MODEL

Pluralism is a consensus theory which analyses the nature and distribution of power in liberal democracies and generally approves of what it finds.

Classical pluralism

This sees power as diffuse, rather than concentrated. Power is dispersed between a variety of interest groups who compete for influence over the government. No single group dominates and the balance between groups is maintained by the government, which is seen as a neutral arbiter of competing claims. The political system which processes the various decisions is seen as legitimate, as are the decisions which are made through it. Interest groups may object to specific decisions, but they accept the rules under which they were made.

Elite pluralism

This has emerged as the result of criticism of the traditional model. The absence of effective interest groups representing the weaker citizens is compensated for by the protection they are given by governments keen to gain their votes.

The restricted access of individuals and groups to the decision-making process is identified as a problem but one minimised by the diversity of policy-making communities, competition between the influential and the independence of government from any single group interest.

Criticism is found in the alternative models below. The failure of pluralism to deal with the issues of agenda setting and ideological legitimation has been pointed out by conflict theories. The pluralist model seems more appropriate to the USA, which has weak political institutions constrained by checks and balances, than to the UK, which has strong party government.

THE ELITIST MODEL

Classical elite theory

This developed as a critical response to Marx. It questioned both his explanation of the concentration of power and his optimism about a post-revolutionary society which would be free of an oppressive state. (See also the Tutor's Answer to Question 1 below.)

The power elite

This was a description of the domination of the weak system of government in the USA by three distinct, but interrelated, elites. Mills was influenced by Marx and Weber rather than by classical elite theory in his criticism of the pluralist analysis of post-war USA. His work lacks the pessimism of theories which see elite rule as inevitable.

Fragmented elitism

This, as with elite pluralism above, has emerged as a compromise to criticism. Elites are fragmented in that they lack some of the characteristics previously thought essential to establish the existence of elite rule. Membership may be closed to the masses, and power exercised in the interests of elites, but they lack the cohesion of a pure elite. Instead, different elite groups form temporary coalitions to achieve particular aims.

Criticism comes in a theoretical form from Marxists, who see the state only as an instrument of power and not as the source of power. Pluralists offer more empirical criticism, showing how decisions are not always made by the few in their own interests.

THE MARXIST MODEL

Marx saw the state as part of the superstructure of exploitative societies. The power of the ruling class derived from ownership, and the role of the state was to maintain the existing relations of production.

The modern Marxists are concerned with three main issues. Firstly, with the autonomy of the state from the ruling class. Secondly, with the increasing importance of the state in maintaining ideological control over the masses. Thirdly, with whether modern capitalism inevitably produces a liberal democratic system.

Criticism has not been confined to the internal Marxist debates but also comes from a variety of external sources. The underlying theory of class has been challenged by Weber and modern Weberians. Pluralists have presented evidence of decisions being both influenced by, and made in, the interests of the working class. Elite theorists have pointed to the continued concentration of power in socialist states. (See also the Tutor's Answer to Question 1 below.)

CLASS AND VOTING

ROSE(1968) argued that there was not an homogenous working class. The more an individual conformed to an 'ideal type' as defined by five characteristics (manual worker, trade union member, tenant, minimum education, and self-assigned working class), the more likely they were to vote Labour.

> Note dates and relate them to election results.

GOLDTHORPE (1978) makes a similar observation about divisions in the British middle class.

GOLDTHORPE ET AL (1969) rejected the Embourgeoisement thesis as an explanation of Conservative electoral success in the 1950s. There has, however, been a revival of interest in the effects of affluence on voting in the 1980s.

PARKIN (1971) predicted a decline in working class support for the Labour party as the isolation of traditional working class communities from the 'dominant value system' diminished. He rejected the view that working class Conservatives should ever have been considered as 'deviant voters' as the prevailing social values were conservative. The real deviants were middle class radicals.

BUTLER and KAVANAGH(1982) noted how the correlation between class and voting, which had been the conventional wisdom since Butler and Stokes' analysis of elections up to 1966, was rapidly breaking down. This was shown by both the working and middle classes abandoning their traditional patterns of support.

ROSE and MCCALLISTER (1983) showed the declining correlation between parents' and children's voting, suggesting that socialisation within the family no longer produced party loyalty.

CURTICE (1987) re-considered Abrams' 1960 question 'Must Labour lose?' He re-examined the possibility of embourgeoisement contributing to three successive defeats for Labour. The affluence of the 1980s was manifested through increased home-ownership and the popularity of the Privatisation share issues. However he cites Heath *et al* (1985) who argued that buyers of council houses, though much more likely to vote Conservative than tenants, were **not** more likely to have switched their vote from Labour to Conservative between 1979 and 1983. Curtice concludes that the working class is shrinking (from one half to one third of the electorate between 1964 and 1983 according to the Goldthorpe scale), so that even if Labour had retained its popularity within the working class they would still have been defeated. However, the Conservative vote is also shrinking, and the future now depends on voters' calculations of personal gain. He also sees the polarisation between North and South operating to the detriment of the Labour party.

POLITICAL ISSUES AND VOTING

HIMMELWEIT (1981) identified individual attitudes (which may or may not be influenced by class, education or family) as the main explanation for voting. The voter is seen as a consumer of the parties policies and promises. This will account for the volatility of voting and suggests an increased importance for the marketing of policies. WHITELY reinforces this view of the well-informed, rational choice replacing loyalty and prejudice.

SARLVIK AND CREWE (1983) introduced the concepts of *class de-alignment* (referring to the severing of links between class and voting) and *partisan de-alignment* (referring to the decline of loyalty to the two main parties in terms of membership, support of policy and voting). They claimed that tossing a coin was as good a predictor of voting as class. The best predictor had become the voters opinion on issues. The success of the Alliance parties (in gaining votes not seats) was seen as continuing a trend towards the support for minor parties.

CREWE (1987) remarked that issue voting had been less significant than the individual's optimism about the economic future. The Labour party was perceived as more competent to deal with three of the four most salient issues.

See *Mass Media* chapter.

DUNLEAVY AND HUSBANDS (1985) adopt a more structural approach to the political attitudes of voters. They echo the work of Parkin in seeing the media as setting political agendas and identifying issues. They also see increased divisions between those who are involved as both consumer or worker in the *public sector* and those who are primarily involved in the *private sector*. This division, rather than class itself, is seen as influencing political attitudes and behaviour.

STUDIES OF POWER

WEBER defined 'power' as the ability to achieve your will against the will of others. 'Authority' was power accepted as being legitimate. He identified three sources of legitimacy, and thus three ideal types of authority.

a) *Charismatic authority*, which rested on affection and personal devotion to the leader, and not to his position.
b) *Traditional authority*, which rested on habit and the acceptance of the social order.
c) *Rational-legal authority*, which depends on the idea that laws can be enacted and changed by an accepted procedure. Obedience is not to individuals, but to bureaucratic rules.

PARSONS introduced a new concept of power which is based on functionalist theory and is less popular among pluralists than Dahl's version of Weber's ideas. Power is derived from the authority given to leaders by subjects to achieve consensual goals. There is thus a variable, not a fixed, sum of power and, like money, more can be created. The functions of the political system include goal attainment as well as integration and social control.

PARSONS provides a functionalist approach to power which is distinct from most pluralist approaches.

GIDDENS criticised Parsons on the following grounds:

a) Power is used to oppress and to exploit and gives access to scarce resources. Thus it does not appear to be an unlimited resource applied to consensual goal attainment.
b) Parsons assumes, but does not demonstrate, the existence of consensual goals. Apparently consensual goals may be imposed by the ideology of the powerful.
c) Unlike Weber, Parsons does not consider the sources of legitimacy.
d) If power is exercised covertly, it cannot depend on the authority granted by the ruled.

DAHL supported the pluralist case by showing how decisions were not made by an unrepresentative minority in New Haven. He also provided a test for the existence of a ruling elite which involved satisfying the following conditions:

a) They must be a cohesive group.
b) Their aims must be against the interests of the majority.
c) Their preferences must prevail.

BACHRACH and BARATZ criticised Dahl for only considering the first face of power, i.e. decision-making, but not the second face which is agenda-setting (or deciding what the issues that need decisions will be).

LUKES adds a third face, which considers who benefits from the exercise of power. Like the Marxists, this view assumes that objective class interests can be identified, even if the group concerned does not recognise them.

MILIBAND wrote a Marxist analysis of the role of the British State. He sees it as the instrument of the ruling class. This relationship is demonstrated by:

a) recruitment being restricted to the ruling class, or to able and indoctrinated outsiders.
b) the ruling class having the resources to win in an allegedly pluralist society.
c) the state supporting capitalism to ensure its survival. Economic growth is equated with the national interest. The state relies on the ruling class to generate revenue.

POULANTZAS offers a structuralist theory of the state similar to that of Althusser. He also points out the increased autonomy of the state from the ruling class, as compared, say, with feudal society. This relative autonomy serves the interests of the whole ruling class by arbitrating between sectional interests and by granting concessions to the working class to maintain ruling class hegemony.

EXAMINATION QUESTIONS

1   Compare and contrast elite and Marxist theories of the nature and distribution of political power.

(AEB 1987)

2   Critically examine the evidence for the assertion that Britain has a ruling class.

(AEB 1986)

3   Compare and contrast pluralist and Marxist explanations of the role of the state in industrial society.

(AEB 1988)

4   Examine sociological explanations of the successes of the Conservative party in the General Elections since 1975.

(AEB 1989)

5   Do the social and political trends of the last ten years (i.e. 1979 to 1988) suggest that the embourgeoisement thesis was rejected prematurely?

(Oxford 1988)

OUTLINE ANSWERS TO SELECTED QUESTIONS

Question 3

This question requires a consideration of both similarities and differences, although the emphasis is likely to be on contrasts.

Diversity **within** each approach should be emphasised, e.g. the distinction between pluralism and elite pluralism and the debate between instrumental and structuralist theories of the state. The theories of the state should be discussed within the broader context of theories of power.

If you wish to deal with the theories in sequence, rather than to make a point-by-point comparison, then the similarities and differences must be made explicit. The straightforward juxtaposition of alternatives without bringing out comparisons would probably produce no better than a D grade answer.

Points of comparison could include:

- Consensus or conflict theory.
- The nature and distribution of power.
- How power is exercised; by consensual goals or class interests.
- The state as a neutral arbiter (pluralism), as an instrument of class domination (Miliband), or as an arbiter between sectional ruling class interests (Poulantzas).
- The relationship between power and authority. Both theories rely on 'consent' but Marxists see this as false consciousness. Discuss hegemony, ideology and ISAs.
- How are political leaders changed and does it make any difference if the class relationships remain intact?

- Both see an expanding role for the state. Although some contemporary Marxists see the superficial withdrawal from areas of possible failure (health, welfare and education as well as privatisation) as an attempt to avoid a 'legitimation crisis'.

Question 4

> Refer to the last three elections. Consideration of earlier results must be linked to the question.

'Successes' could be regarded as problematic. Electoral victories have been accompanied by declining support in terms of membership, loyalty, support for policies and votes.

Interactionists and others identify theoretical and methodological problems in assuming that correlations between voting and other characteristics indicate a *causal* relationship.

A good answer will attempt an *evaluation* of some of the following explanations.

- Class and partisan de-alignment. Particularly the decline in working class support for Labour. The regional divide.
- Changes in the class structure. Embourgeoisement. The shrinking of the working class. The fragmentation of the working class.
- The consumer choice model. (Industrial relations and unemployment in 1979, the Falklands and defence in 1983, but not confirmed by the salient issues of 1987 which indicated success for Labour).
- Economic optimism.
- The ideological explanations (Dunleavy, Parkin and Marxists).
- The rise of third parties and the effects of the electoral system.

Question 5

This is a 'hybrid' question which requires a consideration of class issues as well as political developments. It does emphasise how essential a good understanding of changes in the class structure is to answering voting questions.

- Outline the embourgeoisement thesis in its original 1950s version.
- Outline the refutation by Goldthorpe *et al*.
- Present evidence for embourgeoisement over the last ten years.
  a) Rising real income and consumer boom.
  b) Increasing home and share ownership.
  c) Decline in Union support and influence.
  d) Decline of Labour party support from the working class.
  e) Increased similarity in working conditions and job security for manual and office workers.
  f) Changes in the occupational structure.
  g) Conservative electoral victories.
- Present evidence against embourgeoisement.
  a) The persistence of poverty.
  b) The new 'instrumental' working class as described by Goldthorpe in the earlier study.
  c) The fragmented working class as described by Roberts who saw only a small fraction embourgeoised.
  d) Proletarianisation of office work.
  e) The family does not conform to the middle class ideal described in the 'symmetrical family.'
  f) Alternative explanations of Conservative victories.

TUTOR'S ANSWER

Question 1

Compare and contrast elite and Marxist theories of the nature and distribution of political power.

There are both similarities and differences between Marxist and elite theories. Within each group of theories there is also some variation, as well as many common assumptions.

Both theories adopt a conflict perspective and have a 'constant-sum' view of power. That is, power is seen as being held by one group at the expense of others. This view is also shared by some pluralist writers such as Dahl, but he sees power as being dispersed through a variety of groups and not concentrated in the hands of a minority. Parsons, writing from a functionalist perspective, had a 'variable-sum' view of power. He saw power as being created from the authority which subjects give leaders to achieve consensual goals.

Classical elite theories follow Weber in concentrating on the so-called 'first face' of power. This is the ability to succesfully influence decision-making. Later, as a response to criticism from pluralists, Bachrach and Baratz suggested that consideration be given to a 'second face' of power, where agenda-setting is seen as important in deciding what the political issues will be and which alternatives will be considered.

Lukes identified a 'third face', which is seen as crucial in modern Marxist theory. This emphasises the importance of ideology in legitimising the power of the ruling class. Their interests begin to be seen as the national interest. This Marxist view, namely that gaining the consent of the masses is an important aspect of power, has been developed in the work of Gramsci who introduced the concept of hegemony, where domination is based on the consent of those who accept the ideology of the powerful. Althusser describes the institutions which impose this ideology as ISAs, e.g. the media and the education system. Of course this apparent 'consent' is false consciousness.

In elite theories the concept of legitimation through 'consent' is found in Pareto's distinction between 'lions' who use force and 'foxes' who use guile to rule with the acquiescence of the subjects.

Both Marxist and elite theories see power as being concentrated in the hands of a minority. For Marxists this is the ruling class, whose source of power is ownership of the means of production. Marxist revisionists, like Djilas and Burnham, see *control* over production as the basis of new ruling classes in Eastern Europe and the USA respectively.

Elite theories, some of which developed as criticisms of Marx, identify a variety of sources of power for the ruling elite. Pareto saw the psychological characteristics of individuals as important, whereas Mosca placed greater stress on structural factors, including control over organisation. This emphasis on organisation is also found in Michels' *Iron law of Oligarchy*.

Mills is more accepting of the Marxist analysis than those above. His theory of the 'Power Elite' is not a reaction to Marxism, but a critique of post-war American pluralist theories of power. He argued that the USA was a permanent war economy, where a power elite occupied the command positions. This power elite comprised three groups whose relative power depended on external circumstances such as war, depression or prosperity. They were economic, political and military leaders respectively. The power elite were united by shared aims, common background and an exchange of personnel. They acted in concert, unhindered by weak political institutions.

Lindblom is also closer to Marxist views in emphasising the way in which business elites can veto government decisions because their actions shape the performance of the economy and thus strongly influence the government's chance of re-election.

Functionalists see power as being used to achieve consensual goals and view the moral order as the basis of power. However both Marxists and elite theorists agree that power is not used to further common interests. Marxists see political decisions as reinforcing the existing relations of production and regard the moral order as emerging from ruling class ideology.

Both Westergaard and Resler and Lukes, emphasise the importance of looking at **who** benefits from the exercise of power. The distribution of wealth is seen as evidence of the power of the ruling class. Elite theorists also see power as being exercised selfishly to protect political and economic interests. In contrast to Marxists, wealth is seen as the possible result of power and not as its source. This could be illustrated by the illicit fortunes accumulated by dictators such as Marcos and Noriega, and by the recent exposing of corrupt regimes such as in East Germany.

Modern elite theory, influenced by pluralism, sees fragmented elites competing for power and forming temporary coalitions to gain rewards. The restricted access to such groups distinguishes this theory from conventional pluralist theory.

Explanations of the rotation of power and of the emergence of new leaders distinguishes

Marxist and elite theories. Marxists see the political system as part of the superstructure, and thus only changing when there are changes in the mode of production. Pareto saw elites falling when individuals lost 'their vigour'. Mosca is more influenced by Marx, in that he acknowledges the importance of economic change but also sees changes in other social forces leading to changes in political leadership. The effects of political and religious ideology could be mentioned in this respect.

Finally, both types of theory (and their pluralist critics) see the state becoming increasingly centralised, bureaucratic and important. Elite theories see control of the state as the usual basis for a governing elite. Bottomore thinks this is best illustrated by the political systems of Eastern Europe, although the ability of such elites to maintain power is currently in question.

There are, however, divisions within modern Marxism as to the role of the state. Miliband saw the state as the instrument of the ruling class, making decisions in their favour. Poulantzas has a more structuralist view, emphasising ideological domination. He also argues that the state has become relatively autonomous and that this best serves the general interests of the ruling class. Such a state appears more legitimate to the working class and will grant them the necessary concessions to prevent a legitimation crisis.

STUDENT ANSWER WITH EXAMINER COMMENTS

Question 2

Critically examine the evidence for the assertion that Britain has a ruling class.

> Whether there is a ruling class in Britain is debatable. Marx argues power is held by a particular group in society, the owners of the means of production, at the expense of the rest. The dominant group furthers its interests which are in conflict with the interests of the subject class. If the subject group accept ruling class power as legitimate this indicates they are falsely conscious. Power is used to maintain the existing relations of production.
>
> Westergaard and Resler argue that power can only be measured by its results. They show wealth is concentrated in the hands of about 5% of the population who form the capitalist class. This group monopolises power and is a ruling class.
>
> Marxists argue that privilege and status are gained through inheritance and exclusive education. Those in 'elite' positions are likely to have origins in the upper class. Coates' study of the membership of the 1984 Conservative cabinet showed that 71% were company directors and 14% landowners. Scott's study of undersecretaries and ambassadors showed they came from public schools and 'Oxbridge'. The British ruling class remains a self-recruiting and self-perpetuating stratum with shared political and economic interests. Marxists see these facts as proof that the upper/ruling class actively rule through the state which is the 'executive committee of the Bourgeoisie' and an increasingly important part of the superstructure.
>
> Marx argues that the only way a ruling class will not exist is if a revolution occurs. This has not happened and the gap between the rich and the poor has widened.
>
> Miliband argues that the British state is an instrument of the ruling class and this is demonstrated by restricted recruitment. The wealth of the ruling class ensures they always win. In a supposedly pluralist society the state needs them to generate revenue, even Labour governments.
>
> Poulantzas would argue that, because the ruling class and state are separated, the state is presumed to be an independent, neutral

** Good working definition of a ruling class.**

** Simple supporting evidence.**

** Confuses ruling class with upper class. Good reference to the state.**

** Relevant, but isolated, point.**

** Theories of the state made relevant.**

arbiter so the working class accept its legitimacy. Thus rules are accepted in a way that overt ruling class rule would prevent. There is a debate within Marxism about the independence of the state.

Elite theory is another conflict theory which argues that power in any society is held by an elite minority not a class. Pareto and Mosca used this theory to attack Marxism. Elites owe their position in society to personal qualities of individuals or organisational ability. The elite is a cohesive minority united and organised in the face of the unorganised masses. The utopian view of an egalitarian communist society is seen as an illusion.

C.W.Mills wrote in 1956 that the USA was a permanent war economy dominated by a 'Power Elite' who occupied the command positions in economic, political and military organisations. They act together, with one group sometimes dominating the others. Mills is slightly Marxist in recognising concentration of power as based on other factors as well as economic ones.

Marxists criticise elite theories as failing to identify the source of power in the economy and ignoring the importance of the ruling class by concentrating on their instrument, the state.

Pluralists see power as dispersed, not concentrated, in the hands of a ruling class. Functionalists argue power is a variable sum not constant. Society contains many groups, not just two conflicitng classes. Power is dispersed through elections, shareholders, public ownership, pressure groups, accountability to parliament and the press etc.

Dahl and Hewit claim no one group makes all the important decisions. The government is neutral and balances competing interests. Parsons functionalist view sees power derived from authority not ownership. The distribution of power is based on functional importance of positions. Because power is not a fixed sum you can make more. The more the rulers achieve consensual goals the more power is given to them. Those in power are not at the top because they are a ruling class but because they meet the needs of the system best. Pluralists see this as applicable to any democracy such as Britain. Power is dispersed among a plurality of elites which compete to further their interests.

Critics of pluralism point out that the weak and inarticulate are excluded from the political process. Giddens argues that functionalists assume but do not demonstrate the existence of consensual goals.

"Theoretical criticism of ruling class."

"Theoretical response to criticism."

"Theoretical criticism."

"Brings in evidence but reverts to discussion of power which is not made relevant."

"Theoretical criticism of pluralism not made relevant."

Overall comments

Overall, a well informed and critical account. However the material is not always made explicitly relevant. The candidate needs to bring in rather more empirical evidence about Britain, e.g. using Giddens and Westergaard and Resler.

The answer is worth a C grade, but was potentially a better answer to another question on the nature and distribution of power. The ability to adapt prepared answers to variations on the expected question is important.

DEVELOPMENT, URBANISATION AND COMMUNITY

DEVELOPMENT

COMMUNITY AND URBANISATION

THEORETICAL AND EMPIRICAL STUDIES

GETTING STARTED

This chapter includes a discussion of the concepts of social change, urbanism and community, but is mainly concerned with development. The sociology of development has its roots in the early theories of social change. Its revival into a popular topic at A-level and beyond has been prompted by several influences.

1 Recognition of world economic and political problems has increased. This includes not only concern for the deprived, but also fears about the effects of growth on the environment which would in turn affect the rich.
2 The rejuvenation of the Marxist criticism of capitalism which has been applied on a global scale, and responded to, in the work of Rostow and others.

Examiners give credit for using a comparative appraoch and for applying theories to contemporary examples. This applies to any topic.
  The main themes of questions set on this topic are:

1 **Critical evaluation of theories of development.**
2 **Examining the impact of colonialism.**
3 **Examining the relationship between development and urbanisation.**
4 **Examining different concepts of community and assessing the 'Loss of Community' thesis.**

Definitions

It is important to distinguish the following.

■ The sociology of *development*, which tries to explain why some countries are further up the ladder of progress than others.

■ The sociology of *underdevelopment*, seeks to explain how the development of rich countries is the result of their actively promoting the underdevelopment of other countries, which therefore became (and are kept) poor.

Related topics include health, education, gender and race. Chapter 19 on *Sociological Theories* deals with social change.

ESSENTIAL PRINCIPLES

DEVELOPMENT

Bendix explained development as involving both *economic change* (i.e. industrialisation) and *modernisation* (i.e. cultural and political changes in values and institutions). This view is reminiscent of the Marxist distinction between substructure and superstructure.

Rich and poor countries have been categorised as the First, Second, Third and Fourth world, or as Developed Countries (DCs), Newly Industrialising Countries (NICs) and Underdeveloped Countries (UDCs). Remember that, as in our discussions of the other forms of inequality such as class, gender and race, the writer's political perspective has a major influence on all aspects of their work.

To simplify our consideration of many of the theoretical perspectives on development, we can continue with the idea of a classification based on political values. This amplifies the distinction already made between development and underdevelopment.

The sociology of development

It is assumed that non-developed countries are at a stage prior to (and inferior to) that achieved by industrialised nations. In order to develop they must (either alone or in contact with DCs) acquire the appropriate economic and social institutions and values. Thus aid, trade, investment and cultural diffusion are all potentially beneficial. This approach is exemplified by the work of Parsons and Rostow and is referred to as *modernisation* theory, although Parsons is more accurately a functionalist and Rostow is close to economic determinism.

The sociology of underdevelopment

It is assumed that the underdevelopment of some countries is the direct result of the development of others. The rich became (and stay) rich by exploiting the poor, who are made (and kept) poor by the continued relationship between DCs and UDCs. These theories are more or less Marxist and thus as critical of capitalism as modernisation theories are supportive of it. They tend to suggest revolutionary rather than evolutionary change.

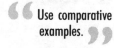
Use comparative examples.

We can identify variations within these broad schools by comparing *internalist* explanations, which focus on the development of a single society, with *global* explanations, which examine the impact of international relations. Again, we can differentiate *determinist* theories, which assume a single and invariable path to development caused by structural changes, from *voluntarist* theories, which see individual decisions as important.

COMMUNITY AND URBANISATION

THE CONCEPT OF COMMUNITY

The concept of community is problematic. The various usages include:

1 Relationships based on locality. Usually a romanticised view of village life.
2 A social system based on a pattern of relationships. This is illustrated by the 'connection' identified by Stacey in her Banbury study.
3 A shared identity which might define an ethnic community.

See *Race and ethnicity* chapter.

The 'loss of community' thesis

This has been **proposed** by those who believe that the feelings associated with a shared identity and a traditional sense of community have been undermined by such social processes as industrialisation, modernisation, urbanisation and bureaucratisation.

The thesis has been **opposed** by:

a) A body of empirical research, which has been able to identify thriving communities, whether in cities, suburbs or among the poor.
b) Marxists, who see the basis of community as being class and the apparent communal ties which cut across class boundaries as merely being false consciousness. Marxist views on racism, religion and nationality illustrate this attitude.

THE URBAN WAY OF LIFE

Urbanisation refers to an increased proportion of a population living in towns and cities. In Western societies, urbanisation has been associated with industrialisation, economic growth and, possibly, imperialism. In Third World countries urbanisation has been associated with independence from colonialism (but perhaps the continuation of neo-colonialism) and population growth, but not so much with industrialisation.

The problems associated with urbanisation in the Third World include:

1 The problem of the rural-urban migrant. This is reminiscent of Wirth's view on the distinctiveness of urban life.
2 Population explosion. However birth rates tend to fall in cities, as compared with rural areas.
3 Degradation of the physical environment, because of the pressures on housing, sanitation, and water supply, and the neglect of social provision, such as education and health care. This is exemplified in studies of 'shanty towns'.
4 Unrest and social disorganisation. This also reminds us of the Chicago schools view of urban life and the functionalist views on social change.

In developed societies, a case has been made for a distinctive urban culture. Wirth claimed the distinctive features of 'urbanism as a way of life' were *size*, *density* and a *heterogeneous* population. These have created a segregation of groups and individuals and helped establish rational, temporary, specialised and superficial relationships.

Critics of the existence of a distinctive urban way of life include:

1 Those who see a rural-urban continuum.
2 Those who do not see the urban-rural distinction as being important. This includes those who have identified inequality and social problems as already existing in rural areas.
3 Those who see industrialisation or capitalism as responsible for shaping social relationships, and not urbanism.

THE EARLY STUDIES OF SOCIAL CHANGE

THEORETICAL AND EMPIRICAL STUDIES

DURKHEIM continued the functionalist tradition of Comte and Spencer, which was later developed by Parsons. His cross-cultural comparative studies led him to distinguish *simple societies*, characterised by *mechanical solidarity*, from *modern societies*, characterised by *organic solidarity* and individualism following the division of labour associated with industrialisation.

MARX provided a comprehensive theory of social change based on historical materialism. Revolutionary changes in the economic substructure produced appropriate changes in the superstructure.

WEBER'S 'The Protestant Ethic and the Spirit of Capitalism' was a comparative study. It sought to explain the rise of capitalism in western Europe rather than in other, apparently equally 'ready', areas. He saw protestant societies as having the enterprising and individualistic values necessary for development. (See Chapter 13, Religion)

There then seems to have been some loss of interest in social change as sociology became the study of modern societies, leaving comparative work on simple societies largely to anthropologists, who in the meantime had 'borrowed' heavily from functionalism.

THE MODERN DEBATE

ROSTOW produced an attack on communism which, nevertheless, had an oddly Marxist flavour. He argued that growth will follow the pattern of Western societies, particularly the USA, and that communism is a 'disease of transition' followed unnecessarily by some nations. (The events in Eastern Europe in 1989 provide belated support for this view.) He proposed five distinct stages of growth which, in turn, are accompanied by changes in the social structure and in values.

PARSONS offered a modernisation theory which is consistent with his functionalist view of social systems. Modern culture 'fits' industrialisation, whereas traditional culture inhibits economic development. Critics see his ideas of a modern culture as an ethnocentric celebration of the USA. (See also the Tutor's Answer to Question 2, below.)

OSCAR LEWIS wrote about how a 'culture of poverty' could inhibit economic progress in Latin America. FRANK, however, responds differently to inequality in the Western Hemisphere.

If we now look at the left-wing perspectives, we can see how modernisation and the approving view of the west is replaced by the notion of dependency and a critical view of capitalism.

GUNDER FRANK'S 'The Sociology of Development and the Under-development of Sociology' re-opened the controversy over development by using Marxist notions of exploitation. But, like BARAN, he saw the work of Marx himself as needing much amendment in order to explain contemporary global inequality. He described the mechanisms of neo-colonialism whereby the imperialistic relations described by Lenin could explain current world poverty (and wealth). Capital accumulation and investment, international trade, and labour markets all figure in his work, explaining exploitation of Latin America by the USA.

HAYTER adds *aid* as a further cause of dependency in her critique of the Brandt report.

ILLICH anticipated 'green' criticisms of economic growth by attacking not just capitalism, but industrialism. He saw the ill-effects of capitalism as including western consumerist culture as well as dangerous products such as arms and drugs.

STUDIES OF COMMUNITIES AND URBAN LIFE

As usual it is worth considering the work of Marx, Weber and Durkheim. Not only have they made contributions in their own right, they have also influenced subsequent writing.

Marx

The development of cities was seen as an inevitable part of the rise of capitalism. Although Marx wrote of the degradation of working class life in city slums, he did see the city as the breeding ground of class consciousness and therefore of revolution. The peasant was seen as essentially conservative. These views have **not** been borne out by communist revolutions in the 20th century.

Weber

He saw the pre-industrial city as the birthplace of the rational ideas which would encourage the birth of capitalism. Trade, a money economy and bureaucracy all arose in the pre-industrial city.

Durkheim

He distinguished between the mechanical solidarity of the pre-industrial simple society and the organic solidarity of the modern society. In the former, integration was based on *consensual values*; in the latter, on *interdependence* created by the division of labour. The social unrest in Paris in the Revolution of 1789, and again in the 19th century, roused fears of anomie in cities, a theory which has subsequently been developed by functionalists. PARSONS saw a similar division between traditional and modern societies based on distinctive 'pattern variables', and MERTON developed the notion of 'anomie'.

Tonnies

Tonnies made a similar distinction between community and society. In traditional rural society he identified intimate and strong *gemeinschaft* relationships. In urban societies he identified *gesellschaft* relationships, which were impersonal, superficial and rational. Even more than Durkheim he was pessimistic about the future of industrial and urban society.

Wirth

Though a member of the Chicago school which dominated urban sociology, Wirth made a distinctive contribution which played down the ecological views of PARK and BURGESS. The distinctive features of urban life mentioned above can be linked to the loss of community thesis by showing how individuals have increasingly superficial ties with family, friends and neighbours.

Redfield

He is credited with establishing the community study as a 'method' rather than particular findings. However there are interesting methodological implications in the contradictory findings by him, and later GANS, when studying the same Mexican village. Whereas Redfield found a well integrated community, Gans found it tense and divided. Arguably it was their expectations, rather than the passing of time, which produced the conflicting results.

Willmott and Young

Like Gans in Boston and New York, they were able to identify a thriving community in the midst of a major city. They explained the tight knit 'mum-centered' community which they found in Bethnal Green in functionalist terms rather than as a hangover from the past. This is reinforced by Willmott's study in Dagenham, which saw an East-End type of community re-emerge after being broken down by re-housing policies.

Pahl

Pahl reminds us that the commuter is evidence of the disappearance of the distinction between the rural and urban ways of life. Commuters from rural dormitory towns and villages have threatened and partly eroded the sense of community in those places. This is exemplified by rising house prices which exclude the children of native residents from competing for housing. Commuting also undermines family and neighbourhood ties.

Rex and Moore

These writers described the lives of ethnic communities based on class. The geographic concentration of ethnic minorities in inner city areas was seen as a result of their weakness in the housing market. PAHL also argued that it was not just the market situation of immigrants which confined them to ghetto areas but the policies and practices of 'urban managers' who allocate resources. These include banks, building societies and estate agents, as well as local authority planners and housing managers.

Castells

Represents the re-emergence of the Marxist tradition in urban sociology. He sees the roots of many urban problems in capitalism, rather than in urban life itself. The nature of the city is explained in terms of the role of institutions in reproducing labour. For example, he looks at public housing, hospitals and transport systems as being used to maintain the health of workers and to provide help for business.

EXAMINATION QUESTIONS

1 'Aid to underdeveloped countries does nothing to reduce their dependency on the developed nations.' Examine this view.

(AEB 1989)

2 Why do some countries remain underdeveloped?

(Cambridge 1988)

3 Critically examine the view that education is 'the major means of achieving modernisation'.

(AEB AS-level 1989)

4 'The problems of the Third World are a direct result of past and present exploitation by the developed nations.' Explain and discuss.

(AEB 1988)

5 Discuss the view that urbanisation inevitably results in a 'loss of community'.

(AEB 1989)

OUTLINE ANSWERS TO SELECTED QUESTIONS

Question 1

This is **not** an invitation to reproduce a prepared answer which merely juxtaposes Dependency and Modernisation theories. A good answer requires an understanding of Dependency theories but also the ability to apply them to the specific issue of aid.

Dependency theorists agree with the view that aid does nothing to reduce the dependency of underdeveloped countries, as they see long-term structural inequality as being based on global exploitation and unaffected by small and short-term aid projects. Aid can be shown to serve the interests of donors and the elites of UEDCs, rather than to contribute to real development. This side of the argument is likely to dominate answers and as well as using studies by Baran, Warren, and Frank, the work of Illich and particularly Hayter are very relevant.

The case for aid is perhaps best argued by examples, looking at the post-war recovery of Japan, Germany, and the UK with US help, and the success of NICs in the Pacific basin. The advantages of intermediate technology and of educational programmes can be cited.

Modernisation theories need not be central to your answer. Indeed they can be used to demonstrate either the irrelevance, or the positive effects, of aid.

Question 3

A good answer will discuss the merits of competing theories of development as well as the possible impact of education on economic growth. All material must of course be made explicitly relevant to the question.

i) Evidence supporting the view can be cited, showing how education can be a key factor in promoting modern values, is an investment in human capital, and can integrate a society threatened by rapid industrialisation and urbanisation. Specific educational programmes for health and birth control could be mentioned. (See Chapter 9)

ii) Arguments can be put forward which accept the functionalist and modernisation perspectives, but which see other factors as being of equal or greater importance, e.g. aid, birth control and investment.

iii) Criticism can be made of the functionalist view of the relationship between education and the economy. Balogh, Foster and Dawes all point out the failure of vocational education in Third World countries to meet their real needs, and suggest the relative autonomy of the education system.

Marxists suggest an alternative relationship between education and the economy. Freire proposes more radical and relevant educational strategies.

iv) The rejection of modernisation theory itself, from the view points of dependency theory or more voluntarist perspectives, can be considered.

Question 5

This question asks you to address the old 'loss of community' debate and to look specifically at urbanisation as the cause of this loss.

i) The problematic nature of the concept of community.
ii) The loss of community thesis. Tonnies, Durkheim.
iii) Urbanism as a way of life. The distinctive features of urban life and the alleged absence of community ties. Wirth, Burgess, etc.
iv) Empirical studies of communities in towns and cities. Gans, Willmott and Young, etc.
v) Conflict views on communities in cities:

- Rex and Moore on housing classes.
- Pahl on the influence of managers.
- Castells' Marxist view of the insignificance of urbanisation as compared with capitalism.

TUTOR'S ANSWER

Question 2

'Why do some countries remain underdeveloped?'

Definitions of development and underdevelopment are problematic and value laden. The general, questionable, assumptions are that industrialisation on western lines is the most advanced, and therefore the most desirable, system. Even if this were accepted, there has been no common pattern of development for industrialised nations and they have not necessarily arrived at the same destination.

Bendix defines development as industrialisation and modernisation, thus considering both economic change (like the Marxist notion of substructure) and social and political change (the superstructure).

In order to simplify many sociological explanations of **why** nations fail to develop we can make a basic division, one based less on a sociological approach than on the author's political stance.

Modernisation theories deal with the sociology of development, whereas dependency theories explain *under*development. Modernisation theories assume non-developed countries are at a stage prior to (and therefore inferior to) development. This desirable goal may or may not be achieved. These views approve of capitalist societies in themselves and see them as potentially helpful to non-developed societies, through aid, trade or even by providing a model of success.

Dependency theories assume the underdevelopment of some countries is the direct result of the development of others, which developed at the expense of the poor and continue to keep them poor. These views are critical of capitalism, which is seen as an international system of exploitation.

We can now critically examine these two approaches, but we also need to note that within these broad political categories there are differences based on ways of diagnosing and solving problems of development. There is the Marx-Weber debate between economic/technological determinism and the more idealistic or voluntaristic models of change. Within the Marxist framework there is the further dispute between internal and global views of exploitation.

Parsons shows how functionalism can explain social change. The various parts of the social system adapt so that modern culture 'fits' industrialisation, whereas traditional culture inhibits it. The pattern variables associated with modern industrial society include nuclear families, mass education, individualism, rational thinking and an emphasis on achievement. Modernisation prompts economic development in an evolutionary way. Therefore UDCs need to modernise in order to develop economically.

Rostow's version of Modernisation theory is both cruder and less sociological. It claims to offer a neutral, but deterministic, view that all societies develop in an identical way, following through five distinct stages. It echoes a vulgar Marxism by claiming that social structure and values change as economic conditions change. Critics dismiss this view as little more than an ideological justification of US capitalism.

Sociological criticism of these explanations of why UDCs remain poor include the following three challenges. Firstly, there has been no single pattern of development. Past UDCs have developed with a variety of social institutions and different values. Secondly, both Parsons and particularly Rostow are accused of over-emphasising structural influences and being deterministic. Weberian schools of social change are more individualistic and voluntarist. Thirdly, the major source of criticism comes from the left. They claim that modernisation ignores both international influences (such as aid, trade and imperialism) and the inevitably exploitative nature of these global relationships.

Frank and Baran have been among the most influential writers who have rejuvenated the sociology of underdevelopment within a Marxist framework. They borrow from Lenin's ideas on imperialism, which introduced the view of global exploitation by metropolitan countries and areas of satellites. Exploitation is imposed by state force (not market forces). Capitalist countries make, and keep, UDCs poor in order to benefit from cheap labour, cheap raw materials and captive markets. Slavery, unfair trade and colonisation are all part of this process.

Frank is more specific when applying this to relations between the USA and Latin America and deals with the flight of both capital and skilled labour to the USA. Other writers note the retardation and destruction of indigenous industry in UDCs and the enforced switch from subsistence to cash crops.

This last point leads us to Hayter's work on the destructive effects of aid, which may inhibit development by destroying local agriculture with free food. Aid is also seen as resulting in debt, which further underdevelops poor countries.

Illich shares the view that some countries are kept poor as a result of relationship with the DCs. He criticises not just capitalism but industrialism itself. His particular targets are the ecological damage caused by industrialisation and the effects of cultural imperialism. ('CocaColonisation').

These views that some countries remain underdeveloped because of the malign influence of global capitalism, can however be challenged. It has been shown that patterns of development vary. In some cases UDCs become NICs with the 'help' of DCs. Exploitation, if it exists, may be domestic rather than international. The importance of UDCs to the developed world may be exaggerated. The major markets for trade, labour, investment and even arguably aid, remain within the rich world. Isolated national development has not been entirely successful (Cuba, China and Tanzania).

The search for a single explanation is perhaps doomed, whether it is a variant of Modernisation or Dependency theory. The more voluntaristic views which allow for a variety of alternatives may prove more enlightening.

STUDENT ANSWER WITH EXAMINER COMMENTS

Question 4

'The problems of the Third World are a direct result of past and present exploitation by the developed nations.' Explain and discuss.

> **Identifies appropriate theory but too many points in one paragraph.**

Frank, a Marxist writer, argues that exploitation of Third World countries is due to the relations they have with developed countries. He argues that the metropolis exploits the satellite to make profits. The cities in the satellites exploit the rural areas so the labourer in agriculture is doubly exploited. He argues that colonialism and imperialism have made these countries poor. The rich are rich at the expense of the poor. The rich make satellites produce cash crops so they cannot become self-sufficient and the dependency on the metropolis will remain. Once these satellites gain independence they cannot become self-sufficient because then they need help and aid from the metropolis because they have no natural resources left.

> **Relevant points which need developing.**

> **Relevant point, but isolated from the argument.**

Hayter argues that the aid and loans the metropolis provides for the satellite are more beneficial to them than the under-developed country. Robbin argued that giving countries loans they cannot repay creates a situation where 'aid is necessary for the system that makes aid necessary'.

Frank argues that the metropolis takes all the natural resources from the satellites and in return gives them a very low price or sells them badly manufactured goods.

> **Too many oversimplified and unrelated points.**

The metropolis exploits human resources, for example, through the slave trade. Underdeveloped countries were left without young and strong men to work in agriculture. Therefore they now require aid. Also colonialism in India destroyed their textile industry.

> **Generally accurate.**

Frank argues that if countries want to become independent they must have a revolution within the country — they must break contact with the metropolis. Frank's arguments are based on the relationships between the USA and Latin America.

> **Worth developing Illich.**

Illich argues imperialism has given under-developed countries false needs (a concept borrowed from Marcuse). He describes this as CocaColonisation. Underdeveloped countries are provided with inappropriate drugs and conventional medicine.

Marx argued that rich countries exploit their own poor. His argument is internalist. He claims that there are fixed stages that all countries go through. These are primitive communism, feudalism, capitalism and communism. Revolution changes the economic structure and thus the whole society. So independence requires a revolution.

> **Needs linking to previous points and the question.**

Parsons proposes a modernisation theory as an alternative to dependency theory. He argues that modern rational societies fit industrialisation but traditional societies do not. So traditional societies must modernise otherwise they will remain undeveloped. Institutions and values related to industrialisation are the nuclear family, individualism, mass education and emphasis on achievement. He disagrees with dependency theory and argues that undeveloped countries can become developed.

McClelland's argument is similar to Parsons'. He says the values of the population must be changed. He argues that change is evolutionary not revolutionary. If under-developed countries come into more contact with developed ones then there will be a diffusion of modern ideas. Also it can be argued that non-colonised countries can be undeveloped which is a criticism of the dependency theory.

Rostow argues that all underdeveloped countries can become developed by passing through five distinct stages. The take-off is the most important and it is when rational scientific society replaces traditional agricultural society.

Weber argues that society is what people make it. This was illustrated by the effect of the protestant ethic on the rise of capitalism. He argues that to become developed these countries need more contact with developed countries. Their ideology must be changed e.g. Iran does not accept Western ideology. Weber argues these countries need a charismatic leader to make them developed.

Criticism of the dependency theory is that there has been no communist revolution in capitalist societies as Marx predicted. Revolution is not due to class consciousness but *vice versa*.

Criticism of the modernisation theory is that even with colonialism ideas of the metropolis have not been transferred to the satellites. Not all countries want to become like the West e.g. the Communists and Arabs. Industrialisation does not always mean capitalism e.g. Communist China is industrialised.

> Reasonable summary of modernisation. Should link explicitly to question.

> Relevant alternatives, but not all suggested by McClelland.

> Not linked to question.

> This is not an accurate summary of Weber.

> Critical, but should be linked to question.

Overall comments

Overall, a Grade D answer. It does demonstrate a critical understanding of different explanations but does not present a clear, logical and coherent argument. The answer lacks a clear structure and material is not always explicitly linked to the question. The terms underdeveloped and undeveloped are not used in a consistent way.

THE FAMILY

FUNCTIONALIST APPROACHES

MARXIST APPROACHES

FEMINIST APPROACHES

OTHER CRITICS

THEORETICAL AND EMPIRICAL STUDIES

GETTING STARTED

Most sociological debates and A-level questions can be seen as arguments between functionalist accounts of the family and a variety of critics. Interest in the sociology of the family has been rejuvenated by the popularisation of feminist and Marxist criticism.

The main themes of questions set on this topic are:

1 **Changes in the structure of the family.**
2 **Changes in roles within the family.**
3 **The causes and effects of family disorganisation.**

The most obviously related topic areas are gender and sociological theory. Useful references to the family can also be made in answers on health and education. Many students criticise functionalists for basing their arguments on white middle class Americans. If you share this view, remember to point out the diversity of family life in your answers.

Definitions

Definitions of the family, and particularly the various types of family, are rather problematic and frequently ideological. Consider the dispute over whether single-parent families are 'real' families or not.

Take care to distinguish 'household' from 'family', and be aware of the diversity which exists in both. Questions may ask you to consider reasons for the existence of 'typical' families.

ESSENTIAL PRINCIPLES

FUNCTIONALIST APPROACHES

The major assumptions made by functionalist writers on the family include the following.

1　The family can only be studied and explained if we examine its relationships with the wider society. This includes its relationships with parts of the social system, like the economy, and indeed with the whole social system. This assumption applies to our examination of the *structure, functions* and *roles* of the family and its members.

2　The family is a 'good' thing. It is functional both for its individual members and for the wider society.

3　The isolated *nuclear* family is the dominant form of family in modern industrial society (because it is this type which is functional). Whereas the *extended* family is typical of pre-industrial society.

4　There is a tendency towards increased equality within the family. This is described as the 'symmetrical family' and functionalists talk of joint conjugal roles.

CRITICS

To simplify matters we can list critics under some broad headings.

1　Marxists.
2　Feminists.
3　Historians.
4　Psychiatric critics.
5　Critics from within the functionalist camp.

MARXIST APPROACHES

The Marxist approach to the family, like the functionalist approach, adopts a structuralist perspective. The family is examined by looking at its relationship with the wider social structure.

The two main themes are:

■ The influence of the economic *substructure* on family life.

■ The role of the family, as part of the *superstructure*, in reproducing the class system.

The family as a product of economic forces

The development of the family through the successive stages of history was traced by Engels and later by Marxists. This Marxist history makes a useful contrast with the 'march of progress' functionalist views.

The family as part of the superstructure

Like other institutions and ideas which form the superstructure, the family serves the interests of the ruling class by maintaining and reproducing the existing relations of production. This is why Marxists condemn the bourgeois family.

a) The family reproduces labour power. This involves the physical and ideological reproduction of the working class by rearing falsely conscious children at no cost to the employer.

b) Married women are a reserve army of labour, available for work when required but not seen as having a right to work.

c) The family is a refuge from the brutality and alienation of working life. It becomes itself a source of alienation as members are obsessed with love, sex, marriage and home comforts.

d) The family provides the consumer base for modern capitalism, as families demand family cars, consumer durables, etc.

(See also the Marxist explanations of gender inequality in Chapter 5, particularly the answer to Question 4).

FEMINIST APPROACHES

There are a variety of feminist views on the family. Most of these owe something to Marxist theory, particularly to Engels' pioneering work. The main themes found in the feminist analysis of the family are:

1　The family is not a voluntary unit based on love and choice, but an economic unit which creates and maintains female dependence.
2　The family is not efficient at performing its functions. Many women, children and old people eventually depend on support and care from state institutions.
3　Childcare is explained, not in terms of family relations, but by its functions in industrial society.
4　Housework is real productive work, and women are exploited by men.
5　Economic dependency makes, and keeps, women falsely conscious.
　　(See also Chapter 5, particularly the answer to Question 1.)

OTHER CRITICS

There are various other critics of both the functionalist approach to the family and the nuclear family itself. Among the most useful for examination purposes are the 'historians' who challenge the inevitability of the nuclear family in industrial society. There is also a collection of writers who have identified the 'dark side of the family' and examined violence, abuse, mental illness and other symptoms of family disorganisation. (See also the Tutor's Answers to Question 3 below.)

THEORETICAL AND EMPIRICAL STUDIES

FUNCTIONALIST STUDIES

Functionalism dominated the sociology of the family for so long, without serious opposition that the task of selecting only a few studies, is rather difficult.

Parsons

Parsons argued that the nuclear family 'fits' the needs of an industrial society and is thus the typical form of family. The family is isolated, socially and geographically mobile, and characterised by different, but complementary, roles for husband, wife and children. It has two basic functions; namely the socialisation of children and the stabilisation of adult personalities.

Willmott and Young

In a series of studies of family life in and around London they identified progressive change, through the following four stages:

a)　The family as a unit of production in pre-industrial society.
b)　The 'Mum-centred' extended family, which provided support for insecure working class families.
c)　The 'Symmetrical family', which is home-centred and tends towards an equal relationship between spouses.
d)　They predict a fourth stage involving a more work-centred nucler family, where conjugal roles become separate again.

Bott

Bott distinguished *segregated* conjugal roles from *joint* conjugal roles. The former she associated with close-knit social networks; the latter with loose-knit networks. The view that roles were becoming increasingly joint and equal is more or less supported by Willmott and Young and Rosser and Harris. Bott's work is a good starting point for a feminist criticism of family life.

Vogel and Bell

These are unusual in offering a critical view of the family from a functionalist perspective. They see the scapegoating of an emotionally disturbed child as functional for the stability of the rest of the family.

Other studies which highlight the **darker** side of family life (usually based on case studies, as was Vogel and Bell's work) include:

Laing and Cooper

In separate and joint studies they criticised family life from a psychiatric perspective, suggesting children are oppressed and family members made 'insane' in both abnormal and normal families.

Dobash and Dobash

They describe violence within the family and claim that it is not abnormal, but rather the predictable consequence of the position of women in marriage and in the wider social structure.(STRAUSS sees children in the same vulnerable position.)

Leach

Starting from an anthropological viewpoint, Leach identified the nuclear family as having detrimental effects on its members and on the wider society.

THE HISTORIANS

The relationship between family structure and industrialisation remains a popular question, linking the topic of the family with social change. The functionalist analysis of Parsons and others can be challenged by using this historical perspective.

LASLETT denied the existence of a typical extended family in pre-industrial times. ANDERSON argued that the extended family became more common in the early days of industrialisation. Both these studies (along with Marxist views on family structure and a variety of other functionalist studies of working class communities) accept that typical families can be explained in structuralist terms.

THE MARXISTS

ENGELS laid down the foundations of the Marxist approach to the family, identifying and explaining the subjugation of women. For this reason feminist writers in the 1970s took up his ideas, blaming capitalism for marital inequality. The work of BENSTON, ANSLEY, MITCHELL and OAKLEY is more or less influenced by the Marxist analysis.

THE FEMINISTS

The family is extremely important to feminists whether seen as the cause of, or only the location of, women's subjugation.

MCINTOSH sees 'the family' as a set of beliefs about the ideal household. However this ideal does not exist in reality, though society is organised as if it did. The consequences include the failure of families to satisfy the needs of women (and, indeed, children, the old and even men).

OAKLEY pioneered the study of housework and the housewife-mother role. Her work is discussed in Chapter 5 on *Gender*, along with that of other feminist writers.

EXAMINATION QUESTIONS

1   'Far from being democratic the family is based on an unequal division of labour and power.' Discuss.

(AEB 1988)

2   'Families in developing and pre-literate societies are extended; families in industrial societies are nuclear.' Discuss.

(ULSEB 1988)

3   'Functionalist accounts of the family underestimate the extent of strain and exploitation in family life.' Discuss.

(AEB 1989)

4   Why is divorce becoming more common in modern society? Does this phenomenon provide support for those who have argued that the nuclear family is 'dysfunctional'?

(Cambridge 1988)

5   Has the family in modern times been stripped of its functions?

(ULSEB 1989)

OUTLINE ANSWERS TO SELECTED QUESTIONS

" Examiners reward comparative evidence, if relevant. "

Question 2

This question, which is taken from ULSEB paper 3, requires a comparative approach.

You should explain the links between economic development and family structure, provide evidence of exceptions and question the whole notion of a 'typical' family.

An outline could be as follows:

1 A brief explanation of the functionalist approach.
2 Functionalist accounts of extended families in pre-industrial societies such as Durkheim or Radcliffe Brown.
3 Parsons' explanation of the fit between industrialisation and the nuclear family. Weber also linked traditional societies with extended families.
4 Marxist views on the development of family structures as part of the superstructure.
5 Exceptions to the generalisations often made from functionalist view points, e.g. Willmott and Young, Dennis *et al.*, Rosser and Harris, Litvak.
6 The historical research of Laslett and Anderson.
7 Evidence of ethnic diversity and other exceptional cases, such as one parent families.

Question 4

There are clearly two parts to this question. Firstly, you must consider competing explanations of rising divorce rates; and secondly, you must explore the consequences of this increase for individual families, the family as an institution, and the wider society.

The list of causes needs to be kept sociological rather than historical.

1 Functionalists point out the decline of the extended family and its supportive functions. This can be linked to the rise of the Welfare State (see also the answer to Question 2 on marital failure, Chapter 17).
2 Changing attitudes and values resulting from secularisation.
3 Marxist and Marxist feminist views on the tensions resulting from capitalism. (McIntosh, Ansley, etc.)
4 Feminists who see rising divorce rates as evidence of women becoming conscious of their exploitation and of possible alternatives to marriage (Bernard).
5 The link between legal and social change can be mentioned.

The debate over the effects of rising divorce rates can be organised by evaluating the views of 'optimistic' functionalists (like Davis and Goode) who explain away divorce as the result of higher expectations of family happiness. They distinguish the disorganisation of individual families from threats to the family as an institution. The popularity of marriage and remarriage is cited as evidence of the continued strength of the family.

Goode sees the family adapting to these changes (rather than threats) by finding better ways of resolving disorganisation. He points out that divorce is seen as even more of a problem than the death of a spouse in the USA, but in Japan, where women can return to the extended family, divorce is not seen as a threat to the family.

These functionalist views can be contrasted with the various studies that do see the rising divorce rate as evidence of the failure of the nuclear family to meet the needs of individuals. (Leach, Laing, Cooper, Dobash and Dobash, Bernard, etc.)

Vogel and Bell deal with the apparent contradiction between the family being functional for society, whilst threatening to its individual members.

Question 5

This question covers similar ground to questions 3 and 4. Morgan wrote that the sociology of the family could be divided into the approving and the disapproving, and the optimistic and pessimistic.

1 Pessimistic functionalists, who approve of the family, compare the security provided by the multi-functional extended family with the less important nuclear family. Leach could be included here, along with conventional functionalists like McIver.
2 Optimistic functionalists see the family as becoming more specialised and performing fewer functions more effectively. Parsons writing about 'fit' and structural differentiation is important in this section, as is Fletcher.

3   Those who disapprove of the family have rather different views as to its continued importance. Marxists see changes in the role of the family as dependent on changes in the economic substructure, but still see it as continuing to reproduce inequality. Feminists see the family as reproducing and maintaining patriarchy and keeping its 'functions' in that sense. The psychiatric critics see the family as failing to be functional, either for individuals or society.

4   Vogel and Bell offer the useful contradiction of the family continuing to perform its social functions, whilst failing some individuals.

TUTOR'S ANSWER

Question 3

'Functionalist accounts of the family underestimate the extent of strain and exploitation of family life.' Discuss.

(This question requires an outline of functionalist theory and of those studies which are relevant to a consideration of 'strain' and 'exploitation'. There are many possible sources of criticism, but whichever are chosen, relevance and evaluation will gain credit.)

Functionalist accounts of the family, though varied, share certain common assumptions. The family must be examined in terms of its relationships with other parts of the social system and indeed with the whole society. The origin, persistence, structure, roles and development of the family can be explained by looking at its functions, i.e. the ways in which it satisfies the system's functional needs of adaptation, integration, pattern maintenance, and goal attainment. In addition to being functional for the social system, it is assumed by most functionalist writers that the family as an institution is beneficial for its individual members.

Many functionalists have produced a list of the functions of the family. These vary but usually include sexual, reproductive, economic, socialisation and affective functions. The diminishing significance of some of these has been welcomed by some, such as McIver and Fletcher who see the more specialised nuclear family performing the most important functions better than ever.

It is Parsons who dominates the functionalist sociology of the family, both as an authority and a target for criticism. He saw the isolated nuclear family as fitting the needs of modern industrial society. This family maintained two basic irreducible functions; the stabilisation of the adult personality and the socialisation of children. The role of the family in performing just these two functions is seen as part of the more general social process of structural differentiation, where institutions become increasingly specialised and efficient.

Although generally optimistic about the future of the family, some functionalists have expressed reservations about the uncritical idealisation of family life. Just as the loss of some functions has been explained away, so too has the threat of rising divorce rates. Davis said they were a reflection of rising expectations of marital happiness and not of increased strain, and Gibson talked of serial monogamy as a new form of family life and not as the undermining of marriage. Goode saw family disorganisation, which he defined as functional or role failure, as a threat to individual families but not to the family as an institution. In any case, problems like divorce and illegitimacy could be accommodated by improving the ways of dealing with family members who were adversely affected, e.g. changes in property laws.

Vogel and Bell describe how certain families use children as scapegoats for their tensions and hostilities, creating emotionally disturbed children. This integrates the family and diminishes its unstable effects on society; it is thus functional for all but the victim.

Leach criticises nuclear families in industrial society by offering what sounds like a functionalist defence of the extended family. This echoes the work of Willmott and Young and Anderson, who suggest that extended families could thrive in industrial society, providing support for the insecure and disadvantaged.

Leach's description of the nuclear family as a breeding ground for suspicion, fear and violence, both within and outside the family unit, is a theme developed by the radical psychiatrists Laing and Cooper. In joint and separate work based, as their critics point out, on case studies of abnormal families, they not only identify the damage done by families to individual members, but also the adverse impact the family has on the wider society. The dark side of the family is a view developed by Dobash and Dobash who add violence to the mental illness described by Laing and Cooper. This violence is seen as institutionalised into society, and not as an individual abnormality. Recent concern about child abuse reinforces this view.

Cooper's work develops various Marxist themes, seeing the family as an ideological conditioning device. Other Marxist writers follow Engels and explain the brutality and exploitative nature of family life by locating the family in the superstructure of capitalist society. Here we are criticising the functionalist view of the family as an institution, rather than the image of individual happy families. The family reproduces the existing relations of production, maintaining the exploitation and oppression of capitalism. It does this in various ways; labour power is physically and ideologically reproduced at no cost to employers; women are part of a reserve army of labour; the family acts as a refuge from the brutalities of working life. This all sounds like functionalism, only in this case the beneficiary is the employer and not the individual or the wider society. The family is not just an escape from alienation, but an actual cause of it! In modern capitalist society the family is a market for goods.

Feminists revived Engels work to argue that the main victims of exploitation were women. Some feminists see the exploiters as men rather than the Bourgeoisie and condemn patriarchal, rather than capitalist, society. There is no clear distinction between Marxist and feminist approaches, rather it is a continuum, with more or less importance attributed to class or gender.

Exploitation of women is seen in the domestic labour process. Housework is seen as real work, done by women without pay or recognition, for the benefit of men. Whereas Parsons and other functionalists saw conjugal roles as complementary and tending towards symmetry and equality, feminists see power concentrated in the hands of men. The measures of inequality of power include decision-making, control over money and violence. Bernard argued that marriage, whilst beneficial for men in terms of career and health, had the opposite effects on women. McIntosh, in 'the anti-social family', argued that the idealisation of family life has harmful effects on society as well as on individual family members. It is assumed, but is not true, that the old, sick and dependent children will be well-cared for within the family so that no other adequate provision need be made.

Finally, a rejoinder to feminist attacks on the family comes from Martin, who sees women as exercising control over relationships with kin and points out that many women enjoy the autonomy of housework compared with routine paid employment.

STUDENT'S ANSWER WITH EXAMINER COMMENTS

Question 1

'Far from being democratic the family is based on an unequal division of labour and power.' Discuss.

" States a clear argument and explains division of labour. "

" Clear argument but does not explain power. "

In both pre-industrial and nuclear families there is evidence that the family is based on an unequal division of labour and power. Boulton's study in 1983 shows that although men claim that the division of labour should be more equal and is more equal, research showed that only 9 out of 50 subjects helped 'extensively' in the house.

Structured inequalities within society have a large impact on family life. Bernard points out that social institutions such as the church, the divorce courts and the social security system have traditionally conferred authority on men in marriage therefore many wives do consider it legitimate even if they argue about the consequences. Men not only have the power but also the authority to get their own way.

Delphy concludes that men exploit women's labour. Like Marx she sees them as a working class, and as men's wages provide the means of production in the home they are like a ruling class. Because most women feel they are responsible for running the home and caring for the children they become or are made economically and socially dependent on their husbands. Final decisions which are seen as important e.g. moving house and financial matters are taken by husbands. Husbands wield far more power than their wives and this power is built into the marital relationship because of the wage earning capacity of the husband particularly when the wife is rearing young children. Edgell explains that men's greater participation in the paid labour market allows them to avoid many household tasks and dominate family life.

> **Good Marxist-feminist analysis. Links exploitation and decisions to the concept of power.**

The continuing importance of male authority in marriage is underlined by the 1980 study 'Violence against wives'. Dobash and Dobash argue that assault on wives is connected to cultural expectations about male authority in marriage. Violent husbands swiftly resort to force when their wives do not provide for their needs, e.g. a hot meal on the table as quickly or in quite the way he wants, or when wives question a husband's actions or opinions.

> **Links violence to division of labour and power.**

Women retain the bulk of domestic responsibility even when they are in full time employment. Rapaport and Rapaport's study of dual career families focussed upon couples where both husbands and wives had professional or business careers. They found that although participants endorsed the dual career pattern, the wife's career was seen as being followed for satisfaction. Both spouses placed upon the wife's shoulders the responsibility for dealing with any demands or problems the family placed on their work.

> **Relevant, but not tied into previous arguments.**

Overall comments

Overall, a C grade answer. The major deficiency is the absence of any awareness of arguments for increased democracy in the family, e.g. the symmetrical family. Rather short for an A-level answer but relevant and conceptually sound. Shows good analytical skills.

EDUCATION

DIFFERENTIAL EDUCATIONAL ACHIEVEMENT

EDUCATION AND THE WIDER SOCIETY

THEORETICAL AND EMPIRICAL STUDIES

GETTING STARTED

The sociology of education is an area in which all sociology students and teachers share some common experiences. It provides students with the opportunity to analyse their own experiences using sociological concepts, and to evaluate theories using their own experiences.

This topic illustrates the relationships between sociology and social policy. Sociological research seems to influence education policy, such as encouraging the expansion of opportunity. On the other hand, social policy has been a topic of research itself and has also influenced the social reality we wish to study. For example, recognition of gender and ethnic inequality has changed the experience of many pupils and their actual levels of achievement. Therefore, note the dates of research studies as apparently contradictory evidence could be the result of studying similar subjects at different times.

The main themes of question set on this topic are:

1   **Examining the relationships between education and the economy.**
2   **Examining the relationship between education and inequality, including consideration of social mobility and meritocracy.**
3   **Evaluating competing explanations of differential educational achievement.**
4   **Examining research on classroom interaction between teachers and pupils and within groups of pupils.**
5   **Examination of the formal curriculum and the 'hidden curriculum'.**
6   **Explaining educational policy and evaluating its effectiveness.**

Definitions:

- *The curriculum.* This is the sum of learning experiences offered by schools.
- *The hidden curriculum.* This is the unofficial consequences of school experience. Not just knowledge, but what is experienced as a result of the organisation of the school.
- *Meritocracy.* This is a system where rewards depend on merit, that is, on ability and effort, and not on ascribed characteristics.
- *Vocational Education.* This is learning that which is seen as directly related to work. It either takes the form of specific training or preparation for employment in general.

Related topics include types of social inequality (class, race and gender), the family, work and development. Subcultural theories of differential achievement reflect similar theories of deviance.

ESSENTIAL PRINCIPLES

DIFFERENTIAL EDUCATIONAL ACHIEVEMENT

A major sociological problem is in explaining the mass of evidence which indicates a correlation between educational achievement and class, ethnicity and gender. The changing sociological explanations reflect developments in sociology in general, such as the rise of interactionist and modern Marxist theories. Explanations can be grouped under four broad headings:

1 Innate ability

This is a psychological rather than a sociological explanation. Functionalist sociologists frequently assume, but do not attempt to demonstrate, natural inequality in order to support the meritocratic ideology. The Liberal sociologists deny the significance of innate differences in explaining the differential achievement of groups, as opposed to individuals.

2 Out-of-school factors

These are generally structuralist explanations, identifying a variety of causal factors under the sub-headings of material deprivation and cultural deprivation. A number of material factors have been mentioned in research, including poverty and bad housing. Cultural influences include parental expectations, values, and child rearing styles, which are seen as class specific, and also language development and usage.

Most of the research in Britain has been on class, whereas in the USA race has always been a major concern. These studies tend to play down the significance of individual differences and the experience of school, and to locate the problem in the family and neighbourhood.

3 In-school factors

Education provision can influence success. Schools vary in the quality of staff and buildings. However, most explanations which identify the school as the most significant factor in explaining educational achievement tend to be interpretive accounts.

Interactionists focus on the teacher-pupil relationship and often draw on labelling theory or refer to the self-fulfilling prophecy. There is also a body of work on the formation of pupil sub-cultures.

Ethnomethodology has criticised the interactionist approach for underestimating the active part played by pupils in making sense of the experience of school.

4 Marxist accounts

Modern Marxists recognise the importance of both out of school deprivation and differential treatment in school. Deprivation is seen as a symptom of socially structured inequality. Thus Bordieu talks of the working class lacking 'cultural capital', which makes them less educable in the majority of schools which conform to the dominant ruling class values.

Differential treatment by teachers is seen as reinforcing existing social categories (occupation, race and gender) rather than as being based on the interaction of individuals. This conforms with the feminist view, that the school reflects and reinforces the prevailing inequalities of the society.

EDUCATION AND THE WIDER SOCIETY

This section deals with the contributions of functionalist and Marxist sociology to the understanding of the role of education. In particular, it is concerned with the relationship between education and the economy, education and inequality, and education and social control. This involves a consideration of both educational institutions and ideas.

THE FUNCTIONALIST APPROACH

Functionalists explain the development of the education system by examining its relationships with other social institutions and the contribution it makes to satisfying the functional needs of the whole system.

The main functions identified are the *economic function*, which meets adaptation needs, and the more general *socialisation function*, which is concerned with integration and social control.

The economic function

Educational systems are perceived as responding to demands for skilled labour and contributing to economic growth. Economic growth, in turn, can provide additional funding for the expansion of educational provision (see also the Outline Answer to Question 3, Chapter 7).

The extent to which education does, or should, provide specific vocational preparation is debatable. The selection and role allocation function is probably more significant. The development of the 'New Vocationalism' in English education could be seen more as the result of political direction than economic forces. A further criticism is that the supply of skilled labour seems to respond to pay, rather than to the provision of places for training. Such places, as in the cases of nursing and teaching, often go unfilled.

The socialisation function

Consensual values are transmitted through the education system either manifestly (for example through religious instruction) or latently (for example the effects on pupils of studying in a hierarchical institution). The distinction between *manifest* (overt and deliberate) functions and *latent* functions (not intentional or even diagnosed consequences) is similar to the Marxist distinction between the official and hidden curricula. The transmission of culture involves the content of the course, the organisation of the school, and the teacher-pupil relationships.

THE MARXIST APPROACH

Marxists see the education system, both the institutions involved and the ideology they transmit, as part of the superstructure of capitalist society. Systems are shaped by the economic substructure and in turn reproduce the existing relationships of production. The role of education is thus to perpetuate capitalism. This involves the preparation of the workforce for its intended role and the reinforcing of ruling class hegemony.

Comparison with the consensus-structuralism of functionalism can be made as follows:

1   Both study education by looking at its relationship with the wider society.
2   Both link education with the economy. Marxism sees education as reproducing capitalism whereas functionalists see it as fitting the needs of industrial society. Functionalists emphasise training and role allocation, whereas Marxists emphasise the production of deskilled obedient workers.
3   Both identify a cultural reproduction role. The functionalists stress the integrative effects of transmitting consensual values, whereas the Marxists talk of ruling class ideology and of maintaining false consciousness.
    (See also the Tutor's Answer to Question 1, below)

EDUCATIONAL ACHIEVEMENT

THEORETICAL AND EMPIRICAL STUDIES

These will be summarised under the headings of class, gender and ethnicity. But first some **warnings** to consider when evaluating evidence.

1   Findings of studies carried out **at the same time** are sometimes contradictory. But this should be distinguished from situations where findings of studies at **different times** disagree. The latter is by no means necessarily contradictory!
2   The nature and extent of differential achievement changes over time. Some groups seen as disadvantaged have subsequently improved their performance.
    Therefore **dates** of studies are highly relevant.
3   Definitions of class, gender and ethnicity are problematic. They are socially defined and their meaning is socially constructed.
4   Classes are divided by race and gender.
5   Ethnic groups are divided by class and gender.
6   Gender groups are divided by class and ethnicity.
7   Different ethnic groups perform differently.
8   The definition and assessment of educational achievement is problematic.
9   Ethnic minorities and females may succeed in terms of examination results, but still be disadvantaged if schools reinforce stereotypes and allow discrimination.
10 If the issue is the existence of a meritocratic society, it must be noted that educational success alone does not eliminate other forms of inequality in the job market.

GENDER

Out of school

The family, peer group and media can socialise girls into early leaving, marriage and 'women's jobs'. This division in the labour market often encourages underachievement with nursing and secretarial work having low entry qualifications as compared with men's professions and skilled jobs.

SHARPE (1976) described how girls learned the priorities of love, marriage, husbands, children, jobs and careers (in that order). MCROBBIE(1978) looked at the content of romantic magazines and their influence on girls' expectations. GRIFFIN (1985) suggested that early leaving was seen by working class girls as an escape from their responsibility for housework, as employment raised their status in the family.

It should be noted that, despite differential treatment at home, girls are raised in the **same families** as boys. Therefore the influence of the family on such things as language will be less significant for gender than for class and ethnic groups.

In school

The influence of curriculum choice and content has been indicated by the following. DEEM (1980) showed how girls were encouraged into 'feminine', and thus low status, subjects by the school. BLACKSTONE (1980) showed how girls were allowed to avoid science in mixed schools, but to a lesser extent in single sex schools. OAKLEY(1982) suggested that the hidden curriculum was a reflection, rather than a cause, of women's position in society.

Teacher-pupil interaction is a significant factor according to WOLPE(1977), who wrote that girls were 'taught' to smile at male teachers, to be passive and to develop self-discipline earlier than boys. DELAMONT (1980) showed how different expectations began in nursery school, and in a subsequent study showed how the YTS pushed girls into feminine jobs. STANWORTH(1983) reported that teachers were more likely to know the boy's names and to interact with them in class, whereas they underestimated the abilities and ambitions of girls. Despite all this evidence, SPENDER found that teachers denied any such favouritism.

Pupil-pupil interaction remains significant in the social control of girls. Both boys and girls share the sexist attitudes of the society in which they live. WHYTE showed how boys denied girls equal access to bricks in nursery school and to science equipment in secondary school. LEES(1988) showed how sexist language such as 'slags and sluts' is used to intimidate and inhibit girls. She also reports physical intimidation of girls in school. SPENDER found that teachers tolerated such behaviour and persisted in the use of 'man-made language.'

ETHNICITY AND RACE

American studies of the 1960s tended to replace the notion of innate intelligence as a cause of black underachievement with descriptions of a deficient culture and a pathological family life. However LABOV (1975) challenged the application of Bernstein-like ideas to black dialects.

REX and MOORE(1967) explained under achievement in class, rather than cultural, terms. Most recent studies have concentrated on the teacher and school as the source of inequality. COARD(1971) saw racism as the explanation of the over-representation of black children in ESN schools, whilst Pakistani children were under-represented. Performance in relevant tests failed to explain these differences. TOMLINSON(1972) found evidence of low teacher expectations for ethnic minority pupils. DRIVER(1981) found evidence that, despite considerable improvements in the numbers getting five or more higher grade CSEs or O-levels and in A-level grades, children of West Indian origin still underachieved. However, girls did better than boys. GREEN showed that white boys got more attention from teachers than girls or ethnic minority pupils.

Separate small-scale studies in London and Bradford in the late 1980s have actually shown pupils from most ethnic minorities achieving more than their white class-mates. These studies need a careful consideration of the class background of the children, as indeed do all studies on this issue.

CLASS

Out-of-school studies have not concentrated on the home in isolation from the school. But they have tended to take the school for granted, seeing it as reacting in a neutral way to children who arrive at school in a more or less educable condition. HALSEY suggested that neither 'material circumstances' (housing, father's class, etc.) nor 'family climate' (parental encouragement, linguistic competence, etc.) have a strong influence, provided children were in the same school.

COATES and SILBURN argued that poverty disadvantaged children in a variety of material and cultural ways. BERNSTEIN, who claims he has been often misrepresented, made language a major area of concern in the sociology of education. He sees differences in the ability of working class and middle class children to use the elaborate code of language favoured by teachers.

In-school studies have looked at the formation of pupil sub-cultures which conform more or less to the values of the school (HARGREAVES 1967, LACEY 1970 and BALL 1981). Sub-cultures seem related to streaming within schools as well as to class. Ball sees the school as offering a 'cooling-out' process where ambition is lowered. WILLIS (1979) describes a similar process, but sees the pupils as playing a more active part.

Teacher-pupil interaction has been described by BECKER, who relates it to labelling theory. NASH emphasises that teachers' expectations are based, not on the 'real' class characteristics of children, but on the teacher's perception of class. KEDDIE identified the way in which teachers offered a different curriculum to low stream pupils and interpreted their questions and behaviour differently.

FUNCTIONALIST STUDIES

Durkheim

Durkheim saw education as the methodological socialisation of the young. It provided them with the general qualities necessary to be members of a society and with the specific skills to fill particular occupational roles. Thus education systems contribute towards satisfying the functional needs of integration, social control and role allocation.

Parsons

Parsons identified the basic values underlying education in the USA as equality of opportunity, competition and individualism. Children cease to be judged by the particularistic standards of the home, which are replaced by the universalistic standards of the whole society. Subsequent inequality is thus legitimised. Education thus reflects the consensual values which integrate the society.

Davis and Moore

Davis and Moore emphasise the role allocation function, seeing education as the mechanism by which the most qualified people are channelled into the most important jobs.

MARXIST STUDIES

Althusser

Althusser described education as an 'Ideological State Apparatus' which reproduces inequality. Both the ideology underlying the curriculm, and the institutions which transmit it, contribute to this reproductive process.

Inequality is legitimised and reinforced. Schools claim to treat pupils in a neutral fashion and teachers and pupils believe this. Althusser sees the process of ideological reproduction as 'unconscious'. This is a common theme in his Marxist-structuralist approach which owes a debt to Durkheim as well as to Marx. The school is mistakenly seen as independent of the economy.

Willis

In contrast to Althusser's structuralism, Willis offers a more action based Marxist analysis. He describes how working class boys are not integrated into the culture of the school which is middle class. The school is seen as offering them nothing which is relevant or useful, and they demand nothing. Thus the school does not 'brainwash' them and has no specific effect, beyond reinforcing the view that education is not for them. They fail, not in their own terms, but in the view of the school.

Bowles and Gintis

In a series of empirical and theoretical studies of schooling in the USA, Bowles and Gintis developed their correspondence theory of education. They argue that there are interdependent relationships between the family, education and work. The work roles of parents influence the socialisation of children, and thus the family influences educational achievement. The school corresponds to the work place and thus work roles are influenced both by socialisation in the family and by achievement in school.

Examples of the correspondence between school and work include:

1   The fragmentation and stratification of school knowledge is similar to deskilled and fragmented work.
2   Pupils rely on teachers for knowledge, as workers rely on managers.
3   Both school and workplace motivate and control through extrinsic rewards.
4   Pupils learn to be submissive to authority.
5   Both school and workplace are hierarchically organised.
6   Rewards appear to be based on merit, which thereby legitimises inequality.

EXAMINATION QUESTIONS

1   'The expansion of educational provision in Western industrial societies is a direct consequence of the demand for an increasingly skilled workforce.' Explain and discuss.

(AEB 1985)

2   Assess the extent to which educational reforms in Britain over the last fifty years have created a meritocratic society.

(AEB 1989)

3   What is meant by the 'hidden curriculum' in schools? How have sociologists contributed to our understanding of this aspect of education?

(WJEC 1989)

4   'The major function of educational systems is the reproduction and legitimation of social inequality.' Discuss.

(AEB 1982)

5   Assess the strengths and weaknesses of interactionist explanations of differential educational achievement.

(AEB 1988)

OUTLINE ANSWERS TO SELECTED QUESTIONS

Question 2

You must start with a clear idea of meritocracy in order to judge the impact of educational reforms. Accurate, if not detailed, knowledge of educational reforms is necessary.

i) Explain meritocracy. The necessary tests of educational reforms should be:
   a) Is education the dominant means of access to highly rewarded positions?
   b) Does educational achievement depend on merit?
ii) Consider the effectiveness of some of the following by referring to relevant sociological studies.
   a) Free secondary education for all.
   b) Comprehensive schools.
   c) Raising of the school leaving age (ROSLA) from 15 to 16.
   d) Expansion of higher education.
   e) 'Vocationalism'.

f) The Education Reform Act: The national curriculum and City Technology Colleges.

The first question is discussed in mobility studies (males only!) particularly by Halsey *et al.* Race is covered by the Swann report and gender by Equal Opportunities Commission publications.

The second question is covered by a wealth of studies including Ford, Ball and Rutter. More recent studies dealing with the YTS etc. make a refreshing change for examiners, e.g. K. Roberts and Parris *et al.*

iii) Marxist criticism, which sees meritocracy as an ideological myth and the educational reforms aimed at reproducing and legitimising inequality. Bowles and Gintis, Willis and Jencks, offer different interpretations of this theme.

Question 3

This question requires an examination of the concept of the 'hidden curriculum' and an evaluation of relevant studies.

i) Provide a definition of the 'hidden curriculum' and distinguish it from the knowledge and practices which comprise the formal curriculum.

ii) Indicate the application of the concept to class, and to race and gender inequality. Mention the organisation of the school, its rules and rituals, the relationships between pupil and pupil, and between teacher and pupil, and the 'hidden' content of school books, e.g. reinforcing nationalism, racism and sexism.

iii) Marxist explanations, which see the 'hidden curriculum' as ruling class ideology and emphasise the significance of economic relations outside the school. (Bowles and Gintis, Althusser and Willis, can be used.)

iv) Interactionist explanations, which see pupils playing a more active and conscious role in pleasing teachers in order to gain rewards. (Jackson and Hargreaves.)

v) Illich provides a similar analysis to the Marxists but uses the concept to criticise the school and teachers rather than capitalist society.

vi) You could include a critical view of the concept comparing it with functionalist views of the latent functions of education. Also point out that what is latent or 'hidden' in one situation, may be overt and formalised in other circumstances; e.g. religious or political education, the promoting of co-operative or competitive games, and the current emphasis on vocational education.

Question 4

The quotation can be seen as Marxist, and relevant Marxist theories and studies can be used to explain and support it. Functionalist alternatives should not be just listed, but **used** to make relevant criticisms. Feminist analysis and reference to race will be rewarded, if made relevant.

Both reproduction and legitimation (i.e. justification) of inequality must be discussed.

1 Brief introduction to the Marxist approach to education, explaining the view of education systems as part of the superstructure of capitalist society.

2 Althusser argues that education is portrayed as ideologically neutral, but actually reproduces and legitimises the existing relations of production.

3 M. F. D. Young emphasised the significance of school knowledge. He sees what is taught, how it is taught, and to whom it is taught as conveying ideological messages. This can be applied to legitimation.

4 Bordieu's notion of 'cultural capital' is an explanation of the reproduction of inequality.

5 Bowles and Gintis wrote the 'correspondence theory of education' and are able to show how the family, school and workplace are all inter-dependent and involved in the reproduction of inequality.

6 Similarities with functionalist theories can be identified. These include the links with the economy and the allocation function. They also offer an alternative consensus explanation for the transmission of culture.

7 The functionalist, critical alternative. Meritocracy as a genuine, not mythical, justification for the unequal distribution of rewards. (Parsons and Davis and Moore.)

Other functions may be seen as equally, or still more important, such as training for jobs or integrating society by transmitting consensual values.

TUTOR'S ANSWER

Question 1

'The expansion of educational provision in Western industrial societies is a direct consequence of the demand for an increasingly skilled workforce.' Explain and discuss.

The growth of educational provision in Western Europe and the USA has occurred throughout the twentieth century and particularly since the Second World War. However the pattern of growth and the nature and extent of increased provision varies between nations. Britain, for example, has a smaller proportion of the population in higher education than most of its competitors.

Both functionalist and Marxist writers tend to explain this expansion by linking it to economic development. Although neither give as narrow an explanation as that offered in the question.

Functionalism explains the origin, persistence and development of social phenomena by identifying their functions. Functions are the contributions the phenomena make towards satisfying the functional needs of the system, thus ensuring the survival and stability of the society. Growth in educational provision would be seen as 'fitting' the needs of an industrial society. Certainly the demand for a skilled workforce is seen as one of those needs. Mass education arrived with industrialisation and, as well as providing suitable workers, could be seen to depend on the economic surplus created by the new methods of production. Advanced industrial societies are characterised by a growth in office, managerial, professional and skilled technological work at the expense of less skilled manual work. These new jobs require educated workers.

This kind of functionalist argument has been used to explain both the expansion of higher education and the development of 'vocational' education. However, functionalists do not see the provision of trained or skilled workers as the sole economic function of education. The selection or allocation function is seen as equally important. The education system provides for the assessment of pupils' abilities and aptitudes, so as to allow the best qualified to fill the most functionally important positions. This is a major theme in Davis and Moore's theory of stratification. Parsons, following Durkheim, also attaches importance to the role of education in integrating society by transmitting consensual values and morality.

Berg has offered critical research which suggests that better educated workers are not necessarily more productive workers. (Although managers may assume that their better workers are more educationally qualified.) Educational qualifications help people to get jobs, but not to perform them well. Debates about education and stratification also raise doubts as to whether the bases for success in education are ability and effort, and thus whether the education system **does** allocate people to suitable positions.

Marxist theories also emphasise the importance of economic influences on the educational system. The organisation of schools and the curriculum are seen as part of the superstructure of capitalist societies. The explanation of the expansion of education lies then, not in the demands of industrial society, but in the effects of capitalism.

Bowles and Gintis, like the functionalist writers, see employment as a major influence on the nature of the education system. Their 'correspondence' theory argues that there are inter-dependent relationships between work, education and the family. The way in which school corresponds to work is the most important element of their study for this answer. If capitalism is to function efficiently, then a disciplined and hard working labour force is required. Possible worker resistance is minimised by the training received in school. Workers are prepared for working for cash in jobs by working for extrinsic rewards at school. They also learn to rely on experts for knowledge and to respect authority. The hierarchy of the workplace corresponds to the hierarchy of the school. Competing for rewards at school prepares the more successful to compete for promotion at work. In both cases, conformity is rewarded.

Other Marxist writers, such as Althusser, also explain the functioning of education by showing how it supports the interests of capitalism. The reproduction of labour power is seen as involving the reproduction of ideology more than suitable skills. Much employment in advanced industrial societies has become deskilled and it is a docile, rather than qualified, labour force which is required. Schools are seen as places which 'cool' ambition rather than encourage competition. Willis explains how pupils play a more active role than many Marxists acknowledge in settling for the same working class jobs as their parents. Clarke and Willis argue that the training schemes of the early 1980s were not set up to bridge the alleged skills gap, but to divert attention from structural causes of unemployment and to locate the problem with the young and the schools.

Marsden has questioned the links between educational expansion and the demand for labour (which is central to both functionalist and Marxist sociology) as well as the stated aims of both Conservative and Labour governments. He sees the education system as responding to other demands, such as equality of opportunity (which is in keeping with functionalist theory). However, he also argues that there is a degree of autonomy, as illustrated by the continued control over the curriculum exercised by the universities and examination boards. Recent government initiatives have challenged this alleged autonomy, and have tried to bring them into line with perceived economic needs.

Collins, in the USA, also argues that the contribution of educational expansion to economic growth has been exaggerated and that the US labour force might be over-educated beyond what is necessary to acquire job skills. In support of this view we could cite the economic growth of the 1950s, which was not driven by educational expansion, and the failure of the expanded Higher Education sector to produce the extra scientists and technologists which the Robbins report advocated. The early 1980s saw a contraction in university places at the same time that the demand for such places was highest. The demand for more higher education for women has not been fuelled by the predicted labour shortage of the 1990s, but by the demand for equal opportunities since the 1970s.

STUDENT ANSWER

Question 5

Assess the strengths and weaknesses of interactionist explanations of differential educational achievement.

> 66 Good start. Not a prepared run-through on differential achievement. Attempts comparison with other explanations. 99

> 66 Relevant studies, but not developed. 99

> 66 Relevant, but not related to ethnicity, class or gender. Not criticised. 99

Interactionist views do not assume that there is any objective social reality. Instead of looking for cause and effect laws they look for the reasons why individuals are defined as successes or failures. They do not use official statistics in their explanations of differential educational achievement seeing them as social constructions. Interactionist sociologists criticise positivist sociologists for their 'out-of-school' explanations of differential achievement because they fail to consider processes in school and are no better than a layman's explanations of sociological phenomena.

Becker saw teacher's views of the pupils as affecting their performance in school. He found by interviewing teachers they had notions of what made an 'ideal pupil'. Cicourel and Kitsuse found that teachers' judgements of pupils, supposedly based on objective factors such as IQ and performance in class, were actually judgements based on the perceived class of pupils. Keddie related this theory to streaming where pupils were judged and grouped according to their perceived ability.

Rosenthal and Jacobson studied the self-fulfilling prophecy in an experiment in a school. They gave the pupils an IQ test to rate their ability and then told teachers that certain pupils were more likely to improve in class. These pupils were in fact chosen at random. They re-tested the pupils after a period of time and found that not only did the teachers perceive the chosen children as being more attentive and better behaved but also the children's actual performance had improved more than other children. Rosenthal and Jacobson found the teachers had forgotten the original list of 'spurters' but their attitudes and attention to the children had improved their performance.

Shows diversity of interactionist approaches. Needs studies.

Ethnomethodological approaches stress the role that pupils play in the classroom situation. They see the pupil's attitude to the teacher as playing an equally important part as the teacher's attitude to the pupil. Whilst following an interpretive approach, ethnomethodologists have criticised other in-school explanations of differential achievement as regarding the pupil as a non-active participant in classroom interaction.

Interactionist approaches have been criticised using positivist out-of-school explanations which show that external influences still affect pupils performance in school. This may be seen more recently where schools have become more equal with more racial and gender equality. It may be seen that when this happens external influences such as class and class-based differences play a greater role in differential achievement.

The Marxist approach is similar to the interactionist approach, in that teachers are seen as treating children unequally, but it also takes into account out-of-school factors.

Shows diversity of interactionist approaches. Needs studies.

Good logical criticism.

Overall comment

Overall, a short but successful attempt to outline and assess interactionist studies. Sound on concepts but thin on evidence. The candidate was either short of time or knowledge. This is a typical last question. The application of a general understanding of relevant concepts to this question deserves credit. Should discuss class, race and gender. Worth a C grade.

CHAPTER

WORK

ALIENATION AND JOB SATISFACTION

INDUSTRIAL CONFLICT

WORK AND NON-WORK

THEORETICAL AND EMPIRICAL STUDIES

GETTING STARTED

There is a considerable overlap between sociology of work and some closely related topics. This applies particularly to the study of both *Stratification* (Chapter 3) and *Organisations* (Chapter 11).

The best guide to what should be covered in this section is perhaps offered by examination questions. However, good answers frequently benefit from, or even require, reference to other topics. The Marxist criticism of 'Taylorism' is a central part of recent debates on the nature of both office and factory work and will be referred to in this chapter, although a more detailed account of Taylor's original work is found in Chapter 11 on *Organisations*.

Apart from Chapters 3 and 11, the other chapters which offer related material include *Professions* (Chapter 12), *Gender* (Chapter 5) and *Education* (Chapter 9).

The major common themes to be found in the various syllabuses are:

1 **Alienation and job satisfaction.**
2 **Industrial conflict.**
3 **The relationship between work and non-work.**
3 **Unemployment.**

Students should show an awareness of the increasing significance to sociologists of studies of women at work (including housework), white collar work and unemployment. The nature of a post-industrial society based on knowledge and information workers, and service type occupations, has implications for stratification and development, as well as for this topic.

Definitions

- *Alienation* is the separation or estrangement of the individual from his true self, from others, and from the world he inhabits. The workplace is seen as the main location and cause of alienation, but the concept is also used in the sociology of religion, the family, race and deviance.

- *Job satisfaction* is often considered as involving *intrinsic* sources of satisfaction found in the work task itself, and *extrinsic* sources of satisfaction, found in working conditions and especially pay.

- *Industrial conflict* occurs in a variety of forms, and not just strikes.

- *Work* is generally seen as paid employment.

- *Unemployment* is the undesired absence of paid employment.

ESSENTIAL PRINCIPLES

ALIENATION AND JOB SATISFACTION

A framework for answering questions on both work satisfaction and industrial conflict can be provided by grouping theories under three headings:

- Conditions in the workplace.
- Marxist approaches.
- Interactionist approaches.

CONDITIONS IN THE WORKPLACE

Conventionally such studies have concentrated on production technology, debating the degree to which technology determines satisfaction (Blauner and critics). We can also consider here the influence of managerial control (Weber and Taylor) and informal work groups (Mayo). There is an overlap with organisation theories discussed in the next chapter.

MARXIST THEORIES

Alienation results inevitably from the relations of production found in pre-communist societies. It is at its worst under capitalism which ' . . . perfects the worker and degrades the man'. The inseparable causes are:

- The wage contract which exploits the employee.
- The nature of factory work (and later office work).

Marxists see the organisation of work as having the dual purpose of maximising profits and controlling the workforce. This results in such alienating conditions as the extreme division of labour, deskilling, mechanisation and bureaucratisation. The worker is motivated solely by pay.

Modern Marxist studies deal not only with factory work, but also with white collar and female workers. These themes are pursued in the discussions about 'proletarianisation' (p.17) and the position of women and ethnic minorities in the labour market (pp. 24 and 34).

INTERACTIONIST STUDIES

These reject structuralist explanations which identify external causes of the workers attitudes and behaviour at work. Instead the reasons for workers experiences are to be found by understanding their motives and the **meanings** they attribute to work. These meanings are influenced by the workers prior experiences, both inside and outside work. Thus, neither capitalism nor working conditions have inevitable and uniform effects on workers.

INDUSTRIAL CONFLICT

The three groups of explanations above can be used to explain both the *extent* and *type* of industrial conflict found in particular firms, industries and countries.

The interactionist approaches concentrate on the meaning which conflict has for the participants, and can be used as the basis for a critical account of strike statistics.

Marxists debate the real meaning behind conflict with the interactionists. The essence of the argument is whether the pursuit of any goal, except that of a change in the relations of production, is to be seen as false consciousness.

A final way to categorise theories of industrial conflict is to distinguish *consensus* from *conflict* theories. The former see peaceful industrial relations as normal and strikes as pathological, whereas the latter sees conflict as normal and apparent peace as evidence of bourgeois hegemony.

Since 1979 the industrial relations climate has changed dramatically in the UK, generally in the favour of employers. Trade union membership has declined, unemployment (though now falling) has risen to unprecedented post-war levels, the occupational structure has continued to change, legislation has curbed trade union power, and previously strong unions such as the miners, printers and dockers have suffered probably irreversible damage.

WORK AND NON-WORK

Definitions of work, non-work and leisure must be regarded as problematic. S. Parker provided widely accepted definitions which were little changed by Elias and Dunning.

- *Work* is paid employment.
- *Work obligations* are voluntary, done outside normal working hours but associated with a job.
- *Existence time* is the satisfaction of needs such as eating and sleeping. *Non-work obligations* are domestic duties, such as childcare and cleaning.
- *Leisure* is free time when people choose activities or inactivity.

McIntosh rejects the work of both Parker and Elias and Dunnings as restricted to men. The degree of choice and separation is not, she claims, available to women.

You might organise your answers by distinguishing the following approaches:

1 Marxists, who see both work and leisure activity as produced by capitalism.
2 Those like Parker, who see work as related to leisure.
3 Feminist critics, who see women's leisure opportunities to be as restricted as their work chances.
4 Interactionists, who see the previous arguments as overdeterministic and are concerned with the meanings attached to work and non-work activities.

Unemployment

The main issues are:

1 Problems of definition, which form the basis of a criticism of the official statistics.
2 Explaining the distribution of unemployment by class, race, age, gender and region.
3 Explaining the causes of unemployment.
4 Examining the effects of unemployment.

THEORETICAL AND EMPIRICAL STUDIES

ALIENATION AND JOB SATISFACTION

In-work studies

BLAUNER sees alienation as the consequence of the type of technology used in industrial production. He distinguishes four types of technology and sees alienation as increasing as technologies become more complex. This trend is (optimistically) reversed when the most modern form of technology is employed. Alienation is measured along four dimensions, powerlessness, meaninglessness, isolation and self-estrangement.

WEDDERBURN, GALLIE and MALLET, in separate studies, all query Blauner's overemphasis on technology. They suggest alternative influences on satisfaction, including managerial practices and the national culture.

WEBER rejects Marx's view that bureaucracy is a form of control exclusively linked to capitalism and inevitably bad for workers. Some aspects of bureaucracy are alienating as they reduce the autonomy of the worker, but others provide him with security and a career. (See Chapter 11 on *Organisations*.)

F. TAYLOR'S theory of 'scientific management' claimed to meet the employers need for efficiency, and the profit this generated then allowed the workers' need for cash to be satisfied.

MAYO'S 'human relations' approach seemed to have discredited Taylorism as early as the 1930s. Social rewards gained from informal work groups were seen as more important than economic rewards gained by individuals. Control was seen as friendlier and more democratic.

TRIST and BAMFORTH pioneered the socio-technical systems approach. This argued that managerial practice can influence satisfaction within the limits set by technology. The reorganisation of conventional car assembly lines by Volvo and Saab-scania followed their recommendations.

Marxists

MARX'S work on alienation developed from his study of philosophy and religion. He predicted an optimistic future for man, who would express his true self through creative work. This can only happen, however, after the fall of capitalism. The alienated worker does not own his product, works only for cash, has no control over production and is isolated from himself, his fellow workers and his employers.

CARCHEDI follows C.W.MILLS in extending the concept of alienation to white collar workers. He writes of the proletarianisation of office work. The causes of this process include: bureaucratisation, fragmentation and the subsequent de-skilling of office workers. Feminisation of this workforce is a contributory factor. Mills extends the argument from routine office workers to managers and professionals. SALAMAN develops BRAVERMAN criticisms of the work of Weber, Taylor and Blauner. The design of work is aimed not just at efficiency, but at controlling the workforce. This is the purpose of the fragmentation of work and of the deskilling of workers. Mayo's proposals are dismissed as simply more subtle forms of control, suitable for higher grade workers or for those likely to resist.

Weberian studies

GOLDTHORPE and LOCKWOOD used their Weberian-influenced 'action approach' to point out the significance of the instrumental attitude to work. Their 'affluent workers' saw work as a means to an end, namely cash, rather than the seeking of intrinsic satisfaction or social rewards in the workplace.

The source of this instrumental attitude was not the boring work, but the privatised family life they experienced **outside** work.

BLACKBURN and BEYNON echo this view. The workers' expectations, and the meaning they give to work, influences the degree of satisfaction they experience. Thus skilled dayshift men, with high expectations, were more alienated than part-time and night-shift women who did less skilled work but had a more instrumental attitude to their jobs.

INDUSTRIAL CONFLICT

In addition to the writers above, the following offer explanations of the extent and type of conflict based on working conditions.

KERR and SEIGEL see integrated communities as more likely to sustain collective conflict, such as strikes, more than fragmented groups. In 1985 the miners of Nottingham and Derbyshire did not, on the whole, support the strike. Unlike other miners they lived in mixed housing in terms of class and occupation.

GOULDNER suggested that organisational change and managerial practice encouraged a strike in a Gypsum mine among underground workers whose work was less suitable for bureaucratic control than that of surface workers.

HYMAN emphasises the need for an 'action approach', while supporting the view that conflict is to be regarded as normal. This point is also made by LANE and ROBERTS in their study of the previously peaceful Pilkington glassworks, where specific demands were formulated by the workers **after** the strike began.

DAHRENDORF agrees that strikes can be seen as normal and argues that the Marxist notion of inevitable revolution has been undermined by the institutionalisation of class conflict in the arena of industrial relations.

TAYLOR and WALTON in a study of industrial sabotage borrow from interactionist studies of deviance to examine the reasons behind allegedly motiveless vandalism.

WORK AND NON-WORK

PARKER reviewed existing studies which linked occupation with non-work activities. He then produced a theory, which suggested three kinds of patterns of work-leisure relationships. These were the opposition, complementary and extension patterns. His work represents a good starting point in answers involving subsequent criticism.

ELIAS and DUNNING largely confirm Parker's classification of work and non-work activities, but suggest the basis of the categorisation should be the *degree of routinisation* involved. Interestingly, they see leisure not as relaxation but as the increasing of arousal. WILENSKY argued that alienation at work spilled over into leisure time.

MARCUSE from a Marxist perspective, saw alienation as being caused by capitalism affecting economic consumption, as well as production. The creation of 'false needs' enslaved workers with 'chains of gold'.

RIGAUER shares DUNNING and SHEARD'S interest in sport, but offers a Marxist view where sport becomes work.

DUMAZEDIER reverses the argument that work influences leisure and sees non-work needs as influencing occupational choice. This reminds us of the instrumentalism described by Goldthorpe and Lockwood above.

Finally, the influence of work on family life has been discussed from a variety of perspectives. Parker cites the work of TUNSTALL and others on extreme occupations, and more recently there has been work on dual-career families by RAPPAPORT and RAPPAPORT, together with various Marxist and feminist critiques, some of which are mentioned in Chapter 8 on *The Family.*

UNEMPLOYMENT

The possible effects of new technology provides one area of debate. C.HANDY predicts the end of full-employment and life-time careers, whereas LITTLER and SALAMAN anticipate a further deskilling of workers, but not necessarily a reduction in employment (see also the Tutor's Answer to Question 1, below).

The following studies are more concerned with the effects of unemployment and with whether these depend on the age, ethnicity, gender and class of the victims.

WILLIS and CLARKE in 'Schooling for the dole' suggest that the school and the unemployed are unfairly blamed for the problem. MUNCIE also argues that the young are unjustifiably seen as a special case who have a training problem, rather than unemployment being the problem as is really the case.

HAWKINS shifts our attention to the old, whose unemployment is seen as a marginal problem.

BILTON *et al* give a good account of the disguised unemployment, not only of the young and old, but also of women. This could be used in an answer criticising official statistics. Studies in the sociology of race indicate how unemployment can be exported, using immigration control and even repatriation.

The Scarman report noted the higher rate of unemployment among ethnic minorities, a trend which seems to have increased as unemployment has risen. FRIEND and METCALFE explore this further, arguing that the Bristol riots of 1980 were not, as characterised in the media, **race** riots but in fact also involved the white unemployed, both young and old.

PAHL argues that it is inappropriate to view the unemployed as a distinct group. People go in and out of employment, particularly the working class whose culture is based on insecure and low paid work.

EXAMINATION QUESTIONS

1   a) Referring to Item A, suggest **two** reasons why the number of A-level leavers available for employment will fall by 1995. (2)
    b) How far do the official statistics of unemployment accurately reflect the number of people looking for work? (6)
    c) Using the statistics in Item C, describe the changing patterns in the occupational structure between 1984 and 1987. (4)
    d) Examine the implications of the statistics in Items A and C for the employment prospects of 18–20 year-olds in the labour market. (6)
    e) Assess sociological contributions to our understanding of the effects of unemployment. (7)

(Total 25 marks)
(AEB, Specimen)

WORK AND LEISURE

Item A ESTIMATES AND PROJECTIONS OF THE CIVILIAN LABOUR FORCE: GB

16–19 Year olds

A–level recruits

Fewer than 20 large employers currently account for the employment of over half of the estimated 27,000 leavers with A–level and Scottish Higher School Certificates looking for work. Employers' demands, if anything, are likely to increase over the next few years. However the numbers at this level available for employment will fall to 22,000 by 1995.

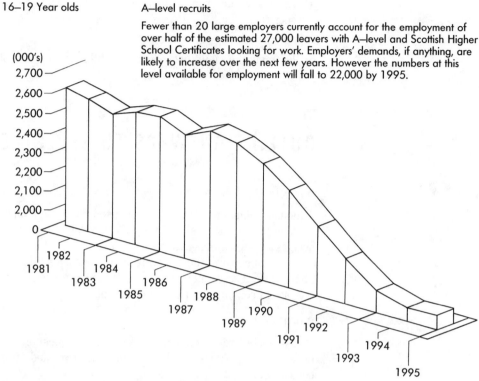

Item B GREAT BRITAIN – UNEMPLOYMENT (seasonally adjusted)

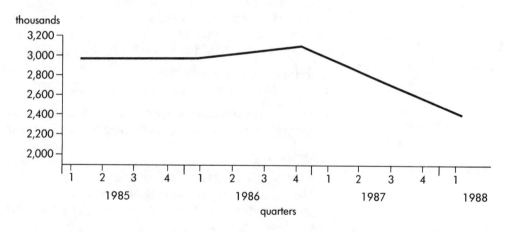

Item C CHANGE IN EMPLOYMENT 1984–1987

	thousands
Agriculture, forestry and fishing	−35.7
Extraction of minerals/manufacture of metals and metal goods	−63.5
Engineering	−64.9
Distribution, hotels and repairs	+235.8
Transport, communications	+65.0
Banking, finance	+428.4

Source: Department of Employment Labour Force Surveys
Reproduced in Labour Market, Quarterly Report, July 1988.

Fig. 10.1

2 Examine the view that distinctions between work and leisure have become increasingly blurred.

(AEB 1988)

3 Evaluate the explanations sociologists have offered for different levels of strike activity and other forms of industrial conflict.

(AEB 1988)

4 Assess the different ways in which sociologists have explained alienation in industrial societies.

(AEB 1989)

5 Examine the view that industrial conflict is an inevitable feature of industrial society.

(AEB 1986)

OUTLINE ANSWERS TO SELECTED QUESTIONS

Question 2

Although definitions such as those used by Parker and Elias and Dunning attempt to distinguish work and leisure they do, in addition, introduce other categories of activity, such as non-work obligations.

You can explore these terms and examine in detail problem areas like sport and housework. The existence of enforced leisure through unemployment and the growth of the black economy can also be discussed.

Question 3

This question requires a different emphasis to question 5, where a more general overview of conflict is permissible. Here, both the level and type of industrial conflict must be considered.

The answer can be constructed using the Marxist, technology and interactionist frameworks outlined above. You should refer to studies of strikes and other forms of conflict which attempt to explain variations in levels, such as community integration, technology, culture, etc.

Types of conflict could be discussed by distinguishing:

a) Individual from collective forms.
b) Overt from institutionalised conflict between employers and unions.

(If you have not prepared the appropriate studies of strikes etc., it is still relevant to refer to the problems of measuring conflict and to examine the official statistics debate.)

Question 4

The key words are 'assess' and 'different'.

The question demands an evaluation of more than one explanation. The framework suggested earlier is suitable for comparing and assessing technological, Marxist, and interactionist theories.

Evaluation can be based on modern Marxists, particularly Braverman and Salaman.
Remember!
'Work' includes office and housework as well as factory work. 'Alienation' can also be discussed outside the workplace. Marxists use the concept to study religion, family and education.

TUTOR'S ANSWER

Question 1

a) Referring to Item A, suggest *two* reasons why the number of A-level leavers available for employment will fall by 1995.

1 There will be a relatively small age cohort owing to a falling birth rate 18 or so years before.
2 A larger proportion of the age group is likely to go into Higher Education.

b) How far do the official statistics of unemployment accurately reflect the number of people looking for work?

The official unemployment figures are based on those who claim unemployment benefit. Thus those looking for work, but not eligible or willing or able to claim, are excluded from the figures. However the figures will also include those who claim benefit, whether legitimately or fraudulently, who may not actually be looking for work.

The statistics can be criticised on the basis of the *reliability*, which is threatened by frequent changes in the basis for collection, and their *validity*, as they reflect current social definitions of 'unemployment' rather than any objective rate. In addition, the government has been criticised by political opponents and professional statisticians for manipulating the criteria of unemployment to make the figures look lower.

Those who may be looking for work, but not eligible for benefit, include those under 18. Muncie estimated 300,000 unemployed youth were hidden in the YOPS training programme. The largest group is married women, who soon cease to be eligible for benefit and may 'disappear' into the home.

This group raises the problem of defining unemployment. Less employable workers, such as married women, the old, the sick and disabled, the unskilled, ill-educated and illiterate, may regard themselves, and be seen, as unemployable rather than unemployed. The Marxist concept of a reserve army of labour reminds us that some groups are seen as available for work when required, but are not seen as entitled to work.

If the definitions and methods of collecting data were kept constant, even if the numbers were inaccurate, there would be a useful indicator of trends of unemployment.

c) Using the statistics in Item C, describe the changing patterns in the occupational structure between 1984 and 1987.

The first two figures indicate a decline in primary (extractive) industry.
The third figure indicates a decline in secondary (manufacturing) industry.
The other three figures indicate increases in the tertiary (service) sector.
The largest change is the increase in office jobs in banking and finance. This, as with the expansion of other service industries, is likely to provide more employment in traditionally feminine jobs.

d) Examine the implications of the statistics in Items A and C for the employment prospects of 18–20 year-olds in the labour market.

Item A indicates a fall in the supply of 18–20 year-old labour. It is also likely that the decline will be proportionately higher among the better educated who are likely to proceed into higher education. Other things being equal, this will enhance the employment prospects of those who are available, particularly the more educated and better trained.

Item C illustrates likely changes in the demand for labour. Those living in rural or mining areas will have to travel, or hope that alternative employment in service industries, e.g. tourism and leisure or 'sunrise' industries, will expand.

Banking and finance remain concentrated in the South East, particularly in London itself. Workers will have to commute and it is possible that demand will be for the more educated.

The other service industries recruit more semi-skilled labour, and this suggests that prospects will be good for levels of employment, if not for those seeking interesting careers with high pay.

The expansion of employment is biased towards the more traditionally feminine occupations. The way in which we view such jobs may change, as employers compete more for workers. Nursing has already anticipated a major shortfall in traditional recruits.

e) Assess sociological contributions to our understanding of the effects of unemployment

Unemployment is claimed to have detrimental effects on individuals and their families. Fagin and Little see the effects in terms of 'loss'. The losses include self-esteem, sense of purpose, routine, relationships and, of course, income. Unemployment correlates with several measures of ill-health. It may be that ill-health contributes to unemployment or that both sickness and unemployment are more common in the lower classes. Caution is necessary when interpreting figures. Lower income can adversely affect diet and housing conditions, affecting the unemployed and their families. Smoking, alcoholism and suicide are all more prevalent among the unemployed (see also Chapter 15, especially the answers to Question 4 and Question 5).

The effects on the wider society are also open to discussion. The Marxist concept of a reserve army of labour would suggest that certain sections of the workforce are more likely to be unemployed. However, despite high unemployment in the 1980s, more and not fewer married women joined the labour market. Unlike Germany, Britain could not 'export' unemployment by limiting the numbers of migrant workers.

The regional nature of unemployment in the UK has led to social and political divisions. The Labour party has lost virtually all its seats in the South, except in inner-London. The Conservative party has lost virtually all its seats in Wales and Scotland.

Union membership and power have declined, although this may be due to legislation and to changes in the occupational structure, as well as to unemployment.

Racial tension in the early 1980s was associated with unemployment, but in the USA the worst violence occurred during periods of prosperity. Crime has also been seen as a result of unemployment, but the crime rates of the 1930s do not confirm this view. J.Young sees relative deprivation as a more important factor.

Finally, Pahl has argued that the unemployed have been stereotyped and are not, in fact, different from other sections of the working class. Working class life has often been characterised by insecurity, unemployment and poverty. The unemployed are not a distinct group, as workers continually move in and out of employment. However, over a quarter of Britain's unemployed have been without work for over two years.

STUDENT ANSWER WITH EXAMINER COMMENTS

Question 4

Assess the different ways in which sociologists have explained alienation in industrial societies.

> Marx said that what singles out humans from other species is the capacity to control nature by creative activity. Work can be an expression of human intellect and creative capacity and through work man can express his true essence. Alienation is the separation of man from his true essence and occurs when work is debased and made a burden. The alienated worker is seen as brutalised and greedy as he works for money.
>
> Marx felt capitalism produced the most alienation. Workers are tied to machines performing meaningless tasks. Labour power becomes a commodity and human activity is bought at the cheapest price. The product of labour is owned and sold by the capitalist and the worker is exploited. Owners design and control the whole work process so creativity and intellect are stifled and controlled by others. The worker has no control over what is made or how, when or at what price.
>
> For Marx the only way to overcome these aspects of alienation is to abolish the economic relations which create it. However, it is not clear whether a communist society could sustain abundance through high productivity and still abolish alienation and allow men to realise their true selves.
>
> Marxist theory concentrates on factory work rather than office work and so do other theories.
>
> Weber, Taylor, Mayo and Blauner all feel alienation is caused by conditions within the workplace. Unlike Marx, Weber feels bureaucratic control is not exclusively a feature of capitalism nor is it necessarily harmful but it will persist because it is efficient.
>
> Taylor pioneered Scientific Management which involved minute

❝ Successful description of alienation. ❞

❝ Capitalism identified as cause; design and control point good. ❞

❝ Modern Marxists do discuss deskilling and proletarianisation of office work. ❞

> **Not directly linked to alienation or question.**

division of labour, the separation of the worker from the decision maker and payment by results. Mayo indicated informal social relations were more important to workers than economic rewards.

Weber, Taylor and Mayo all suggest ways in which work can be organised efficiently, i.e. profitably, and their ideas have been applied to the workplace. Alienation is seen as the unfortunate product of efficiency.

> **Good brief summary.**

Blauner also disagrees with Marx's assumption that alienation is a product of capitalism. He feels it is caused by production technology. Blauner measures alienation along four dimensions: powerlessness, meaninglessness, isolation and self-estrangement. He divides technology into four types. Craft, machine-minding and assembly line work produce increasing amounts of alienation. However the fourth most modern type, process production, is less alienating and caused Blauner to be optimistic about the future.

> **Nice reference.**

Blauner's description of alienation has been used by women to describe housework. Oakley interviewed 40 housewives who described their work in similar terms as assembly line workers.

> **Salaman should be linked to Marxist ideas. A quote about design and control has been used in a past question.**

Salaman disagrees with the idea that alienation is caused by working conditions. He claims the most important cause is the design and control of the work which can be explained by the capitalist system. Work is organised by owners or managers to meet two interrelated needs. These are profit and control. Sometimes one is seen as more important than the other.

Braverman also stresses the control of the proletariat. It is easier to control the workers when they are under one roof. This, he claims, was the main reason the factory system replaced domestic production. Deskilling and fragmentation ensures that only the boss knows the whole process. This reduces the worker's bargaining power and cheapens labour. This may have the effect of either fragmenting solidarity or the opposite of increasing class consciousness.

In contrast to those sociologists who see alienation caused by capitalism or conditions in the workplace interactionists feel that alienation is an individual response which depends on the attitude of the workers. Workers' experience of work depends on the meaning they attribute to work which is influenced by the workers present and past experience both inside and out of work. Individuals respond differently to the same objective conditions.

Goldthorpe and Lockwood's Luton Studies found workers had an instrumental attitude to work. They worked for money not job satisfaction. Therefore if financial rewards were high they were not dissatisfied. The source of the instrumental attitude was thought to be outside in the privatised family.

Blackburn and Beynon agree, finding that part-time women workers and night-shift men had low expectations of job satisfaction but worked for the pay. They were generally satisfied despite their boring jobs. However, day shift skilled men, despite having more interesting jobs, were dissatisfied because of higher expectations.

> **Good use of studies.**

McKinnon conducted a similar study in Canada but concluded that instrumental attitudes were a response to boring work not a reason for choosing high paid but alienating work.

Overall comment

Overall, a sophisticated and critical account with a variety of relevant studies. An A grade answer.

Odd parts could be directly related to the question explicitly.

The candidate would be rewarded for considering alienation in other contexts apart from the context of work, e.g. religion or family.

ORGANISATIONS

BUREAUCRACY

FORMAL AND INFORMAL ORGANISATION

MANAGEMENT THEORIES

CAN ORGANISATIONS BE DEMOCRATIC?

THEORETICAL AND EMPIRICAL STUDIES

GETTING STARTED

Some students, or even teachers, find this a rather dry topic, perhaps because most of the literature on the subject is about work organisations. You might find this chapter more relevant if you try to relate what is often dated and remote material to your own experiences. You may not have direct experience of even part-time work, but you will have been a customer, client, patient, and certainly a student, of bureaucratic and other types of organisation.

The main themes of questions set on this topic are:

1 **A critical view of bureaucratic organisations.**
2 **The need to study informal as well as formal organisations.**
3 **A critical evaluation of management theories, particularly 'Scientific Management' and 'Human Relations' theories.**
4 **Can organisations be democratic?**

The most obvious related topics are work and the study of professions, professional associations and trade unions.

Definitions

- *Organisations* are groups with a structure and values, set up to achieve specific goals.

- *Informal organisation* describes the social order which emerges from a work group, rather than being imposed from above.

- *Formal organisation* describes the planned allocation of authority and tasks.

- *Bureaucracy* is a form of organisation based on rational principles. It is hierarchical, impersonal and governed by rules.

- *Effectiveness* refers to success in achieving goals.

- *Efficiency* refers to minimising costs.

ESSENTIAL PRINCIPLES

BUREAUCRACY

Weber saw *rational-legal* or *bureaucratic authority* as increasingly typical for government and business organisations in modern industrial societies. His ideal type of bureaucratic organisation is easier to remember and analyse if we use LITTLER's scheme, which divides the characteristics into two categories.

1   Bureaucratisation of the structure of control. This includes the division of labour and the hierarchical control over jobs rather than individuals. This is sought by leaders in order to maintain control.

2   Bureaucratisation of the employment relationship. This describes the career of individuals, where appointment, salary and promotion are based on rational and not personal criteria. This is often sought by workers to provide security.

The case for bureaucracy

66 **Is bureaucracy bad?** 99

It is suited to the efficient management of large-scale organisations in predictable conditions. Its technical superiority can be likened to mechanisation in factories. Action is 'rational' (i.e. individuals can calculate the best means to achieve ends) rather than effective or traditional.

The case against bureaucracy

Weber himself recognised certain limitations: inefficiency in times of crisis; 'specialists without spirit' efficient organisations with evil purposes. Either now, or at the end of the chapter, try and illustrate these points, both from the studies and from your own knowledge and experience.

Later critics develop these and other points. The main themes are:

1   Ineffectiveness and inefficiency in achieving goals.
2   Adverse effects on staff in terms of job satisfaction.
3   Adverse effects on inmates, patients and clients.

FORMAL AND INFORMAL ORGANISATION

You need to:

1   Define organisation.
2   Distinguish formal from informal organisation.
3   Explain why informal organisation develops, despite being unplanned.
4   Offer both Marxist and interactionist perspectives on informal organisation.

Remember that formal organisation can usually be equated with bureaucracy as it involves the planned and rational allocation of tasks and authority. Informal organisation describes actual, rather than ideal (i.e. desired by management), behaviour. Authority and control exist in informal organisations but are often 'traditional' rather than rational. Mayo suggests that norms emerge because of the structure of the work group, whereas interactionists see order as negotiated.

MANAGEMENT THEORIES

These can be arranged into the various schools which have criticised the work of F. Taylor.

Taylor's basic assumptions were:

1   Workers want high wages.
2   Bosses want low production costs (i.e. efficiency).
3   Scientific Management could satisfy both bosses and workers.

Taylor's critics include:

■ Mayo and the Human Relations school who deny Taylor's view of cash motivated individuals. They accept his aim of efficiency for profit but suggest a variety of more participative and democratic management methods.

■ Marxist critics who challenge the possibility of consensual aims between employer and worker. More specifically, they are concerned with the alienating effects of the fragmentation of tasks and the deskilling of workers.

■ Action theorists who deny the view shared by these essentially structuralist writers. Namely, that the organisation can be seen as a social system which exists independently of the members and which can determine their attitudes and behaviour. Instead, organisational order is seen here as being negotiated by individuals.

Consideration of the issues raised by this question should go beyond a discussion of MICHELS' work. The meaning of 'democracy' in this context could be outlined. Generally it implies the sharing of power and the participation in decision making.

We can look at democracy inside the organisation and examine the extent of participation rather than imperative control. We can also look at the effects which the organisation has on outsiders, such as clients, patients and the wider society.

Whereas Michels and, in a different way, Marxists see organisational democracy as impossible, other writers suggest the possibility of democracy, either for some kinds of organisations rather than others or for some individuals in the organisation rather than others.

BUREAUCRACY

BURNS and STALKER, GOULDNER and GROZIER all suggest that bureaucracy is inefficient in unstable and unpredictable circumstances, such as scientific research, mining and factory maintenace.

BLAU showed how rule-breaking in a bureaucratic organisation enhanced efficiency in the work of employment agencies. ROY made a similar case for rule-breaking in a factory, where workers saved unnecessary journeys by taking more tools from a store room than were allowed.

SELZNICK argued that bureaucratic organisations develop their own internal needs, such as survival and expansion, which can conflict with their stated goals. The effects of this are described in MICHELS' work.

MERTON'S criticism takes the form of identifying the *dysfunctions* of bureaucracy. As above, he sees it as inappropriate for conditions of change or flexibility. In addition, he sees the possibility of 'ritualism' developing, where workers become obsessed with means (rules and red-tape) rather than ends. All the above critics have taken the organisation's goals for granted and concerned themselves with the issue of 'efficiency.'

Marxists see bureaucracy as an organisational form which is part of the superstructure of capitalism and has inevitably adverse and alienating effects on both individuals and the wider society. Neo-Marxists, such as BURNHAM and DJILAS, see the top managers and administrators who control, rather than own, the means of production as forming new ruling classes in the USA and communist Eastern Europe, respectively.

SILVERMAN and other interactionist critics reject the bureaucratic approach, not on the grounds of its inefficiency nor of its alienating effects, but because it fails to explain the workings of organisations. It is individual actors, not organisations, who have needs and goals. Social order is not imposed by impersonal organisation rules nor through ruling class hegemony but *negotiated*, as individuals attribute meaning to the behaviour of themselves and others. GOFFMAN shows the very 'real' effects of this interaction process on inmates of Total Institutions, such as psychiatric hospitals.

FORMAL AND INFORMAL ORGANISATION

WEBER'S model of bureaucracy can be used as the dominant example of a type of formal organisation.

BLAU explains how informal organisation develops in order to achieve organisational aims.

DITTON'S 'Fiddling bread salesmen' and the illegal price-fixers described by Geis show how organisations tolerate and even reward law breakers who serve their own and organisational interest. (You might consider the 'insider trading' scandals of 1988 in this light.)

ETZIONI summarises interactionist criticism of the approaches above which over-emphasise the possibility of harmony and fail to consider non-business organisations. These interactionist approaches (see SILVERMAN above) are more concerned with the processes by which order is negotiated rather than imposed by either exploitative or enlightened managers.

MANAGEMENT THEORIES

TAYLOR'S work was completed before the 1st World War but remains influential, despite its early apparent discrediting by the human relations school. Marxists argue that its principles remain the basis for the organisation and control of work in capitalist society, and subsequent management theorists see his work as a benchmark to be rejected or amended.

The main principles are:

1 Scientific work-study can find the best ways for engaging in the work activity.
2 'Suitable' workers should be selected and trained to work scientifically, motivated by cash incentives.
3 Management should be separated from workers and should also be governed by scientific principles.
4 Piece-rates can be scientifically calculated and should not be reduced if workers earn a lot; they should share in the firm's prosperity.

MAYO: the studies at the Hawthorne Works led him into laying the foundations of the 'Human Relations' school of management, which perhaps even now dominates academic writing and the ideology of management in the workplace. The studies emphasise the importance of informal work groups in setting norms of production and the significance of social as well as economic rewards. Managers are advised to seek consensual solutions to problems and to develop structures and skills which enhance the communication between workers and managers.

BURNS and STALKER argued that there is **no** ideal management system and instead suggest a 'contingency approach', where technology, markets, human skills and motivation are all considered. They distinguish *mechanistic organisation* (similar to Weber's bureaucracy) from *organismic organisation*, which is more flexible, less hierarchical and more suited to conditions of change. Their main example is in the field of electronics, where firms require continual research and development.

EXAMINATION QUESTIONS

1 Assess the proposition that all organisations are inevitably oligarchic.

(ULSEB 1989)

2 'Scientific Management and Human Relations are different approaches to the study of organisations but they share the same aim of controlling the workforce.' Discuss.

(AEB 1988)

3 'Informal social processes reduce the efficiency of organisations.' Examine this view.

(AEB 1988)

4 Examine the view that Bureaucracy is always an efficient form of organisation.

(AEB 1987)

5 'Organic systems of organisation may be effective in innovative high-technology firms; they are unlikely to be effective in large-scale manufacturing industry.' Discuss.

(Oxford 1986)

OUTLINE ANSWERS TO SELECTED QUESTIONS

Question 1

This question occurs in the politics section of the paper. It requires reference to wider political issues and not just a narrow critique of bureaucracy, although this is relevant.

The essence of the answer should be an evaluation of the theoretical and empirical arguments for and against Michels' 'iron law of oligarchy'.

i) Explain and illustrate Michels' proposition. He can be seen as an elite theorist critical of Marxist views on the liberating effects of a revolution.

ii) Subsequent studies which support Michels can be cited, e.g. Selznick on the TVA. Include criticism of the governments of socialist countries, but perhaps mention the democratisation of Eastern Europe in 1989.

iii) Subsequent studies which criticise him can be cited. Include Gouldner's theoretical criticism, where he points out the need for leaders to get the consent of workers or subjects and sees oligarchy not as inevitable, but as in competition with democracy. Collective bargaining in British industrial relations is an example. Other studies can be used, such as Lipset *et al*, who see the possibility of democracy in unions but are generally pessimistic. Marxists see the cause of oligarchy in class relationships, not in the organisation itself. Etzioni sees some organisations as democractic.

Question 3

There is the opportunity here to use material on bureaucracy in answering questions on informal organisation.

i) Define and distinguish formal and informal organisation.

ii) Define effectiveness and efficiency.

iii) Ask 'efficient for whom?' and discuss at this point, or later, the Marxist analysis of organisations and their emphasis on control (Braverman etc.)

iv) Consider Weber's view that rationally planned organisation (usually bureaucratic) is the most efficient.

v) A variety of studies from different perspectives can be cited which support the proposition in the question. Taylor and Walton's interactionist study on industrial sabotage, Beynon on resisting management control of the pace of work, and studies of working to rule (easily linked to criticism of bureaucracy). Ditton, Mars and others who have studied theft in the workplace, note how theft from customers may be permitted, encouraged or even institutionalised into work roles. However this threatens the employer when the techniques are applied to theft from the organisation.

vi) The other side of the argument can be examined, i.e. that informal social processes could enhance organisational efficiency. This is found in studies by Blau, Mayo, Etzioni and Roy. Separate studies of receptionists and nurses in a dressings clinic show how people develop unofficial, but sometimes approved of, discretionary powers in order to make their jobs more interesting and more efficient.

Question 5

This is a more **specific** variant of those questions on organisations which are concerned with the effectiveness and efficiency of bureaucracy, formal organisation and particular methods of management.

i) Outline Burns and Stalker's work. Their mechanistic type of organisation can be equated with Weber's bureaucracy to provide greater opportunity for criticism.

ii) The effectiveness of mechanistic forms in mass production is supported by Weber and Taylor and also by those critics of bureaucracy who see it as unsuitable in unpredictable circumstances but efficient in large-scale manufacturing.

iii) The need for less bureaucratic types of organisation has been argued by Handy, who sees more organic forms as suitable for the development of new technologies. Drug manufacturers mass produce but are also dependent on continual research and development. The place of scientists in such organisations varies, from a leadership role to being outsiders working on research contracts.

iv) The development of the atomic bomb pioneered the bureaucratisation of scientific research, which Burns and Stalker later argued was inappropriate.

TUTOR'S ANSWER

Question 4

Examine the view that Bureaucracy is always an efficient form of organisation.

For the purposes of this essay, a bureaucratic organisation will be defined as one which conforms more or less to Weber's ideal type. Efficiency will be looked at from the managerial viewpoint of achieving goals at minimum cost. This can be distinguished from effectiveness which is measured by the extent to which goals are achieved.

Weber saw bureaucracy as proliferating in modern industrial societies because of its 'technical superiority' in maintaining social order and in achieving goals. Bureaucracy is based on rational rather than effective or traditional social action. The rational actor calculates the best means to achieve deliberately chosen goals. Bureaucracy then avoids arbitrariness, both in the treatment of staff and clients (or patients, inmates or subjects depending on whom the organisation serves). This ensures that the most suitable staff are appointed and promoted. Control is ensured by making behaviour conform to rules, and thus be predictable. The results of actions can be calculated in advance. This permits continuity for the organisation, since individuals become dispensable as the rules apply to their *positions* and not to them personally. Such information is kept in files, and not by individuals. Weber saw bureaucracy as ensuring efficiency by reducing both personal and material costs, because of the strict subordination of staff to rational rules.

Gouldner is better known for his criticisms of bureaucracy, but he does identify four positive functions which enhance organisational efficiency. Firstly, the 'explication function' where desired behaviour is made explicit by managers to subordinates. Secondly, the 'screening function' where the manager is protected from resentment by the impersonality of the rules. This reliance on bureaucratic authority also helps solve the problem of replacing the sometimes charismatic founder of business and other organisations. Thirdly, the 'remote control function' where individual managers need not be present to supervise work as the rules substitute for close observation and control. Gouldner cites the example of the forest ranger who follows state rules and procedures whilst working in isolation. Finally, there is the 'legitimate punishment function' where rules allow punishment for rule breaking without provoking unmanageable personal tensions.

So far it has been argued that bureaucracy can be efficient, at least in some circumstances. However Weber, himself, recognised certain problems. He saw it as 'inefficient in times of crisis' as well as having adverse effects on staff, or being used to achieve evil aims, albeit efficiently. This last point acknowledges the Marxist view that the bureaucratic state is used as an instrument of class domination. (See *Power and Politics*, Chapter 6)

The theme of inefficiency in the face of crisis, or even of unpredictability is common to a number of critics. Grozier, in a study of a tobacco factory, noted that the mass production of a standardised product was ideally suited to bureaucratisation. However the unpredictable nature of *machine failure* meant that the work of *maintenance staff* could not operate under a bureaucratic system. Some organisations have adopted planned maintenance schemes, where routines are followed whether or not such work is actually necessary. Critics see this as a ritualistic attempt to ensure that workers at least look as though they are working.

Gouldner, in the study of attempts to bureaucratise a gypsum mine documented the conflicts which arose when a new manager was appointed. The new manager had to contend, not only with the unpredictable nature of mining, but also with resistance from a workforce which had integrated into the local community to such an extent that supervisors were not prepared to enforce rules against theft against their neighbours, friends and relatives.

Burns and Stalker use different terminology but again emphasise the unsuitability of bureaucracy (or mechanistic organisation) for work where initiative, creativity and flexibility is required. They argue that organismic organisation is more appropriate for successful research and development in the electronics industry. The difficulties faced by scientists and other professionals working under bureaucratic control has been described by Cotgrove, Merton and (in a more Marxist context) Mills, who sees alienation resulting, together with the failure of the professional, to serve the needs of clients.

Blau showed how the actual breaking of bureaucratic rules could enhance organisational efficiency and increase the job knowledge of federal employment inspectors. This suggests either that the particular rules were unsuitable, or that bureaucratic rules cannot be produced for some situations.

If we regard the term 'efficiency' as problematic, we can ask efficient for whom? Goffman's study of a psychiatric hospital does not take the existence of bureaucracy for granted, but does see social order emerging from the negotiation of reality by the 'actors' involved in the situation. However, he also sees those with most power, namely the staff, imposing rules on the patients. The effects of imposing these rules is the opposite of the purpose of the organisation, which is therapeutic.

Marxist and other conflict critiques of bureaucracy see efficiency as always being judged from the point of view of the employers or the state. The organisations will then have alienating effects on staff, clients and subjects.

Efficiency does not always imply effectiveness. The NHS uses short waiting lists and short stays in hospital as indicators of efficiency. This disregards the fact that patients drop off lists if they cannot attend the hospital on the nominated day, even if never treated. Early discharge from hospital may inhibit recovery or even encourage return for further treatment. Similar observations can be made about prisons, where harsh (and cheap) regimes may encourage re-offending.

Michels saw the tendency towards oligarchy, even in organisations with democratic aims, as inhibiting effectiveness and efficiency. Similarly, Selznick saw organisations developing their own survival and expansion needs to the detriment of efficiency.

STUDENT ANSWER WITH EXAMINER COMMENTS

Question 2

'Scientific Management and Human Relations are different approaches to the study of organisations but they share the same aim of controlling the workforce.' Discuss.

> Scientific Management was an idea developed by F.Taylor in 1912. Its principles reflect Weber's contemporary writing on bureaucracy. Weber's theory is based less on technology and more on methods of organisation and control. Weber rejects the Marxist view that bureaucracy is a form of capitalist control which has ill effects on workers.
>
> Taylor, like Weber, suggested that the optimum efficiency of the workers would only be achieved by treating them as an extension of machines or organisations and as isolated individuals. This was opposed to treating them as a united work force with thoughts and minds of their own. Taylor advised standardisation and specialisation of tasks and removal of all intellectual work from workers. Decision making and control should be placed in the hands of managers. He thus pioneered the ideas which were later taken up by Ford such as deskilling, fragmentation of work and mass production on an assembly line.
>
> Taylor also advocated payment by results. He decided the workers were motivated solely by money and would produce more goods more efficiently if paid piece rates.
>
> In direct conflict with Taylor's theory Mayo produced the Human Relations theory. He carried out a series of studies at the Hawthorne works of Western Electric in Chicago. He wanted to test Taylor's theory that there was an optimum illumination level to maximise productivity. He discredited Taylor's theory by discovering that illumination itself had no effect but the fact that the workers knew they were being studied did. When they were aware of being observed productivity increased. Mayo then argued that social factors affected workers performance.
>
> Mayo carried out follow up studies in the 'bank wiring room'. He studied fourteen workers for six months. They were paid by a productivity bonus scheme. He discovered that despite being paid

66 Clever links with Marx and Weber. **99**

66 Brief but thorough account of Taylor. **99**

by results there was a unity among the workers not to individually maximise their production for extra bonuses but instead the group established its norms of production. There was group disapproval against those who produced either more or less than the norm. The Human Relation theory also argues that people need security, companionship and identity. They need to feel that they can communicate with the management. These people have to work with one another, on a collective basis, otherwise the worker will experience alienation and this will lead to a fall in productivity.

> **Brief but adequate account of Mayo.**

Braverman and Bowles and Gintis suggested that although the Human Relations theory was preferable to Scientific Management they both shared the common aim of controlling the proletariat. They said management serves two main purposes, these are efficiency and profitability and secondly to control the workers thus inhibiting the development of workers autonomy. Braverman says that the decline of domestic production was not due to new machinery but because the bourgeoisie had a vested interest in keeping the proletariat controlled in one area, that is, the factory. He also suggests that the fragmentation of tasks and the deskilling of workers makes them easy to replace and reduces their bargaining power as the manager knows the whole process and the workers do not.

> **Good critical use of writers; should identify as Marxist.**

Salaman agrees with Braverman that Taylorism is a form of organisational control but he also believes that Human Relations is a way of concealing exploitation. The sympathetic treatment of workers keeps them falsely conscious. Salaman explains the design of work in Marxist terms arguing that bureaucracy is not, as Weber claimed, inevitable but a product of capitalism not industrial society. Both management theories control workers but in different ways using different forms of rewards.

> **Accurate and relevant. It is he, not Braverman who criticises human relations.**

Modern Marxists claim Taylorism is still used today despite the view that Mayo discredited it in the 1930s. The evidence is found at the lower end of the job market where workers are deskilled and are extensions of the production line. Mayo's theory is used more with higher level and managerial workers where the need for social rewards is greater.

> **Apt comment.**

We can conclude that both theories are indeed just ways of controlling the work force and means of exploitation, but Human Relations is less insensitive and thus preferable.

> **Forceful, if arguable, conclusion.**

Overall comments

Overall, this is a succinct and well argued account. It shows the differences between Scientific Management and Human Relations and successfully identifies the Marxist criticism of these in the question.

Worth a grade B. Could be improved by clarifying the Human Relations section and by linking the Braverman study more explicitly to Taylor.

CHAPTER

PROFESSIONS

THE ROLE OF PROFESSIONS IN SOCIETY

PROFESSIONAL ASSOCIATIONS AND TRADES UNIONS

PROFESSIONALS IN ORGANISATIONS

THEORETICAL AND EMPIRICAL STUDIES

GETTING STARTED

Questions on the professions are set regularly. They frequently require you to challenge the view that they are distinctive occupations with a particular commitment to public service.

Criticism has tended to come from conflict theorists, but it is interesting to note the more recent attacks from the 1987 Conservative government. The government's commitment to market forces, competition and efficiency, has encouraged challenges to the restrictive practices of lawyers, to the professional autonomy of doctors and to the job security of university lecturers.

The main themes of questions set on this topic are:

1 **A critical evaluation of the role of professions in society**.
2 **A comparison of professional associations and trade unions**.
3 **The problems experienced by professionals working in bureaucratic organisations**.

Related topics include:

- *Stratification*. Some critics examine professions in class terms.
- *Work*. We could examine attitudes to work and the relationship between work and non-work.
- *Organisations*. Professionals are increasingly salaried employees rather than fee earners.
- *Health, education, welfare, science* and even sociology itself all provide employment for professionals.

Definition of the key term 'profession' is problematic and is indeed part of the answer to the most popular questions (See pp 102–103). Professions can either be seen favourably as special occupations, or more critically, as a class or classes.

THE ROLE OF PROFESSIONS IN SOCIETY

ESSENTIAL PRINCIPLES

We can summarise the various approaches as follows:

- **Consensus perspectives**:
  - Trait approach.
  - Functionalist accounts.
- **Conflict perspectives**:
  - Marxist accounts.
  - Weberian accounts.
  - Illich.
  - Feminist accounts.

This provides a useful framework for some answers.

CONSENSUS PERSPECTIVES

These offer an approving view of the professions, demonstrating the special contribution they make towards satisfying the needs of individuals and the functional needs of the social system.

The trait approach

This defines professions in terms of their possesion of distinctive traits or characteristics which make up an ideal type. This allows us to distinguish real professions, such as medicine or law, from semi-professions, such as teaching and nursing.
A typical list of traits is:

a) Altruism. A commitment to serving the client and society.
b) A specialist body of knowledge acquired during a long period of education and training.
c) Control over training, qualification, recruitment and expulsion.
d) A code of ethics.
e) Fee earning.

These five characteristics all enhance both individual and occupational autonomy.
   (**N.B.** You might use this list of traits to structure an essay. You could examine each one from both consensus and conflict view points.)

Functionalist accounts

These see the professions as playing a unique role in meeting the needs of the social system. The professional's work deals with important values, where the client lacks expertise and thus has to rely on the professional's integrity and skill. Professional norms, such as those found in their code of ethics, protect the client from exploitation and ensure that the public interest is served. The high status and rewards enjoyed by the professions are explained by their functional importance (see the functional theory of stratification: Davis and Moore, Chapter 3).

CONFLICT PERSPECTIVES

Marxist accounts

These see professionals as serving the interests of the ruling class. They tend to consider not just the traditional professions but also managers and bureaucrats. Professional knowledge is seen as part of the superstructure of capitalist society, e.g. the law or definitions of health.

Weberian accounts

These emphasise the ways in which the traits of professions can be used as strategies to maintain or improve their market situation. The key Weberian concept employed is *social closure*, this means restricting access to both the rewards, and the opportunities for achieving them in order to maximise those rewards.
   Although the state may help secure a monopoly for a profession the relationship is not a

simple one. Some professions (or even levels of a particular profession) are more supported by, and in turn support, the state than others.

Illich

The distinctive contribution of Ivan Illich has been to examine in detail the **harm** done by professions to individual clients and to the wider society (see Illich on health, Chapter 15).

Although he shares some common ground with other conflict approaches, he does not attack capitalist or patriarchal society in general, but rather the professions themselves.

Feminist accounts

Feminist critiques of the professions are concerned with two main issues. Firstly, the exclusion of women from high status and highly rewarded professions, or at least the higher ranks within the occupations. Secondly, the harm inflicted on women as clients, for example the medicalisation of pregnancy. (See also Chapter 5 and 15.)

PROFESSIONAL ASSOCIATIONS AND TRADES UNIONS

Generally, consensus theorists see the two types of organisation as quite distinct, and are uncritical of the role of professional associations. On the other hand, conflict theorists see them as essentially similar, but explain the 'apparent' differences as attempts to legitimise the privileged position of the professions.

Questions which require comparisons are best constructed by choosing a **particular** characteristic and then considering it from the viewpoint of the two institutions (or in other cases, the theories, approaches or methods) to be compared. This works much better than just describing the two institutions in separate parts of an answer.

You could compare their:

- objectives
- memberships
- methods
- values and ideologies

(See also the Tutor's Answer to Question 1, below.)

PROFESSIONALS IN ORGANISATIONS

The major issue is the effects which follow from professionals losing their traditional autonomy by becoming salaried employees of organisations rather than fee earners.

There are a variety of possible relationships between the professional and the organisation (see Hall below).

These may produce a number of problems:

1 The more bureaucratic, and thus less professional the employing organisation, the more likely is the possibility of *role conflict*. Involvement in work becomes less moral (i.e. based on shared values) and more calculative (i.e. instrumental) or even alienated.

2 The organisation's *efficiency* and *effectiveness* can be adversely affected if decision makers are less knowledgeable than the professionals they control. Judgements of competence are now made by managers, and not by peers. Weber failed to anticipate the split between bureaucratic authority and the professional authority which is based on expert knowledge, and not rank, and which is not confined to the needs of the organisations.

3 The professional-client relationship may be undermined. Potential **solutions** to these and other problems lie in:

   i   Separating professional tasks and personnel from bureaucratic tasks and officials.
   ii Professionals themselves adapting to bureaucratic needs.
   iii Changing the organisational structure, so that professionals are granted more autonomy.

THEORETICAL AND EMPIRICAL STUDIES

THE ROLE OF PROFESSIONS IN SOCIETY

DURKHEIM sees professions as a stabilising force, integrating industrial society where social solidarity is threatened by the division of labour. He emphasises their commitment to community, and not to class or selfish values.

BARBER, writing in post-war USA, repeats this point about the altruism of professionals, describing them as dedicated to community interests.

PARSONS illustrates the above, describing how scientists employ their knowledge rationally to solve community problems. He also identifies the functional role of the doctor, who authenticates the sickness, thereby allowing the patient to temporarily abandon work and other responsibilities (see Chapter 15).

DAVIS and MOORE explain the high rewards enjoyed by professionals in terms of their functional importance and the need to attract and motivate the most able recruits.

The following *conflict theorists* tend to see the professions in class terms, rather than just as an occupational category.

T.JOHNSON points out that different professions and, just as important, the different ranks within a profession, enjoy various levels of occupational control and reward. This inequality is a result of the changing class structure of capitalist society.

ALTHUSSER shares the Marxist view, and emphasises the importance of professions in transmitting ruling class ideology and their role in both ISAs and RSAs (see also Chapter 9).

NAVARRO explains state intervention in medicine by pointing out the need for a healthy (i.e. fit for work) workforce to serve employers.

MILLS anticipates the proletarianisation of professionals, together with other white collar workers (see also Chapter 3).

FRIEDSON sees the importance of state intervention in professional activity from a Weberian, rather than a Marxist perspective. Professional autonomy is dependent on restricting knowledge and the state can protect or undermine professional monopoly.

PARRY and PARRY show how professionals try to maximise rewards by restricting competition. Professionalism is an occupational strategy which can only be understood in relation to the class structure.

ILLICH specifically identifies the harm inflicted by doctors and other health professionals on individual patients and society. He describes *iatrogenic* illness, which is caused by medical intervention.

PROFESSIONAL ASSOCIATIONS AND TRADES UNIONS

PARKER offers a clear comparison between the two types of organisation.

T. JOHNSON shows how different sociological perspectives could be applied to the comparison, particularly how conflict perspectives blur the distinction.

J. JACKSON describes the process and the effects of the professionalisation of both occupations and society.

PROFESSIONALS AND ORGANISATIONS

HALL proposes four types of relationship between professionals and organisations:

1 Private practice (e.g. traditional partnerships).
2 Professional-led organisations (decisions made by experts, e.g. US hospitals).
3 Heteronomous organisations. (Organisations of professionals under external control, e.g. English hospitals and schools.)
4 Professional departments within bureaucratic organisations (the professional is in a subordinate position serving the needs of the organisation; e.g. lawyers employed by commercial companies).

MERTON identifies role conflict for scientists employed in large organisations.

COTGROVE sees scientists in industry as abandoning professional values and serving organisational goals by becoming instrumental rather than private professionals.

MILLS sees lawyers as serving the interests of corporations, and not the public, and the increased bureaucratisation of professions.

BURNS and STALKER suggest that *organismic* rather than *mechanical* organisation is better suited to solving scientific problems (see also Chapter 11).

EXAMINATION QUESTIONS

1   Examine the similarities and differences between Trades Unions and Professional Associations. Illustrate your answer with examples.

(AEB 1989)

2   Compare and contrast consensus and conflict approaches to the study of 'professions'.

(AEB 1983)

3   Assess sociological explanations of the high income and status associated with professional occupations.

(AEB 1988)

4   Describe and explain the differences between 'professions' and 'semi-professions'!

(AEB Oxford 1987)

5   Examine the relationship of professions to bureaucratic organisations.

(Author's question but the wording comes from the new AEB syllabus)

OUTLINE ANSWERS TO SELECTED QUESTIONS

Question 3

Critical analysis, not just description, of the competing explanations is required for a good answer. Do not just outline different approaches to the professions, but focus on 'high income and status'!

Reference to more general explanations of inequality by the various approaches will add theoretical depth to the specific studies of professions.

■ Trait approaches see professions as distinctive and superior occupations. You should critically evaluate the distinctive features asking whose interests are served in each case. Also regard the term 'professional' as problematic.

■ Functionalist approaches share the approving view of professions but explain their high status and rewards as a necessary mechanism for ensuring effective role allocation and performance to functionally important positions. Select relevant criticism of Parsons and Davis and Moore to challenge this view.

■ Conflict theories tend to derive from Marxist or Weberian explanations of inequality. The former emphasise the ideological role of professions and the latter the occupational strategies that restrict competition.

Remember that positive, as well as the more obvious negative, criticism scores marks.

Question 4

Some detailed description of the characteristics of professions as perceived by the various approaches is obviously required. However, as in all answers, credit is given not just for remembering descriptive material but more importantly for the ability to analyse and evaluate arguments.

We can, as above, use consensus and conflict approaches as the framework for the answer.

Trait theories distinguish degrees of professionalism, on the basis of the possession of a list of distinctive traits. Traditional professions have most of these traits, whereas semi-professions have fewer. Give illustrations and perhaps explain development in terms of the historical role of the State. Functionalism explains the professionalisation of society and occupations and sees full professions as performing the most valued tasks, and employing the rarest skills.

Marxist theory sees the relative status and rewards of different occupations (and ranks within an occupation) as reflecting the needs of a developing capitalist class structure.

Weberian theories see the distinction between real and semi-professions as no more than their respective ability to control competition through closure strategies.

In conclusion, it is worth pointing out that any distinction between professions and semi-professions should not be seen as fixed. All the above theories see the possibility of threats to traditional professions, e.g. bureaucratisation and the increased professionalisation of other occupations.

Question 5

The instruction to 'examine' requires a detailed and critical analysis of the various relationships which can exist between the professions and bureaucratic organisations.

You could use Hall's four types of relationship to organise an answer, and in each case consider the problems that are likely to occur. Alternatively you could write separate sections on problems for the professional, the organisation and the client. Hall's types could then be offered as potential solutions to conflict.

A good answer is likely to put the process of bureaucratisation in a theoretical context, refering to Marx, Weber and Durkheim.

TUTOR'S ANSWER

Question 1

Examine the similarities and differences between Trades Unions and Professional Associations. Illustrate your answer with examples.

There are three main views as to the similarities and differences between Trades Unions (TUs) and Professional Associations (PAs).

Firstly, despite acknowledging that both are organisations of workers, they are seen as distinct in terms of their role in society, objectives, methods, ideology and membership.

Secondly, they are seen as essentially similar, but the public acceptance of professional ideology conceals this so that PAs seem superior.

Thirdly, both similarities and differences are recognised and a tendency for a degree of convergence between the two identified.

Definitions of the PAs and TUs must be regarded as problematic, because their characteristics are changing rather than fixed and their role is perceived differently from the various sociological perspectives.

Those writers who see the two types of organisation as largely different tend to accept at face value their 'ideal types' and to be uncritical of the distinctive traits of the professions.

I shall now contrast the two by distinguishing their objectives, methods, membership and values. The main stated goal of PAs is to serve the client and community through the rational application of their particular expert knowledge and the maintenance of high standards of practice. They are thus committed to social service rather than to the selfish interests of the members. In contrast, the TUs are seen as defensive and not altruistic, organisations. They try to redress the bargaining disadvantage of individual workers in their relationship with employers.

The methods used by each to achieve their objectives can also be contrasted. PAs strive for, and in many cases achieve, autonomous job regulation. They gain this independence by exerting control over recruitment, training and qualification. They also may devise and enforce their own code of ethics. The main methods used by TUs are collective bargaining (backed up by sanctions such as strikes) and joint consultation (or even participation) with employers at plant, company, industry and national level. This co-operation at national level with employers, and also with government, has been diminished in recent years by the current government's distaste for 'corporatism'.

Perhaps the most superficial distinction can be made by looking at membership. PAs are organised on an occupational basis and comprise highly educated recruits to, and usually from, the middle classes. TU membership largely consists of manual workers, organised perhaps on an occupational or craft basis but also possibly as an industrial or general TU.

The total membership of TUs has declined dramatically since 1979, but the non-manual membership has risen, both in proportional and real terms. This distinction is thus diminishing, particularly as some white collar unions seek professional status and some PAs adopt TU methods.

In terms of values and ideology, considerable differences are perceived. PAs are individualistic in outlook, despite a sense of community based on their positive attitude to work. Whereas TUs are collectivistic in outlook their solidarity being based on tradition or instrumentalism. (These concepts are developed in the work of Lockwood and Goldthorpe.) TU members see society in class terms ('them and us') whereas professionals see social inequality as based on individual achievement. The PAs are seen as conservative, supporting the status quo but generally above partisan politics, whereas the TUs in most industrial societies are associated with leftwing parties.

If, in the second part of the answer, we argue that the two types of organisation are essentially similar, then the professions must be looked at more critically.

From a pluralist view, both can be seen as secondary work organisations which bargain in the industrial relations system and represent members interests in the wider political system. However, a better case for similarity is found if we adopt the conflict perspectives argued by Marxist and also Weberian writers.

The objectives of PAs are seen here as either serving ruling class interests or as being intrinsically selfish, but legitimised by ideology. Their methods are similar to, but often more effective than, those used by TUs. The closed-shop, restrictive practices, pressurising of government and using industrial muscle are all employed by PAs. The autonomous job regulation which was effectively destroyed by Rupert Murdoch of Fleet Street is virtually unchallenged on Harley Street. However both dockers and university lecturers have lost job security in the 1980s.

The special traits which define the professions can be negatively evaluated to argue they are merely strategies of 'closure' used by PAs to maintain or improve the market situation of professional workers.

If we now, for the third part of the answer, argue that the similarities and differences cannot be regarded as fixed but develop in response to wider social changes, then some tendency to convergence can be argued.

Professionalisation of individual occupations and society as a whole has been remarked upon by functionalists and Weberians. This process is explained by the increased rationalisation of society and the successful application of scientific and other expertise to societies problems. Functionalists see the effects as stabilising the social system, Weberians as increasing efficiency and improving the rewards of professionals.

Marxists have predicted the 'proletarianisation' of professionals along with other white collar workers. Unionisation of lower professionals, such as teachers and nurses, and the bureaucratisation of the employers of higher professionals, such as doctors, are threats to the autonomy described above. Those professions, or ranks of professions, which have been most 'feminised' in membership are perhaps the most vulnerable.

Braverman saw TUs emerging and maturing as a response to Taylorism, which led to the loss of occupational self control of craft workers through deskilling. Similar threats to the control of knowledge and technique enjoyed by professionals may lead PAs to develop TU tactics.

In conclusion, it might be wisest to abandon attempts to argue that TUs and PAs are either identical or distinct categories, but instead to see a continuum between the two which is changing and not fixed.

STUDENT'S ANSWER WITH EXAMINER COMMENTS

Question 2

Compare and contrast consensus and conflict theories to the study of the 'professions'.

> The role of people in the professions is seen by functionalists as satisfying the functional needs of the social system. Davis and Moore state that certain positions in society are more important than others and require special skills which only few people have

the talent to perform. Therefore the high rewards for the professions are one way of making sure that important positions are filled by the best people.

However, Marx argues that they are servants of the ruling class keeping the working class falsely conscious and using their positions to legitimise power and rewards of higher income and prestige.

Many of the long established and influential professions have bodies which have a legal right to test the competence of prospective members. Such bodies as the BMA and the Law Society control the right of individuals to practice and can therefore control the number and type of practitioners in a particular field.

Whereas functionalists would say that this system maintains standards and protects clients by preventing exploitation, conflict theories suggest it is their way of restricting entry. By controlling members it creates a closed shop.

Marshall and Barber respectively see professionals as unselfish and dedicated to the interests of the client and the community, but in fact the client is rarely given the opportunity to express satisfaction or dissatisfaction with service received. Professionals usually insist that only fellow professionals are qualified to assess their performance. Their own ethical codes may prohibit one professional from criticising another.

One important characteristic of professionals as seen by functionalists is that they have a distinctive body of knowledge acquired through formal training which is expertly applied. Marx says the language used in training denies access to the working class making it difficult to understand. Today in some professions, e.g. lawyers, it seems easy for them to demand large sums of money from the working class to translate complicated vocabulary in documents drawn up by themselves

Weber thinks the professions are part of the redistribution of power to bureaucratic organisations which increasingly employ professionals. The upper and middle classes providing a service for themselves.

Durkheim, however, says the professions integrate modern societies by serving the community not themselves. They bridge the gap between capitalism and the extension of the bureaucratic state by being dedicated to community interests.

Professionals are seen by some Marxist revisionists as part of a new ruling class rather than just servants of it. This new ruling class controls, rather than owns, the means of production. Parsons, however, argues that scientists serve the community rather than class or selfish interests.

Women's health seems to be controlled in most cases by doctors. Statistics show that far more women are patients than men. Feminists feel that in most cases such as pregnancy women are able to take care of themselves.

Illich attacks the professions as selfish occupations not part of a particular class. For example in 'de-schooling society' teachers are seen as obstacles to education. They control pupils through the monopolisation of knowledge. We can all be made into potential patients by doctors.

Sidebar comments:
- Should identify functionalism as a consensus theory.
- Not clear if the income of the professional or the ruling class is referred to.
- Sounds more like Weberian than Marxist analysis.
- Good comparative point.
- Functionalism and critics, but not identified as such.
- Not clear if it is the client or the prospective professional who is excluded by language.
- Yes.
- Yes.
- Djilas and Burnham and criticism.
- Feminist critique of professions could be developed.
- More to be said on Illich and critique of medicine.

Overall comments

Overall, a competent and critical account, worth a C Grade; it could be improved by:
1 Developing the Weberian views of Parry and Parry to discuss the self interested behaviour of professions, using concepts like market situation, status and power. The potential for exclusion should be pointed out.
2 Explaining more clearly the distinction between consensus and conflict theories.
3 Distinguishing Marx from Marxists.

CHAPTER

13

RELIGION

MARXIST PERSPECTIVES

FUNCTIONALIST PERSPECTIVES

THE SECULARISATION DEBATE

THEORETICAL AND EMPIRICAL STUDIES

GETTING STARTED

The sociology of religion is concerned with the role of religion in the wider society and the way in which religion helps people make sense of the world. The intention of sociology is neither to affirm nor challenge religious belief but to examine religion from the point of view of social actors or to identify the impact of religion on social behaviour.

The main themes of questions set on this topic are:

1 **Critical evaluation of the major theories of religion of Marx, Durkheim and Weber.**
2 **Comparison of the major theories and their application to issues such as social order, social change and social inequality.**
3 **The secularisation debate.**
4 **The significance of the growth of sects.**

Credit will be given for comparative material and for the ability to apply theories to contemporary events.

Definitions

- *Religion*. There is no agreed definition, but sociologists are concerned with these three aspects of religion:
- *Religious belief.*
- *Religious practice.*
- *Religious institutions.*
- *Secularisation*. Involves the decline in the influence of religion on the wider society and the reduction in the spiritual content of religious belief. Any definition must be regarded as problematic.
- *Sects*. According to Wilson, these are 'Exclusive bodies which impose some test of merit . . .faith, knowledge or obedience . . . .
- *Cults*. Are arguably, religious groups, whose beliefs and practices are more concerned with this world than with more spiritual matters.

Related topics include *sociological theory, development, stratification* and other areas which are concerned with *belief, knowledge* and *ideology*.

ESSENTIAL PRINCIPLES

Certain shared assumptions about the role of religion in society are to be found in the work of Marx and in subsequent Marxist accounts.

1   Religious beliefs and institutions are part of the superstructure of exploitative (pre-communist) societies.
2   Changes in the economic substructure produce changes in religion.
3   Religion helps to reproduce the existing relations of production.
4   Religion is a form of alienation. It was made by men to ease their suffering, but also perpetuates it.
5   Religion is the 'Opiate of the masses'. Firstly, it eases the pain produced by capitalism and secondly, it distorts reality so that the source of pain is concealed. The working class is kept falsely conscious. Suffering, deprivation and poverty are seen as divinely ordered. Justice will come to the righteous and meek in the next world. Some religions await imminent devine intervention which cools revolutionary fervour.

Critics

Weber attacked the alleged economic determinism of Marx. He saw religious belief as influencing the economic organisation of society, rather than vice versa.

Functionalists recognise similar effects of religion on the wider society, e.g. Durkheim saw it as diminishing the significance of social stratification and Malinowski saw it as easing emotional stress. However they emphasise the positive, integrative effects of religion, rather than seeing it as reproducing inequality.

Functionalists, following Durkheim, include social anthropologists like Malinowski and Americans like Parsons and Davis and Moore. They share certain common assumptions about the nature of society and the role of religion in society. The origin, persistence and form of religion can be explained by identifying the contribution it makes towards meeting the needs of the social system.

The functional needs satisfied by religion are:

1   *Integration*: shared beliefs, rituals and sacred objects provide a basis for social order based on consensual values. Durkheim saw religion as the worship of the moral order which makes up society.
2   *Social control (pattern maintenance)*: religion provides divine backing for important rules and the certainty of justice in the next world.

Critics

Critics question both the desirability and existence of social solidarity based on consensus. Even if these were demonstrated, religion could be the cause of disharmony and disunity.

WEBER

WEBER'S study 'The Protestant Ethic and the Spirit of Capitalism' is seen as having a wider significance than its explanation of the substantive issue of the rise of capitalism in Western Europe.

1   It provides a critical view of the Durkheimian approach to sociology, whereby the scientific study of social facts is advocated. Weber shows how the social meanings given to behaviour offer an alternative topic of study.
2   It is more obviously a critique of Marxist economic determinism. Whereas Marxists see ideas emerging from the substructure, Weber argues that ideas and beliefs (i.e. the Protestant ethic) can influence the economic organisation of society. Whereas Marxists see religious belief as inhibiting social change, Weber saw religious belief as a potential cause of change.

Weber's study argued that protestant beliefs contributed towards the rise of capitalism in certain specific cases. It was a necessary, but not a sufficient, cause and was not an example of a universal social law.

The basis of the argument is that the protestant beliefs associated with Calvinism, such as concern with deeds in this world and predestination, encouraged thrift and individualism which in turn encouraged the development of capitalism. The individual is seen as working hard, in a rational manner, and investing the proceeds in order to improve productivity and profitability.

Critics

Marxists maintain that the apparent link between protestantism and capitalism is not, as Weber suggests, an 'elective affinity' but the result of protestantism being a suitable ideology to legitimise inequality.

Other critics, whilst accepting the possible relationship between religious belief and economic development, argue that a variety of other factors may have been more influential in explaining the rise of capitalism and are therefore more appropriate explanations of economic development in general. The alternative causal factors include religious freedom, liberal democracy, and the influence of 'marginal groups' such as immigrants.

THE SECULARISATION DEBATE

Marx, Durkheim and Weber are all concerned with the relationship between religion and the wider society. They emphasise the effects of religion on various aspects of social life, such as social change. All three, in fact, predict the emergence of more secular societies and see the rise of modern industrial or capitalist society as an influence on this process.

The main sociological issues involve the problems of:

- defining secularisation.
- assessing the extent of secularisation.
- attributing meaning to behaviour, particularly attendance at religious ceremonies.

Sects

The early studies of sects were concerned with the categorisation of religious organisations, in particular with distinguishing sects from churches. The major emphasis of most studies was on Christian sects. Subsequently, interest has shifted to explaining the links between religious movements and other aspects of social life. The origin, growth and future development of sects and cults has been explained in a variety of ways, relating changes to other aspects of social change. Non-Christian sects and non-religious cults have been studied and their roles in society examined (see p.109).

THEORETICAL AND EMPIRICAL STUDIES

MARXIST STUDIES

Modern Marxists are far less interested in religion than Marx himself was. This is because there now appear to be more effective ways of reproducing ruling class ideology, e.g. education and the mass media (see Marxist sections of Chapters 9, 14 and 19). Althusser and Gramsci are certainly interested in notions of hegemony and ideological control, but primarily acknowledge the effects of secularisation rather than religion in Western capitalist societies.

FUNCTIONALIST STUDIES

DURKHEIM provided the basic ideas which are found in modern functionalist approaches and which were outlined above. He did offer the distinctive view that religion was, in fact, the worship of society, or more specifically the moral order. In describing religion in aboriginal society he said 'the God of the clan is the clan itself'.

Durkheim offers the rather Marxist sounding view that religion can integrate societies by making inequalities seem less significant and making people feel less aggrieved by them.

MALINOWSKI, like Durkheim, applied the fuctionalist approach to the study of religion in simple societies. He does not accept Durkheim's view that religion is the worship of society. He offers, instead, the view that the functions of religion apply to more restricted areas of social life than the establishment of the collective conscience. Religious beliefs and rituals integrate societies when solidarity is threatened by emotional stress, e.g. following death or by uncertainty resulting from the inability to predict nature, e.g. the impact of bad weather on fishing.

HERBERG offers a functionalist account of the role of religion in contemporary American society which, incidentally, indicates the way in which religion itself can become secularised. Religion helps to integrate an immigrant society by:

a) providing churches which cut across ethnic divisions.
b) providing organisations to which individuals in a competitive individualistic society feel they can belong.
c) 'Americanising' the major denominations of Christianity and Judaism.

Religion and Social change

Both marxists and functionalists see religion as essentially a conservative influence on society. There are, however, various studies which challenge this view.

THOMPSON identifies the roots of English socialism in the Methodist Church, not in Marxism, and thus sees the potential for religious beliefs to support social change.

WORSLEY, in a study of 'cargo cults' in the South Pacific, suggests that religious movements can be transformed into radical political groups challenging imperialism.

FRIERE, in discussing the rise of 'liberation theology' within the Roman Catholic Church in Latin America, argued that authentic Christianity involves the 'critical analysis of social structures'.

The role of religious movements in the struggle for civil rights in the USA and against apartheid reinforces the reformist, or arguably revolutionary, potential of religion. Islam is identified as a conservative influence in some societies, and as a force for change in others.

Studies of sects

WILSON explained the growth of sects as a response to secularisation, unlike Martin's view that they were evidence against secularisation as they represent a movement towards pure and fervent religion. Wilson sees sects as attracting seekers of mystery, ecstasy, a stable social order, a sense of identity and a feeling of belonging. In addition they attract those who reject the impersonal, rational, bureaucratic and wicked world. He does not accept that all such groups would be regarded as religious in the everyday sense of the word.

Wilson distinguished eight types of sect and cult based on their attitude to the wider society which influences their beliefs, practices and organisation. He sees significant differences between 'conversionist' and 'withdrawn' groups and also between 'world affirming' and 'world rejecting' groups.

WALLIS explained the development of various kinds of new religions and new cults in terms of their members rejection of modern industrial society. He identified the alienating effects of work, curbs on individual freedom, secularisation and materialism. The new converts were frequently adolescents who sought success or peace of mind in this world, or an escape from it. The reference to secularisation is similar to Wilson's earlier views. Wallis also offers a view, influenced by Merton's anomie theory of deviance, suggesting that blocked opportunities to achieve consensual goals by legitimate means, encourages membership of world affirming groups such as Scientology or Christian Science.

Wallis distinguishes cults, which offer success in this world, from the new religions which may also be world rejecting or world accommodating. The new religions include:

a) Fundamentalist sects of Jewish-Christian origin, which tend to be evangelical and puritanical.
b) Imported sects of Eastern religions, which are puritanical and reject materialism.
c) Hybrids, like the 'Moonies' (the subject of a participant observation study by Barker) whose church is an amalgam of Eastern and Western religions and is pro-capitalist.

Studies of secularisation

WILSON has argued for the secularisation thesis (see also Tutor's Answer to Question 4). He cites as evidence:

a) The decline in religious practice, such as church attendance, observing rules and participation in rites of passage.
b) The decline in religious knowledge and belief.
c) The decline in the influence of religious institutions, particularly on secular matters such as politics and education.

d) The declining numbers, influence and prestige of an ageing clergy.
e) The growth of sectarianism.

MARTIN has presented an opposing view, questioning the validity of the behavioural measures listed by Wilson. He claims that religious beliefs and meanings continue to have considerable influence on people's lives. He sees people and religious organisations as becoming more, not less, religious.

BELLAH has argued that the declining influence of religious institutions is not evidence of secularisation, but simply a change to a more individual form of religious belief and practice. Martin saw this as the natural development of the protestant tradition of individualism.

PARSONS sees the persistence of religious belief and values in the secular morality of Western societies. He is concerned with the integrative and social control functions of religion. Fellow functionalists, Davis and Moore, see a minimal amount of religiosity as 'indispensable' because of the functions associated with religion.

EXAMINATION QUESTIONS

1 Examine the view that religious ideas and institutions are necessarily conservative forces.

(AEB 1987)

2 'The growth of religious sects and cults can be understood mainly as a response to social and economic deprivation'. Examine this view.

(AEB 1989)

3 Does the growth of new religious movements throw doubt on the idea of secularisation?

(Oxford 1988)

4 What problems do sociologists face in attempting to define and measure secularisation?

(AEB 1987)

5 Compare and contrast Marxist and Weberian explanations of relationship between religious belief and social change.

(AEB 1986)

OUTLINE ANSWERS TO SELECTED QUESTIONS

Question 1

This question requires a critical discussion of the role of both religious belief and organisations in the wider society. The simplest organising framework is to use the three classic theories and some modern examples. Note the different interpretations of the term 'conservative' and their implications for the answer.

1 Marx and the Marxists:
  Religion is conservative in the sense that as part of the superstructure of exploitative societies it helps to maintain the existing substructure. The opiate of the masses keeps the working class falsely conscious.
2 Durkheim and the functionalists:
  Religion is implicitly conservative in that it helps to maintain the equilibrium of the social system. It stops people feeling aggrieved and makes inequality less noticeable. Note the similarity with Marx. Change if it occurs, is evolutionary rather than revolutionary. Religion integrates society and helps maintain social order. Herberg suggests that religion integrated US society.

3 Weber:
   Religion is not necessarily conservative. Calvinism helped promote the rise of capitalism. The Islamic revolution in Iran, the Liberation Theology of the RC Church in Latin America, and Worsley's 'Cargo Cults' all illustrate similar changes encouraged by religion.
4 You could also discuss whether churches are conservative whereas sects are not (this is a generalisation to be challenged).

Question 2

You must explain, criticise and offer alternative views to the claim that deprivation is the main explanation of the growth of sects.

1 Social and economic deprivation does not explain growth:
   a) Marx sees all religious beliefs and institutions as part of the superstructure.
   b) Weber writes of a Theodicy of suffering.
   c) Glock and Stark see the development of religious groups as a response to deprivation of various kinds, including social and economic deprivation.
   d) The success of Black Muslims in the ghettoes of the USA is an example of responding to deprivation.
2 Alternative explanations of the growth of religious groups:
   a) Wilson suggests that sects arise as a response to secularisation.
   b) Martin sees sects as evidence of a religious revival.
   c) Niebhur sees sectarianism, and the subsequent consolidation of some sects into denominations, as a recurring process.
   d) Wallis offers a variety of possible factors encouraging new groups, including alienation, anomie and the rejection of materialism.
   e) Glock and Stark suggest other forms of deprivation, such as ill-health, which sects compensate for.

Question 3

This is not an uncommon question and it requires consideration of material both on sects and secularisation.

Yes:
1 Churches have lost members and influence but new movements have thrived indicating religion is developing, not in decline (Martin).
2 This is a continuation of historic tendencies towards sectarianism to regain purity and/or follow a charismatic leader (e.g. Christians and Sikhs).

No:
1 Sects are a response to secularisation, not evidence against it (Wilson).
2 Growth is explained by social disorganisation and change (Wallis).
3 Growth is explained by social and economic deprivation (Glock and Stark).

TUTOR'S ANSWER

Question 4

What problems do sociologists face in attempting to define and measure secularisation?

Sociological debates about the extent of secularisation in modern industrial societies focus more on the problems of definition and assessment than on the 'facts' about religious events. Definitions of both religion and secularisation are disputed, and in the absence of a consensual view of what specularisation would involve there can be no agreement on the extent of the phenomenon.

Durkheim saw religion as a unified system of beliefs and practices about sacred things. The emphasis on unity suggests that the influence and functions of religion decline when there is religious diversity or scepticism. Wilson suggests that we should see religion as the behaviour and organisations which are 'in the everyday sense of the word religious'. He is trying to avoid the problem of perceiving any novel magical, mystical or supernatural belief and practice, as evidence of some kind of religious revival.

The major arguments against secularisation in Britain have come from Martin. He sees secularisation as referring to firstly, changes in thought, attitude and belief, and secondly, changes in institutions, custom and practice. Secularisation would involve the declining importance of religion at both the institutional level and the personal level. His concern with belief, as well as practice, is central to the problem of assessment.

A less partisan position is taken by Shiner who, in an attempt to unravel the complications caused by the term secularisation being used in so many different ways, offers a simplified view. Based on a review of the literature, he suggests that there are two dominant themes. Firstly, the secularisation of society, which involves a decline in the influence of religion over the wider society. Secondly, the secularisation of religion itself, which involves religious ideas and institutions becoming less spiritual and more wordly.

A final view, from an interpretive perspective, comes from Berger and Luckman. They saw religion as providing a 'universe of meaning' whereby individuals made sense of the world. Religion legitimises beliefs and institutions. They are doubtful whether more rational beliefs could explain ultimate mysteries, such as death.

Assessment of the extent of secularisation usually involves consideration of three dimensions of measurement of religion. These are: religious belief, religious behaviour and religious institutions. The reliability and validity of such measures will be considered below.

The main problems of assessing the extent of secularisation can be summarised as follows:

Firstly, the problem of agreeing on definitions so that sociologists can decide what should be observed and measured. This has been discussed already but one outstanding issue is the extent to which change in religious belief, practice or institutions should in itself be regarded as evidence of secularisation.

Secondly, the problems of identifying the meaning behind behaviour. Even if the reliability of, say, church attendance statistics could be taken for granted, the significance of church-going as a measure of religiosity could be disputed. There are of course technical problems involved in the gathering of church attendance figures, such as which institutions should be included, as well as problems of interpretation.

Thirdly, there is the problem of assessing the degree of *past* religiosity which is of course necessary in order to compare the current position with the past. Such a comparison is to demonstrate the decline or otherwise of religion. Many of those who simultaneously describe and deplore the trend towards a more secular society may have a romanticised view of some non-existent 'golden age' when religion flourished.

These problems can be illustrated by considering some of the major disputes over interpreting events which, it has been argued, are evidence of secularisation. The most important of these is the problem of the motives and meanings attributed to religious behaviour. There has been a decline in church attendance and in participation in rites of passage. This could be taken at face value, or the meaning of this could be questioned by pointing out that religious belief does not require church attendance and that individual practice, for example in the home, still flourishes. Conversely, religious practice may have alternative meanings; for example, people may follow dietary rules for secular reasons and church attendance may be motivated by the desire to participate in social activities.

The declining influence of religious institutions has been cited as evidence of secularisation. However, Parsons has argued that the withdrawal of churches from political and educational roles is evidence of structural differentiation and that the churches are now more religious. Martin sees the declining influence of the church as a natural progression of the individualism of the protestant tradition, which he supports.

The development of rational, secular ideas in politics, the sciences and professions, seems to represent a threat to the traditional religious ideas. Marx, Freud and Darwin have all been used to challenge religious beliefs. Durkheim, Weber and Marx all predicted the decline of religion in more rational industrial societies. Critics have suggested that the secular alternatives are no more rational than religious belief. Berger talks about 'scientism' as an ideology involving unquestioning faith in the ability of science to explain the universe. However, as stated above, Wilson pointed out that not all irrational beliefs could be regarded as authentic religion.

The view that religion itself has become secularised by accommodating itself to the various changes in society, has been used to sustain the secularisation thesis in the USA where religious identification and practice remains at high levels. Examples can be found of the bureaucratisation of religion, the development of business aims by religious organisations and the modernisation of religious beliefs and practices to conform to the secular values of a secular society. However it is also the case in the USA, and throughout much of the Islamic world, that there has been a revival of religious fundamentalism which challenges the secularisation thesis.

Thus, it can be seen that the debate over secularisation is as much a debate over the appropriate definition of concepts and methods of assessment, as it is a dispute over evidence.

STUDENT ANSWER WITH EXAMINER COMMENTS

Question 5

Compare and contrast Marxist and Weberian explanations of the relationship between religious belief and social change.

❝❝ Suitable introduction. ❞❞

❝❝ Should link history to social change. ❞❞

❝❝ Insert 'help' before create. ❞❞

❝❝ Good on ruling class. How is inequality legitimised? ❞❞

❝❝ Insert 'or possibility' after need. ❞❞

❝❝ Insert 'may' before cause. ❞❞

Two completely different concepts in sociology are Marxist and Weberian explanations of religion. Marx believed the relationship between religion and social change was that religion inhibited and suppressed social change. Weber, on the other hand, believed that religious belief could and did cause social change.

However, before we compare and contrast these two views, it must be said that both Marx and Weber adopted different approaches to the study of religion. Weber attempted the interpretive understanding of social action and employed the comparative method. Marx believed that action is constrained by the economy. Many Marxists believe history is a mechanical process directed by economic forces.

Marx sees the role of religion as supporting ruling class interests. Religion creates a falsely conscious society, unaware of its exploitation and fitting the needs of capitalist employers.

The falsely conscious society is created by easing the pain of exploitation. The working class are led to believe that their suffering is a virtue and that they would be rewarded in the next world. Their exploitation and inequality is justified by God. It is not only the working class who are influenced by religion but also the ruling class. However, for them religion is a force which can justify their wealth at the expense of the workers.

Therefore Marx believed that religion acted as an opiate to dull the pain produced by oppression. It creates a distortion of reality and provides many of the deceptions which form the basis of ruling class ideology. Religion does not solve the problem of exploitation but is instead a misguided attempt to make life bearable. As the workers are under the influence of religion and falsely conscious they see no need for social change. Therefore, religion acts as a restraint over any type of reform and smothers thoughts of revolution.

Weber sees religion as a dynamic force which causes social change rather than discourages it. In 'The Protestant Ethic and the Spirit of Capitalism' Weber concentrates on the effects of Calvinism on the promotion of capitalism. He describes how Calvinistic beliefs encourage individualism. Instead of trying to attain success in the next world they attempt to find success in this world. Rather than putting their energies into religious activities, as some religions do, the Calvinist puts a lot of effort into economic production. The profits gained from production are saved and invested in new ventures rather than lavishly spent.

Weber concludes that Calvinism underlies the practice of capitalism and that making money becomes both a business and a

> The need for religious belief declines as profit becomes an aim in itself.

religious ethic. As evidence of his theory Weber points out that where Calvinism did not prevail economic development was slower than in protestant Western Europe.

Therefore, unlike Marx, Weber believes that religious belief encourages social change. Although, in itself, religion is not able to do so, it does provide individuals with the right attitudes and values to adopt social change.

The major contrast between Marx and Weber is that Marx believed that religion was shaped by economic factors but Weber rejected this view and believed that religion was able to influence economic behaviour.

However, both Marx and Weber did agree that ultimately religion would be wiped out. In Marx's case a communist society would banish exploitation therefore the need for religion and superstition would vanish as there would be no pain to ease. Weber sees the growth of science and rational thinking as leading to the decline of religion.

> These three paragraphs contain good comparative material.

> Why does protestantism particularly suit capitalism?

Marx believed that protestantism particularly suited capitalism. As part of the superstructure it met the requirements of the ruling class. Weber saw protestant beliefs as a necessary ingredient in the rise of capitalism.

Both Marx and Weber can be criticised by the functionalist view of religion. Durkehim saw religion as reinforcing social norms and promoting solidarity not false consciousness. He believed that religion forms a collective consciousness, not individualism. This creates order, control and social stability.

> Appropriate critical use of Durkheim.

> Should deal with belief.

Marx can be criticised by the fact that religion continues to flourish in Eastern Europe. Also church leaders have been involved in protest e.g. Martin Luther King and Desmond Tutu.

Weber's work is harder to criticise as he claims that Calvinism is not the only cause of social change and the rise of capitalism but that many factors were involved. However, England was never like the Western European countries Weber describes as its religious beliefs were not Calvinistic. Also many believe that early capitalism actually preceded and largely determined protestantism.

> Not 'determined' may be encouraged.

Therefore, we can see that Marxist and Weberian explanations of the relationship between religious belief and social change are contradictory. However, Weber's theory did come about as a direct attempt to criticise Marx.

Overall comments

Overall, a good C grade answer. It needs to deal more specifically with belief rather than religion in general. The link between Calvinist beliefs and the rise of capitalism could be explained more clearly.

Comparative points must be made explicit throughout the essay.

There are better modern examples of the relationship between religious belief and social change, e.g. the influence of Islam on the Iranian revolution.

GETTING STARTED

Sociological interest in the mass media has developed through a series of focal concerns which often reflect more general developments in sociology. However public interest remains concentrated on the issue of the adverse effects of the media on anti-social behaviour. The need for censorship and control because of the perceived effects of sex and violence in the media is still on the political agenda. It is an issue which has produced an unlikely alliance of feminists and traditional moralists. The government announced another research project in December 1989 which will begin by reviewing existing research.

The main sociological interests have shifted to the ideological role of the media in relation to class, gender and ethnic issues. Both sociologists and politicians remain interested in the partiality of TV news, for example the rows over the reporting of Northern Ireland and the American bombing of Libya.

The mass media provides a fruitful source of subjects for student research and hopefully this chapter will suggest some suitable hypotheses for further investigation.

The main themes of questions set on this topic are:

1 **Explanations of the relationship between ownership, control and output of the media**.
2 **Critical examination of bias in the presentation/selection of the news**.
3 **Examination and explanation of media representation of gender, ethnicity, age and class**.
4 **The role of the media in the amplification of deviance**.
5 **Evaluation of studies of the effects of the media on attitudes and behaviour**.

Definitions

- *The mass media* is the system of communication which transmits messages to large audiences. It includes TV, radio, newspapers and magazines. Some writers would also consider including discs and tapes as well as popular design in the definition.

Related topics include *deviance, race, gender, politics* and *stratification*.

THE MARKET MODEL

THE MASS MANIPULATIVE MODEL

THE INTERACTIONIST MODEL

THEORETICAL AND EMPIRICAL STUDIES

ESSENTIAL PRINCIPLES

Early research on the mass media emphasised the effects of media output on attitudes and behaviour. The methods and explanations were frequently influenced by psychology.

The shift from studying short-term effects to more general cultural effects has been accompanied by attempts to place the media in a broader social context. The main concern has become the relationship between ownership, control and output. There often seems to be more interest in analysing the content of the media and in making various assertions, than in demonstrating possible effects on the audience. The various relationships between ownership and production have been evaluated by Cohen and Young, who favour the interactionist model explained below.

THE MARKET MODEL

This is the model which conforms to the principles of a liberal-democratic society with a market economy. The audience is seen as made up of consumers who thus influence the output of the media by providing profit for the owners. Owners, and thus controllers and producers, seek audiences. They compete to provide what is demanded. There is no conspiracy between owners or government. A wide range of opinions are offered, and only the illegal and the unsellable are excluded. Events in the news are seen as having an objective reality and are selected for broadcasting or publication by journalists and editors on a professional basis. In the USA the free press is seen as an important watchdog, helping prevent state abuse of power.

Criticism

This comes from Marxists who raise the issue of oligarchic control of the media, and from liberals who claim state interference and control.

THE MASS MANIPULATIVE MODEL

This is seen by Cohen and Young as being the opposite of the market model in that the audience, instead of being the major influence on the media, are the passive and uncritical receivers of media messages. The Christian 'right', epitomised by Mary Whitehouse and the American 'moral majority', still support the pre-war 'hypodermic syringe' view and see a conspiracy to corrupt conventional morality through the portrayal of sex, violence and other challenges to traditional morality. The Marxist version of this model is much more common among sociologists. There is an internal Marxist debate (found also in the sociology of the State) between instrumentalists, such as Miliband, and structuralists, such as Althusser and Marcuse (see also Chapter 6). The former view sees fairly direct control over media production by the ruling class, whereas the latter view sees journalists and editors as being influenced by ruling class ideology, and willingly conforming to the interests of capitalists.

Criticism

Coming from *both* liberals and interactionists it suggests that the evidence of concentration of ownership, or even bias in output, is insufficient to demonstrate particular effects on the audience.

THE INTERACTIONIST MODEL

This combines some elements of the previous theories. The media is seen as reflecting the existing attitudes of the audience, as well as helping to create and reinforce a consensual view of the world.

The prevailing consensus is identified by writers within this perspective as pro-capitalist, sexist and racist. Thus this model has become associated with the left, at least in Britain.

The selection and presentation of news is seen as being influenced by both technical and ideological factors. In this sense 'the news' is seen as socially constructed, rather than a neutral description of real events. The process is described by Cohen and Young as the 'manufacture of news' and the outcome as 'agenda-setting'.

Criticism

This has come from ideological opponents who accuse them of political bias in their selection and interpretation of broadcasts.

Ethnomethodologists see the interpretation of news by academics as a similar process to the manufacture of news by journalists. Sociologists like other viewers and readers interpret media output according to their own 'commonsense assumptions'. Meanings are read into stories and images according to the audiences expectations.

EFFECTS OF THE MASS MEDIA

KATZ and LAZARSFELD rejected the 'hypodermic syringe' model which had developed both in academic and popular circles to criticise the effects of Hollywood films on the young. They replaced it with their two-step flow model which saw the audience as made up of *groups* influenced by opinion leaders, rather than as on undifferentiated and uncritical mass.

MCQUAIL, BLUMLER and BROWN emphasised the different uses people made of the media, which therefore satisfied different needs.

BELSON conducted in-depth interviews with adolescent boys to assess the effects of TV violence on their behaviour. He claimed that a high exposure to TV violence increased the degree to which they engaged in serious violence.

Among a variety of methodological criticisms of his study is the problem identified by MURDOCK and MCCRON of using the boys' memories as sources of data, on both the exposure to violent programmes and the committing of violent acts.

EYSENCK and NIAS supported the view that the media can cause violence. Their approach and methods are psychological, but they are worthy of note as authorities for those who seek evidence for extending control over the media.

Thus a series of studies, using methods such as case histories, interviews, surveys and laboratory experiments, have produced inconsistent and contradictory results. Imitation, desensitisation to violence and cathartic effects have all been noted.

POLITICS AND THE MASS MEDIA

BLUMLER and MCQUAIL (1959 election) and BUTLER and STOKES (1964 election) minimise the short term effects that the media have on political attitudes and electoral behaviour. The earlier study even suggested that the partisan press might repel support. The latter study saw a friendly press as preserving loyalty during a difficult period for the government.

GOLDSMITH'S media research group conducted a study of press reporting of London councils. They claim that a negative campaign damaged Labour's vote in the 1987 election. They investigated a series of invented stories which discredited councils and reinforced the perception of them as 'loony left'. They claim that stories which portray councils as obsessed with minority interests had the following effects: they distracted electors from real social problems like employment and housing, they divided the Labour party, they marshalled support for control of council spending, and they fuelled a dislike of minorities and of those involved in equal opportunities policies.

THE GLASGOW UNIVERSITY MEDIA GROUP (GUMG) criticised TV news coverage of the Falklands Campaign. The main charge was weakness and laziness in the face of a Ministry of Defence policy of managing the news to maintain public support.

INDUSTRIAL RELATIONS

THE GUMG, in a series of studies based on a detailed analysis of the presentation and selection of industrial relations reporting, saw evidence of a systematic bias against employees and Trades Unions.

M.HARRISON, in *TV news: whose bias?*, accused the GUMG of the very selectivity and bias they themselves saw in news broadcasts. The GUMG claim the mantle of 'social scientists', but are no less subjective than journalists.

PALMER and LITTLER described management as 'invisible heroes' in media reporting of industrial relations. They point out the frequency of reports of Trades Union and TUC statements which give the workers views and the apparent absence of employer statements. This is because the employer viewpoint is often presented as an objective one, not requiring attribution. They also noted the emphasis on **symptoms** of disorder and conflict, rather than **causes**.

RACE

HARTMAN and HUSBAND described how the media helped to create a 'framework for thinking' about race relations. The media did not define the situation in isolation, but within the existing culture, with its imperialist legacy.

They provide some useful data on media effects on school children, as well as explaining the media output in terms of 'news value'. Race is newsworthy when familiar negative stories can be written about violence and immigration.

TROYNA, in a study of press reporting of race in 1974, found different **attitudes** in the *Guardian, Times, Mirror* and *Express*, but agreement on the **issues**. The agenda comprised immigration control, hostility and discrimination, legislation and Enoch Powell.

GENDER

MCROBBIE, in a study of the girls' magazine *Jackie*, suggested that the presentation of femininity as attractiveness was tied in to the need to fall in love. The magazine reinforced traditional gender stereotypes with romantic love as the motive force.

TUCHMAN, in an article based on content analysis, argued that women were 'symbolically annihilated' by the media through their absence, condemnation and trivialisation. Perhaps the most hostile reporting of women came with the Greenham Common story, where the peace issue became an attack on feminism.

FERGUSON, in study of women's magazines, showed the persistence of themes like 'getting your man' and 'self-improvement', but also the change in emphasis over a 25-year period.

DEVIANCE

DITTON and DUFFY demonstrated the over-reporting of violent and sex crimes. Though only a small proportion of the total extent of crime, they dominate the crime stories in newspapers. This, and the sensationalisation of crime, helped promote fear of crime.

HALL looked at the role of the media in reinforcing ideological views on law and order. The media helped promote hegemony when the perceived 'right' of the ruling class to lead was being undermined by economic crisis. The need to be more coercive was legitimised by the combined threats of race, youth and crime.

COHEN explained the role of the media in the amplification of deviance. The alleged seaside 'riots' of the 1960s were, in fact, initially only minor disturbances and they were described as such in local papers. The hostile social reaction, fuelled by the media and their predictions of trouble, helped to increase the levels of perceived and real deviance.
(See also Chapters on *Race, Deviance, Gender, Work* and *Politics*).

EXAMINATION QUESTIONS

1   What factors influence the content of 'the news' in the mass media?

(Oxford 1987)

2   Critically examine sociological explanations of the effects of the mass media on their audience.

(AEB 1989)

3   How have sociological approaches to the study of the mass media changed over the last forty years?

(AEB 1989)

4   Assess the extent to which the ownership of the mass media can influence the content of the mass media.

(AEB 1988)

5 'The mass media may not tell us what to think, but they do tell us what to think about'. Explain and discuss.

(AEB 1986)

6 a) What part is played by the mass media in the formation of public opinion in the United Kingdom?   (13)
   b) To what extent does television provide balanced information for citizens?   (12)

(*Total 25 marks*)

(SCE 1988)

OUTLINE ANSWERS TO SELECTED QUESTIONS

Question 1

This is a similar question to 4 except for its more narrow focus on 'the news' rather than media output in general. The issue of ownership will, of course, be considered but need not dominate the answer. The concept of 'the news' should be treated as problematic. The framework of the three basic approaches, identified above, can be used and this offers different interpretations of what is newsworthy.

i) The 'market' model offers a liberal-democratic view of news reporting. The selection and presentation of real-life objective events is influenced by a combination of consumer wants and professional judgements. Critics provide evidence of interference by owners, and particularly government, and cite examples of bias. Supporters point to the diversity of views and resistance to censorship.

ii) The 'mass manipulative' view can propose both Marxist views on hegemony and evidence of censorship or even direct control by governments. Marxist approaches tend to assume rather than demonstrate effects, but there is plenty of evidence of interference by governments.

iii) The interactionist view provides much empirical evidence of bias. The content of the news is seen as the product of both ideological and technical influences. Critics suggest that the bias is frequently in the eye of the beholder. Harrison's critique of the GUMG analysis of the Falklands news reporting is a good illustration.

Question 2

The best answers will evaluate the explanations from theoretical and methodological standpoints, as well as criticise findings. The answer could be based on the chronological development of explanations

i) The 'hypodermic syringe' model suggested that a passive audience might react immediately to suggestions in the media. Crime and violence were favourite themes. The underlying theory assumes the development of a 'mass society' and the favoured methods are influenced by social psychology. Despite the criticism which follows, the model remains popular with the public and politicians and some researchers such as Eysenck and Nias. Research based on case histories, experiments and surveys has produced conflicting results.

ii) The 'two-step flow' model developed as a criticism of the hypodermic syringe model. In particular it rejects the portrayal of audiences as uncritical and 'sponge-like'. The theory emphasises the importance of 'opinion leaders' within small social groups and plays down the effects of the media. Critics have pointed out that the effects may be long-term, rather than immediate, and that the issue of ownership must be addressed.

iii) The 'uses and gratification' approach is very similar to the market model described above. The audience is seen as diverse and 'using' the media for a variety of purposes. The influence of psychology is apparent in descriptions of human needs and motivation.

iv) The absence of convincing evidence of media effects has led to researchers looking at the role of the media in the creation and reinforcement of cultural images, norms and values. This kind of approach has been supported by Marxists, interactionists and feminists among others. Choosing appropriate research methods to measure long-term effects seems to be a problem.

Question 3

This is a very broad question, where the candidate must provide the focus if a coherent answer is to be developed in 45 minutes. The best answers will trace changes in approaches to the study of the media and try to link them with the development of sociology in general.

i) Early studies influenced by psychology concentrated on assessing the effects of the media on audiences. The attempts to utilise scientific kinds of methods could be linked to the predominance of the positivist paradigm in sociology and behaviourism in psychology. Apart from violence, the effects of TV on political attitudes was a popular issue as TV was becoming the dominant medium.

ii) Cohen and Young edited a selection of studies on the 'Manufacture of News' which were more or less influenced by the rise of the Interactionist approach. These studies concentrate on the output of the media, rather than on the effects on the audience. The interest in deviance and social problems is apparent in work on moral panics (seaside riots and mugging), race relations and strikes.

iii) The 'rejuvenation of Marxist' analysis is reflected in media research which concentrates on the issue of the relationship between ownership and output. Often a reference to the media is only a part of more general and critical views of the role of the State in capitalist societies, as found in the work of Althusser, Marcuse, Miliband and Westergaard and Resler.

iv) The influence of *semiology* (the science of signs), popularised by Barthes, can be found in media studies which concentrate on the representation of youth, ethnic groups and women in the media. Stereotyping is often seen as ideological by Marxists and feminists. The choice of women or ethnic minorities in such studies reflects the rising interest in sociology (and in society in general) in such issues.

Question 6

a) A good answer will emphasise the absence of academic consensus on this issue. The advertising and public relations industries are evidence that government, political parties and business all see the media as influential.

i) Hypodermic syringe model: explain and illustrate with a current example.

ii) Two-step flow model: criticise the view of an uncritical mass society and point out the importance of opinion leaders.

iii) Consider Hartman and Husband's view that the media provides a framework for thinking about issues, but does not form attitudes and opinions.

iiv) Consider the Goldsmith's media group claim that adverse press reports damaged the support for the Labour party in 1987.

b) It is worth briefly considering the difference between 'balanced' and 'objective'. Balanced implies allowing more than one view on an issue, whereas objective suggests that reporting could be value free.

This part of the question specifies television and it is likely, but not essential, that news broadcasting will be the major issue. In addition, documentaries, current affairs programmes and drama could also be considered.

i) Studies of the impartiality of the news by Cohen and Young and the GUMG on industrial relations and the Falklands.

ii) Consideration of government interference with news and current affairs, e.g. the arguments over bombing Libya and interviews with the IRA.

iii) Consideration of the way that television drama represents groups or ideas, e.g. race and gender.

TUTOR'S ANSWER

Question 4

Assess the extent to which ownership of the mass media can influence the content of the mass media.

There is no single pattern of ownership of the mass media, either internationally or even within the UK. There are, however, recognisable tendencies for concentration into fewer hands. This means corporations do not simply accumulate more newspaper titles but also extend ownership over different kinds of media. Golding and others have documented this process of accumulation, citing the Murdoch and Maxwell multi-nationals as examples. Obviously any Marxist interpretation of such accumulation is open to criticism, but the pattern of ownership itself is more varied than such an analysis suggests.

The BBC is a public corporation financed by a government set licence fee and the extent and manner of interference is disputed. Independent TV is currently owned by shareholders who have temporary franchises awarded by publicly responsible bodies and are subject to scrutiny from them. It may be that the conglomerates expand their empires into press, TV and news media, like satellite and cable TV, but new technology and the changing industrial relations situation in the newspaper industry has led to the publishing of new independent titles, such as *The Independent* and *Today*.

Examination of the content of the media can take various forms. Marxists focus on very general effects on the audience, which is seen as relatively passively soaking up messages which maintain false consciousness. Content of media production is read in this light. Other, equally critical, studies focus on more specific issues, such as industrial relations, race and gender stereotyping or political bias. Cohen and Young, in the 'Manufacture of News', suggested that most analyses of the relationship between ownership, control and production of the media can be seen to fall into three broad categories.

First, the market model, which assumes the working of economic forces in a free market. Owners will seek to maximise profits. The sources of profit include the cover price of the paper, the cost of hiring cable or satellite facilities, and advertising revenue. The content of the media is thus indirectly determined by readers and viewers, as owners and editors seek to maximise audiences (in the case of tabloids and popular TV) or to reach a selective audience (as in the case of quality papers and specialist TV or magazines). Within this model, there is the possibility of editors and journalists satisfying both owners and the public by operating as independent professionals with a commitment to quality and truth. This might be exemplified by Woodward and Bernstein taking on President Nixon. The audience can use market forces to gain their preferences, which are sufficiently varied to ensure that there is a broad spectrum of opinion.

Second, the mass manipulative model, which is predominantly, but not necessarily, Marxist, reverses this causation. Instead of audiences influencing content through owners, the owners influence the audience (which is seen as passive and sponge like) through the content of the media.

Marxist theory would not isolate the particular issue of ownership of the media as being especially important. The owners of the means of production will control the media, whether they are in private or state ownership. Althusser sees the mass media as increasingly important as an ISA, reinforcing ruling class hegemony. Miliband sees the process of control as more subtle than a simple conspiracy. He identifies four control mechanisms:

1 Direct ownership and control.
2 The use of advertising revenue to determine content.
3 The use of the state to control output openly or covertly.
4 The ideology of the personnel who produce the content. This high conspiracy view sees control over journalists and editors as implicit. They willingly accept bourgeois ideology or benefit from co-operating, e.g. tame lobby correspondents. Those who dissent can be excluded (journalists had to be approved to accompany the Falklands task force or to be admitted to briefings).

Golding and Murdock saw the Fleet Street papers as opinion making flagships, which made losses for their conglomerate owners. Now, of course, most are very profitable.

The third model follows an interactionist approach and emphasises the existence of a 'consensual paradigm' which shapes media content. This consensual paradigm is a limited framework for thinking about issues, which is therefore both a cause and effect of media output. Thus, neither audience nor owners determine the content of the media in isolation, as claimed by the previous explanations. Content reflects the prevailing culture of society. This is not seen as genuinely consensual but as influenced by the powerful. The output also helps create and reinforce this consensual paradigm. Thus selection and presentation are identified as the key processes influencing output, and ownership is only one influence to be considered.

The GUMG emphasise the role of ideology, whereas Cohen and Young see technical influences as also significant. These include decisions about the placing of cameras and the influence of deadlines. The news, then, is 'manufactured' in the sense that it is preplanned. Hoggart reinforces this theme by talking of four filters through which TV news must pass. These are the effects of time and resources, the news value, the visual value, and the prevailing culture. Again, there is mention of both ideology and practical considerations in the setting of agendas.

A final alternative to these three views is suggested by Tunstall, who sees the influence of media professionals as being of more significance than the other models suggest. He accepts many of the points made in the interactionist view, such as Cohen and Young's view of the importance of periodicity (time scales) and consonance (fitting in with existing views of what is newsworthy). Organisational and professional needs can be divorced from the issue of ownership. However, editors and journalists do get sacked.

STUDENT ANSWER WITH EXAMINER COMMENTS

Question 5

'The mass media may not tell us what to think but they do tell us what to think about'. Explain and discuss.

> ❝ Good exam technique; straight into answer. ❞

> ❝ Cohen and Young use the term 'consensual' in a critical way. ❞

> ❝ Perhaps too much detail for exam. Good conclusion. ❞

> ❝ Selection and presentation are key processes. ❞

> ❝ Agenda setting is a key concept. Sophisticated theory. ❞

The interactionist approach argues that the media reflects existing attitudes and values. The content of the media is explained by the wider society i.e. the prevailing consensus. Hartman and Husband judged the effects of the media on attitudes and the way the audience 'defined the situation' in a study about race relations. They conducted a comparative survey of school children in areas of both high and low immigration and in schools within these areas with high and low numbers of immigrants. They found the rate of immigration was perceived as high, rising and threatening. There was little awareness of either the real rate of immigration or immigration controls. In areas with many immigrants competition for jobs and housing were seen as problems but in areas with few immigrants riots were seen as a problem. Where the media and not experience was the main source of information then conflict was more likely to be perceived. They conclude that attitudes are neither formed nor changed by the media but the media interact with cultural values to produce a 'framework for thinking' about race relations. The framework may be hostile due to society being hostile because of the imperial legacy and the news value of conflict.

Interactionists argue that the media help create and reinforce consensual values. Items are selected and presented to conform to these beliefs. Media output is in line with the prevailing consensus and can thus be examined for bias. 'Bad News' by the GUMG is a left-wing critique of industrial relations reporting alleged bias against workers. Selection is illustrated by the editing of a speech by Harold Wilson on the economy. The initial news item was restricted to the BL strike and a later item omitted criticism of management. Presentation bias is identified in language e.g. bosses make 'offers' and workers make 'demands' and usually bosses are in offices whilst workers are on picket lines. The framework here is industrial action as threatening and disruptive. Similar to the selection as news of high immigrant birth rates and omission of falling immigration. Reports used words like 'invade' when forty illegal immigrants were found.

Cohen and Young in the 'manufacture of news' show how much of the news is planned agenda setting. News does not therefore consist of real world objective events but is a social construction which tells us what issues to think about.

Only critics talk of race
relations 'industry'.

Not linked directly to
question.

Good introduction.

Not entirely clear, but
good points.

Good conclusion.

The CRE showed conflict and bad news dominate reporting of race. The race relations industry is seen as composed of villains who discriminate against the white community. Content analysis showed how black unemployment and blacks as victims of crime are not considered newsworthy.

Goldsmith's Media Research Group linked race to anti-left stories in media coverage of the GLC e.g. *The Sun* reported the banning by Camden council of the word 'sunshine' and *The Star* reported the banning of 'Baa Baa Black Sheep' by Hackney. The reports were fabricated by journalists.

All this research shows how the media form a type of framework of particular issues. But Marxists argue that the media is part of the superstructure reinforcing the existing relations of production (not consensus). Althusser argues institutions such as the media promote false consciousness through ISAs rather than coerce the working class.

Cohen and Young argue that 'the Manufacture of News is largely an elitist endeavour' i.e. for the purposes of the bourgeoisie to control and tell the masses what to think about. The output promotes false consciousness which therefore demonstrates who controls it and therefore sets limits on thought by (a) lies and distortions in the news (b) the opium of the masses (c) creation of false needs as argued by Marcuse. The bourgeoisie replace the chains of iron with chains of gold.

Miliband argues that because of the function the mass media plays in this economic and political context it can only affirm and not challenge existing patterns of power and privilege. Therefore it is an instrument in the hands of the ruling class.

The Marxist account argues, unlike the interactionists, that it is the ruling class not consensual values of society that tell us what to think about.

Overall comments

Overall, a thorough and conceptually sophisticated answer. Occasionally material is not made explicitly relevant. Not enough on the difference between 'what to think' and 'what to think about'. Hartman and Husband do illustrate just this point as do some modern Marxists.

There are of course studies on attitude formation and change which are neither Marxist nor interactionist. This is worth a B grade.

HEALTH

THE TRADITIONAL MEDICAL MODEL

POSITIVIST APPROACHES

INTERACTIONIST APPROACHES

CONFLICT APPROACHES

FUNCTIONALIST APPROACHES

THEORETICAL AND EMPIRICAL STUDIES

INEQUALITIES IN HEALTH CARE

GENDER AND HEALTH

MENTAL ILLNESS

GETTING STARTED

This relatively new topic is a useful vehicle to discuss broader issues in sociology, such as theories, approaches and methods. It makes a refreshing change from suicide and crime in the critical discussion of positivism and the use of official statistics. It is also a good topic to use to illustrate interactionist theory and provides material to discuss social policy issues.

The main themes of questions set on this topic are:

1 **The social definition and construction of health**.
2 **The social distribution of health chances and health care by class, age, gender, ethnicity and region**.
3 **Relationships between doctors and patients**.
4 **The development and effectiveness of health care by the NHS, private sector, community and family**.

Most questions focus on the social distribution of health, but it is wise in any question to treat health and related concepts as problematic. The best answers do not rely on journalistic accounts of inequality or even on the amassing of sociological research studies, but instead apply and evaluate sociological approaches.

Related areas include:

1 The *professions*; particularly doctors but also nurses.
  Poverty and the *Welfare State*.
3 *Deviance* and *Suicide* are studied in similar ways, and *Mental Illness* in particular links them to the study of health.
4 *Class, age, gender* and *development* are all related to the *social distribution* question.
5 *Sociological theory* and *methods*.

Definitions

Definitions are problematic and are often a critical issue in questions.

- *Disease* is a pathological abnormality with an objective biological cause (you have a disease).
- *Illness* is a patient's subjective response to real or imagined disease. It involves the experience of pain, discomfort or abnormality (you feel ill). Disease and illness need not coincide.
- *Health* can be defined as the absence of sickness (either disease or illness), or in a more positive way as a sense of well-being. Good health is falsely assumed to be normal, in fact a 1978 survey indicated the reverse, that health problems were normal;

ESSENTIAL PRINCIPLES

The sociology of health can be simplified by regarding it as a series of familiar sociological approaches applied to a range of sociological issues.

The issues include:

1   The definition of health.
2   The social distribution of health chances and health care.
3   The role of health professionals and others who care for the sick.
4   The effectiveness of the NHS.

The approaches to be considered are:

1   The traditional medical model.
2   Positivist.
3   Interactionist.
4   Conflict.
5   Functionalist.

THE TRADITIONAL MEDICAL MODEL

This non-sociological approach has been the basis of the public's commonsense view of health and health care for some time, although it is increasingly challenged as lay experts and the general public become better informed or more critical of experts.

Disease is seen as the cause of ill-health and disease is often equated with external attacks on the body by micro-organisms, i.e. bacteria and viruses. Good health is perceived as normal and ill health as an objective state producing predictable illness behaviour in individuals who are either seen as unfortunate or perhaps inadequate. This moral dimension of 'getting sick' is treated somewhat differently by the functionalists below but in this approach getting sick can be seen as the result of choosing a bad diet, smoking, poor personal hygiene or sexual misdemeanours.

Medicine is seen as treating individual symptoms in a professional and rational way and advances in health as depending on finding cures.

POSITIVIST APPROACHES

The major difference between this and the non-sociological approach above is the view that ill-health can have social, rather than purely individual, causes. Thus the emphasis is on the comparative method to identify social and economic patterns of ill-health. These approaches are strongly influenced by Durkheim's 'Suicide'. Definitions of health and sickness are seen as objective and tend to be taken for granted. Studies seek to establish the biological or social causes of disease. Health statistics are seen as a useful source of data. Explanations of the inequalities in health revealed by positivist research involve either examining the different lifestyles of the rich and poor or examining differences in the availability of health care. Conflict theorists use positivist studies to attribute blame for sickness to socially structured inequality rather than to individual misfortune.

INTERACTIONIST APPROACHES

These present similar criticisms of positivism to those found in the sociology of suicide and deviance. Health statistics, which record differences between the mortality and morbidity of different social groups, are seen as a social construction. In the same way that police and judicial processes produce crime statistics, and coroners' verdicts are the source of suicide statistics, it has been argued that health statistics are produced by doctors diagnoses.

Studies of disease, and particularly mental illness, may adopt the labelling approach popularised by BECKER. Health, disease, illness and even death are seen as social constructions. There are no 'real' rates of ill-health to be discovered. Such rates are seen as a result of the interaction between doctors, patients and others. The negotiation of reality by doctors, patients, relatives and the media can be used as part of functionalist, Marxist, feminist and other conflict approaches. The conflict approaches tend to stress the importance of power in these interactions.

CONFLICT APPROACHES

MARXISTS

Marxists argue that disease is caused by capitalism and not just industrial society. Direct causes include pollution, dangerous products and the stress and poverty caused by exploitation.

Definitions of ill-health and the institutions which are involved in the treatment of the sick, are seen as part of the superstructure and thus help to reproduce the existing relations of production, e.g. health has been equated with being fit to work. The views that ill-health is the result of individual misfortune or that the solution to health problems lies in medical treatment and scientific breakthroughs which will produce miracle cures, are seen as false consciousness.

Doctors and the NHS are seen as serving the interests of the ruling classes by keeping the working class 'fit' and docile. Medical care is seen as a form of social control, e.g. the definition of mental illness and the control of patients with drugs or in locked wards. The health industries divert attention away from the real causes of ill-health by focusing on cures rather than prevention. The Welfare State, through the tax system, transfers the cash of the working class to private industry, such as drug companies and hospital builders and suppliers.

FEMINISTS

Feminists argue that disease results from the inequalities of patriarchal societies. Women are seen as being at greater risk of disease than men because of inequalities in the home and at work. An additional cause of stress is the role many women play as unpaid and unrecognised providers of primary health care within the family, whether nursing the temporarily sick or the permanently infirm or disabled. Feminists see doctors as exercising control over female bodies and feminine behaviour.

ILLICH

Illich specifically criticised doctors and drug companies for the 'medicalisation of life' which produces *iatrogenic* illness. This means illness caused by health care. The source of the problem is seen as lying in industrial, rather than specifically capitalist, society. He distinguishes three forms of iatrogenesis:

1 *Clinical iatrogenesis* is the result of harmful medical intervention in the form of unnecessary or incompetent surgery, side effects or addiction to drugs and accidents in hospital.
2 *Social iatrogenesis* describes the medicalisation of life, e.g. fertility, pregnancy or unhappiness. Social problems, such as abortion or 'mercy killing', become technical problems and are left to doctors rather than to politicians or priests to resolve.
3 *Cultural iatrogenesis* involves individuals giving up independence and allowing experts to control their lives. A similar process is described in his critique of education where teachers are seen to be preventing the education of children in the same way that doctors 'expropriate health' (see also Chapter 12).

FUNCTIONALIST APPROACHES

PARSONS work on the functional effects of the 'sick role' is not based on the coincidence of consensus perspective and positivist approach we have come to expect after Durkheim. The patient's adopting of the sick role is legitimised by doctors. It results from a negotiation between the two parties. it is functional as it allows the patient to temporarily drop out from responsibility without challenging consensual norms.

Doctors are seen as competent professionals, committed to the public good and to the interests of their patients. Their high rewards are justified by their functional importance (see also Davis and Moore on *Inequality*, Chapter 3, and *The Professions*, Chapter 12).

THEORETICAL AND EMPIRICAL STUDIES

INEQUALITIES IN HEALTH

This was the title given to the Black report, a study of the social distribution of health commissioned by the Labour government in 1974 and published in 1980 amidst some controversy. It reviewed the research of others and summarised the explanations for the continued correlation between health and class under four headings. Criticism of the explanations can be found in the Black report itself and in later research such as 'The Health Divide', 1987.

The artefact explanation

This suggested that there was no real evidence that low income caused ill-health. The apparent relationship was based on the fact that definitions of class based on occupation concentrated on the old (and thus less healthy) in the lower classes, because there were fewer new recruits to the shrinking ranks of unskilled manual workers. Criticism in a later study called 'The Health Divide' indicates that poorer civil servants are less healthy than richer ones.

The selection explanation

This argument reverses the causation in the relationship between class and health. Instead of poverty being seen as the cause of ill-health, ill-health is seen as a cause of downward social mobility and good health as contributing to upward mobility. A similar argument has been offered to suggest that the unhealthy are more likely to be unemployed.

Criticism of this view has been based on longitudinal studies which demonstrate that only 3% of the seriously ill are downwardly mobile and that only 10% of the differences in infant mortality between the classes can be explained in this way.

The cultural deprivation explanation

This is reminiscent of the culture of poverty argument put forward by LEWIS and others, which is alleged to blame poverty on the poor. In this case disease is blamed on the inadequacies of the poor who choose an unhealthy lifestyle involving smoking, drinking and too many chips (former Health Minister Edwina Currie's famous speech). In addition, the lower classes are seen as failing to use effectively the available health care.

Critics see poverty and ill-health as the result of socially structured inequality, rather than of cultural deficiency. Also the evaluation of culture depends on time, place and power. What is regarded as unhealthy eating habits may depend on **who** displays them. For example when potatoes were the food of the poor whilst the rich ate meat, the latter was held in higher health regard; since then the relative values of these foods have been re-examined.

The material deprivation argument

This was the explanation preferred by Townsend who was on the Black committee. It was also the implications of this that probably led the government to dismiss Black's recommendations as unrealistically expensive. Numerous studies have suggested that the following can have detrimental effects on health and that the lower classes are more at risk.

Bad housing has been linked to stress and contagious diseases. Unemployment has been linked to stress related diseases, suicide, increased drinking and smoking, and of course the effects of reduced income to eating a less nutritious diet. Working conditions can also provide risks, such as accident, exposure to toxic substances and stress.

'The Health Divide' was able to offer only minimal criticism of this view, by largely supporting the cultural argument. Poorer civil servants, for example, do indeed have worse smoking and dietary habits.

INEQUALITIES IN HEALTH CARE

The social distribution of health may depend on access to health care as well as on inequalities in health chances. Internationally, it is evident that there are enormous differences in the availability of medical treatment. In general, developed countries have healthier populations and certainly spend more on health care.

In the UK, there is an ideological commitment to equality of treatment and to free care, at least for acute problems. The extent to which the NHS fulfils this commitment, and who is to blame for any inequalities in health care provision, is of course a party political issue.

The two main concerns are:

1 The provision of health care, which depends on the allocation of resources.
2 The effective use of health care, which may be inhibited by practical or cultural barriers.

There are methodological problems in assessing the effective use of services.

1 The needs of groups to be compared must be held constant. That is, the age structure and other risks must be controlled in order to see whether provision is fair.

2 Measures of use are problematic. Quality of care is as important as the frequency of visits to GPs, or the duration of stay in hospital.
3 Health statistics may be seen as a social construct, with the 'need' of groups only assessed by using the previous diagnoses of doctors.
4 More expensive care may not be better care. The cost of patient care will be increased if the prices of drugs or hospital buildings rise, without improving quality.

PROVISION OF HEALTH CARE

Private health care is available for individuals who can, and wish, to pay. Employers provide private health insurance for key workers and perhaps from their families.

Allocation of resources within the NHS is also an influence on the care available to different groups. The allocation of resources can be based on social policy, political decisions and market forces. We can explain the allocation of money in different ways.

Marxists would consider the benefits to the ruling class of, for example, spending on health in order to keep the workforce fit. Illich would see the emphasis on high technology hospitals oriented towards cures, rather than prevention, as evidence of the medicalisation of life. Doctors may prefer to spend time and resources on those who can be cured, rather than on, say, the care of the terminally ill.

Successive governments have planned to re-allocate spending to even out spending patterns between regions. In the past, the south and urban areas were better provided for than the north and rural areas; this does not reflect a simple class bias. The majority of spending is still on hospitals rather than on community care, and within the hospital sector geriatric, psychiatric and disability attract less funds than acute medicine.

Research in 1990 claims that the quality of care is a major influence on the survival of cancer patients, and that the provision of such care varies considerably between regions.

THE USE OF SERVICES

Even where services are open to all, the middle classes have been shown to use them more effectively. The working class in general uses the NHS more, but by most measures they are less healthy and thus have a greater need. The middle classes use preventive care more, including screening of cancer, dentistry, immunisation, ante-natal care, and family planning.

The middle classes seek earlier treatment, get longer consultations, and are able to communicate more effectively with GPs. HOWLETT and ASHLEY overcame some of the methodological problems mentioned above by studying prostate operations (prostate disease occurs more or less equally in all classes of men) and finding that the middle classes were more likely to seek early treatment and gain admission to teaching hospitals. The working class male was more likely to wait until the condition was chronic and go to less well-equipped general hospitals.

GENDER AND HEALTH

The main concerns are:

1 Women as providers of health care.
2 The influence of gender on health. This involves consideration of the differential health chances of men and women and also the differences in the extent and type of health care used by men and women.

As with most gender issues the emphasis in recent research has been on women rather than men.

WOMEN AS PROVIDERS OF HEALTH CARE

This can be related to the study of housework and inequalities within the family (see pp. 35–36).

Most paid NHS workers are women, but they are under-represented in the higher status and higher paid jobs.

Women as mothers, wives and daughters provide unpaid health care within the home.

This is rarely recognised by the social security system which does however provide support for men to employ care where wives are not available. This responsibility contributes to the perception of mothers as less suitable employees.

WOMEN AS USERS OF HEALTH CARE

NATHANSON wrote that 'Women get sick but men die'. Despite their longer life expectancy, women use the health care services more than men. This is not the cause of their living longer, nor is the extra health care the reason they live longer. The most intensive use is whilst women are fertile, between the ages of about 15 and 44.

Mental illness rates are twice that for men, as calculated by GP diagnoses, and 50% higher if admission to hospital as an in-patient is used as a measure. The type of mental illness diagnosed is different for women, with more depression and less psychosis.

Explanations

1   Women are biologically more at risk, particularly whilst of childbearing age.
2   Women are socially more at risk, because of their role within the family. GRAHAM found that marriage in effect depressed the class of women by reducing their access to resources. As compared with single women, she found that married women ate less well than single mothers living on lower household incomes. BERNARD found that marriage itself had an adverse effect on health.
3   Interactionists argue that the illness behaviour of women is different. Women are more likely to go to the doctor, perhaps because they are less likely to be in paid employment. They are also encouraged to seek medical explanations for, and solutions to, problems associated with housing, poverty, marriage and sex.
4   Women are diagnosed differently from men. They are more likely to be perceived as mentally ill and are more willing to accept a diagnosis which allows temporary respite from household stress through hospitalisation or drugs. Men can often avoid stress through absence from work, and mental illness may be concealed as it is deemed harmful to one's career. ILLICH has described how the concept of the medicalisation of life can be applied to the fertility and pregnancy of women.

MENTAL ILLNESS

Positivist studies of mental illness have largely accepted the medical model of mental illness and followed Durkheim's positivist methodology. Interactionist critics have questioned the possibility of an objective definition of mental illness (or indeed any other kind). Conflict theorists are concerned with **who** defines people as mentally ill and for **what purpose**.

LEMERT distinguishes primary and secondary mental illness, the latter resulting from social reaction; this also applied to deviance. He argues against the medical view that paranoia is the result of delusions and claims that the social misfit is in fact excluded from normal interaction and that this produces increasingly deviant behaviour.

GOFFMAN'S 'Asylums' is a useful study of organisations as well as of the 'career' of the mental patient. He describes how 'total institutions' produce rational responses to the rules, which are often perceived as madness, e.g. hoarding or wishing to leave. This last point is demonstrated by the difficulty encountered by ROSENHAN and others who faked the symptoms of schizophrenia to study a psychiatric hospital from the inside and needed legal help to get out. Getting out requires the patient to accept the sick label and then, after treatment, to conform to a model of 'well behaviour'.

SZASZ dismissed mental illness as a myth and psychiatry as a form of social control. He comments on the role of the law in defining madness and the custodial role of psychiatric hospitals. Deviance is redefined as illness and is alleged to be capable of scientific diagnosis and treatment; e.g. until the 1960s the American Psychiatric Association defined homosexuality as an illness. His work is a largely conservative attack on 'the therapeutic state'.

EXAMINATION QUESTIONS

1   To what extent would you agree that what constitutes health and illness is a matter of social definition?

(ULSEB 1988)

2 How might sociologists contribute to our understanding of the relationship between doctors and patients?

(AEB AS 1989)

3 'The availability of good medical care tends to vary inversely with the need for it in the population served' (HART, The Inverse Care Law) Explain this view and assess the evidence for it.

(AEB AS 1989)

4 'Whether people are sick or healthy is not a chance occurrence but something produced by the society in which they live'. Explain and discuss.

(AEB 1988)

5 Examine sociological explanations of class, gender and regional variations in the distribution of health and illness.

(AEB 1987)

OUTLINE ANSWERS TO SELECTED QUESTIONS

Question 1

This is similar to those questions which ask you to consider the extent to which deviance, suicide, madness, genius, old age, youth or gender can be regarded as objective categories or as socially defined and constructed.

i) Traditional medical model: where health and illness are objectively defined in physiological terms.
ii) Positivist approach: following Durkheim, illness is seen as abnormal and differential patterns of ill-health explained by identifying social causes.
iii) Interactionist approaches: see health, disease and illness as socially defined and constructed. The negotiation of reality between doctors and patients is emphasised. Parsons functionalist explanation of the adopting of the 'sick' role can be included here.
iv) Marxist approaches: often use positivist explanations of disease but also point out the ideological nature of definitions of health and sickness.
v) Feminists: echo the views of Illich on the 'medicalisation' of life. Doctors have medicalised fertility, pregnancy and childbirth.
vi) Other non-Marxist conflict theorists: these have argued that the definition of mental illness is a form of social control.

Question 2

This is a general question where a variety of good responses are possible. The general rule to remember is that credit is given for evaluating, as well as for examining, the sociological contributions.

The different approaches provide an appropriate framework for an answer, which could deal with a variety of material depending on your knowledge of this and related parts of the syllabus.

One outline could be:

i) Interactionist theories influence all the following approaches. Each suggests different reasons why doctor-patient interaction has particular outcomes. Explain the theoretical approach and illustrate. Examples include GIBSON, GOFFMAN, LEMERT and DUFF and HOLLINGSHEAD.
ii) PARSONS on the functions of the sick role. Perhaps other functionalist views on professions.
iii) Marxist approaches emphasising the role of medicine as a form of social control. This is found in non-Marxist conflict theory, e.g. SZASZ and ZOLA.
iv) Feminist approaches where (male) doctors control women, e.g. through the medicalisation of pregnancy.
v The work of ILLICH on iatrogenic illness.

Question 3

Explaining the question requires examination of both 'need' (i.e. health chances) and 'availability' of health care.

Assessment requires you to evaluate various sociological explanations of inequalities of health.

You will be rewarded for regarding both 'need ' and 'good medical care' as problematic and socially defined.

Answers could be based on the different approaches, or on dealing separately with need and care.

i) Need can be discussed by evaluating evidence on the health chances of class, ethnic and gender groups. Positivist, Marxist and interactionist approaches can be applied, where appropriate.

ii) Care should be discussed both in terms of provision and use.

iii) The difficulties of measuring the quality of care should be considered, e.g. the meaning behind the frequency and duration of visits to GPs and hospital.

iv) The allocation of resources by market forces and social policy should be examined.

v) The use of services, including preventive care, can be considered

TUTOR'S ANSWER

Question 5

Examine sociological explanations of class, gender, and regional variations in the distribution of health and illness.

Explanations of the social distribution of health and illness must consider the problematic nature of health statistics which can be seen as socially constructed. Morbidity and mortality statistics record doctors' diagnoses and coroners' decisions and thus variations (as in suicide and crime rates) may not represent the real rate of sickness, if indeed there is a real rate. The three variables mentioned in the question can be separated logically, if not in practice. Regional differences may be influenced by class, and within classes there are gender differences. Separate explanation of each variable requires that the other two be held constant. In each case, the distribution of health and illness will be influenced by both the health chances of each group and the availability and use of health care.

There is as much variation within regions as between them. Localities within regions may have characteristic patterns of ill-health. Separate studies by Harrison in Hackney and Skrimshire in Newham, both in east London, indicate low standards of health. Harrison identified access to care as a major cause, whereas Skrimshire blamed industrialisation in Newham compared with rural Oxfordshire for high rates of bronchial and respiratory disease.

Unemployment is related to ill-health. This may be the effect of unemployment itself or the effects of loss of income. Certain categories of people are more at risk of unemployment, such as ethnic minorities, women, the lower classes and the unfit. Unemployment is concentrated in particular regions of the U.K., such as N. Ireland and Scotland which also have the worst health records.

Cultural differences may be regionally based. Ethnicity may influence diet, smoking and drinking habits, family size and the experience of violence. Doyal's Marxist study 'The Politics of Cancer' suggests that industrial processes are a causal factor and industry is of course concentrated in particular regions. For example, high levels of radioactivity, whether manmade or natural, have been linked with cancer.

Gender also correlates with ill-health. 'Women get sick but men die' (Nathanson). Woven live longer, but use health care more. Most of the extra use is not in old age, but during the fertile years. Women have higher rates of mental illness and have different kinds of mental illness.

There are a variety of related explanations for these variations. Feminists identify social causes: Bernard blames marriage itself and Graham suggests that women get less than their fair share of family resources. The comparatively confined lives led by women means that their chances of death through accident or violent crime are less than those for men.

Sex, as well as gender, may be influential, with women's reproductive capacity exposing them to health risk. This last point can be seen from an interactionist view. Illich's claim that fertility and pregnancy have been 'medicalised' explains the more frequent contact with doctors. Similarly, women may be more likely to be diagnosed as mentally ill and more likely to accept the diagnosis. Women are encouraged by the family, school and media to seek medical resolutions for emotional and social problems, such as poverty, housing, sexuality, marriage and unhappiness.

There is a massive amount of available data on class and ill-health. Both internationally and within the UK health correlates with class. This can be explained by looking at both health chances and health care. Within the UK, the NHS is supposed to offer equal care, but Titmus and Anderson argue that the middle class has more access to, and makes better use of, the available services. Resources are allocated on the basis of the market and social policy. Marxists see the decisions as serving the interests of the ruling class, concentrating on getting workers fit for work. Howlett and Ashley have shown how the middle class seek earlier treatment and are more likely to use preventive care.

The Black report on inequalities of health suggested from possible links between class and health. Two of these explained away class differences as either 'artefact' because lower classes had a higher average age or the result of ill-health causing downward mobility and unemployment. Evidence published in 'The Health Divide' in 1987 refutes these explanations, as few of the ill are downwardly mobile and poor civil servants are less healthy than rich ones.

The other explanations focused on the material and cultural deprivation of the working classes. This includes housing, diet, smoking and drinking habits, etc.

Doyal and Pennel offer a thorough Marxist analysis of the social distribution of health, identifying capitalism as the cause of ill-health. Thinking of ill-health as a random event is regarded as false consciousness. The actual causal mechanisms are identified as poverty, industrial accidents and diseases, pollution and unsafe and unhealthy products. Health care is seen as diverting attention from the real causes of disease, transferring public funds to big business, and as a form of social control.

STUDENT ANSWER WITH EXAMINER COMMENTS

Question 4

'Whether people are sick or healthy is not a chance occurrence, but something produced by the society in which they live'. Explain and discuss.

Straight into the answer. Not elegant style, but practical exam technique.

> Marxist theories suggest that ill-health is caused by capitalism and for working class people to think it is a chance occurrence is false consciousness produced by capitalist ideology. Poverty, accidents at work and diseases developed from occupational hazards mean ill-health is a result of capitalism.

Relevant arguments demonstrating social causes.

> Statistics indicate that mortality and morbidity rates show better health for higher than lower classes. Within the UK health is unequally distributed in terms of getting sick and getting care. The Black Report 1980 found that 'material deprivation' i.e. low income, which has an effect on diet and housing, and 'cultural deprivation' among working class people contribute to ill health.

> The public's commonsense view is that ill-health is an objective state and needs to be cured. Medicine is seen as treating symptoms in a professional scientific way.

This is where the other side of the argument should be presented. She misses the opportunity. Ill health is seen as objective and as a chance occurrence, e.g. random infection by bacteria or virus.

Good explanation of the social construction of health with examples.

> Interactionists challenge the medical system by saying good or bad health is diagnosed by labelling and is a social construction resulting from the negotiation of reality between doctors,

CHAPTER 15 **STUDENT ANSWER** 133

patients and their relatives and the media etc. Lemert found in his studies that the socially inadequate were made paranoid by real not imagined exclusion. Homosexuality, not screaming, and the absence of skin disease, have all been socially defined as forms of illness.

> **Class influencing care is adequately explained.**

The middle class have had better access to and made better use of available health care services conclude Titmus and Anderson. They use preventive care, e.g. screening, dentistry, antenatal care, immunisation and family planning. They seek earlier treatment get longer consultations and are better known to doctors. Private health care is more available to people who are better off because they can afford it and employers usually offer it to valued employees.

> **Should be Marxists not Marx.**

Marx sees medical care used as social control e.g. mental illness and control of women's fertility. Treatment is promoted to keep workers healthy. Illich uses the term iatrogenic illness to describe sickness induced by medical care. He believes that health care causes disease through side effects of drugs prescribed, immunisation, unnecessary operations and has led to the 'medicalisation of life' producing changed definitions of health and illness behaviour. Screening and preventive health education are seen as ineffective and increasing the number of patients. Being pregnant, wishing to control fertility, being old, ugly, unhappy or mad have been medicalised, seen as ill health and requiring medical treatment.

> **Better to start new paragraph for Illich. Good description though.**

He states that improvements in morbidity and mortality rates are due to public hygiene or higher living standards. Unemployment, class and ill-health seem to be related. Unemployment is more common in lower classes and ill health is too. Sickness causes downward mobility e.g. the ex-mentally ill patient cannot get the same position in the job market. 'Fit for work' is a social not a medical category and depends on the labour market.

> **Completes Illich; should be in same paragraph.**

> **Relevant argument.**

Women use health care more often than men; according to Nathanson women get sick but men often die. Mental illness rates are twice male rates for diagnosis by GP and 50% higher than males for in-patient admissions. Explanations could be that they are biologically more at risk (fertility) and socially because of stress in the family. Women are encouraged by the media and their families to seek medical resolutions to social problems like housing, marriage, poverty and sexual problems.

> **Good material; extends discussion from class to gender. Could have developed the social construction issues.**

For ethnic minorities racism, racial discrimination and racial harassment may cause stress related diseases and access to medical care may be hindered by language and cultural differences.

> **Several relevant points, but no studies.**

Overall comments

Overall, a well developed but one sided account. The theoretical issues could be developed further and the discussion needs to be more critical. A well informed answer showing knowledge and understanding of this topic. Worth a B grade.

DEVIANCE

DURKHEIMIAN THEORIES

INTERACTIONIST THEORIES

MARXIST THEORIES

THEORETICAL AND EMPIRICAL STUDIES

GETTING STARTED

It seems that, somewhat in common with Sunday newspapers, sociology examinations are more concerned with deviance than with social order. As deviance helps us to identify rules which might otherwise be taken for granted, this topic is a useful source of examples for many sociological issues. The value of a comparative approach to sociology, which is emphasised by some examination boards, is highlighted by the culturally specific nature of deviance.

The main themes of questions set on this topic are:

1 **The relationships between power, social control and deviance.**
2 **Evaluation of sociological explanations of deviance.** Questions may cite particular theories by name for you to consider, or may present you with a problem to explain, such as differential conviction rates.
3 **Discussion of specific forms of deviance.** These may include football hooliganism, drug abuse, white collar crime, etc. **suicide** and **ill-health** are discussed in other chapters.

Related topics include:

- *Suicide*. This develops in detail the debate over positivism.
- *Media* and their role in deviance amplification.
- *Methods questions*. Deviance studies offer a rich source of examples to evaluate methods and to illustrate theoretical problems in doing research.
- *Health*. The debate as to whether health can be objectively defined or whether it is a social construction, is the same as that over the definition of deviance.
- *Sub-cultural* theories of deviance contribute to discussions of *education* and *youth-cultures*.
- As expected, *class, race* and *gender inequalities* manifest themselves in the sociology of deviance.

Definitions

The definition of *deviance* is problematic, and is itself a central issue in some questions, as we shall see later in this chapter.

ESSENTIAL PRINCIPLES

The best way to organise answers on this topic is to use a simplified grouping of theories, approaches and studies. This provides the framework for comparative and critical answers.

The three main headings used here are:

1   DURKHEIMIAN
2   INTERACTIONIST
3   MARXIST

There are differences **within** these broad groupings, but some common assumptions which apply to most studies can be identified.

DURKHEIMIAN THEORIES

The general perspective is consensus structuralism. The major theories are functionalism and sub-cultural theories. The dominant approach to research is positivist.

Deviance is defined as breaking consensual rules and deviants as rule breakers. The main question is 'why do some people break the rules?'

A common method of enquiry is to compare the biographies of known deviants with those of normal people, and to see the differences as causes of deviance. Crime statistics are seen as a useful resource which can be used in comparative studies.

The police and courts are not seen as problematic, but as neutral. The role of the media is to reinforce consensual values.

The main types of deviance studied are crime and other serious offences.

Critics

Interactionists challenge the definition of deviance, the positivist approach and related methods.

Marxists deny the existence of genuinely consensual values.

INTERACTIONIST THEORIES

The shared perspective is individualist rather than structuralist. Some writers acknowledge the influence of power in the creation of social order. The major theoretical influences are symbolic interactionism and ethnomethodology. The dominant approach is anti-positivist. It is this that unifies these various studies.

A deviant is not seen as a rule-breaker but as someone who has been processed as a deviant, i.e. successfully labelled deviant. The main question is 'why are some people more likely to be so labelled?'

The methods associated with this approach try to describe the interaction or negotiation between 'offenders' and various forms of social institutions and agencies such as the police, the courts and the media. Crime statistics are not seen as a useful resource, but as a subject to study. It is suggested that they describe police and judicial procedures, rather than the criminals. The role of the media in amplifying deviance and causing moral panics can be a question in its own right. Minor non-criminal deviance, or even non-offenders, are studied as well as crime, e.g. mental illness, stuttering and the innocent.

Critics

Positivists claim that interactionists avoid the most important issue which is explaining crime.

Marxists share the view of differential law enforcement and the problematic nature of crime, but criticise interactionists for not considering the influence of structural inequality on justice.

MARXIST THEORIES

The shared perspective is conflict structuralism. The major theories are varieties of Marxism. The sociological approach may be positivist. Deviants are seen as real or alleged breakers of ruling class law. The main questions are 'who makes the rules and how does their enforcement serve ruling class interests?' The results of research, whatever the method, are interpreted in a Marxist light. Crime statistics are seen as a device to blame social problems on the working class and as evidence of unequal enforcement. The police, courts and the law itself are seen as part of the superstructure. The media reinforce ruling class ideology. Studies often describe crimes of the powerful and the policing of the working class.

Critics

The possibility of genuinely consensual norms and values is avoided. As with interactionist approaches, there is the tendency to excuse or even glorify offenders and to ignore victims.

Interactionists see Marxist studies as overdeterministic: the effect of structural influences being exaggerated.

THEORETICAL AND EMPIRICAL STUDIES

DURKHEIMIAN STUDIES

DURKHEIM saw some deviance as potentially functional. It tests the usefulness of current norms and reinforces the collective consciousness. The causes of deviance include too much or too little integration. 'Suicide' provides the model for studying deviance.

ERIKSON followed Durkheim and argued that the authorities created crime waves to clarify and reinforce norms. He cites witchhunts as examples.

MERTON developed Durkheim's concept of *anomie* to explain deviance in the USA. The socially disadvantaged lacked the opportunities to achieve consensual norms by legitimate means and therefore some rejected either the means or the ends themselves. This produced four kinds of deviance.

SUBCULTURAL THEORIES

These present an 'internal critique' of Merton. They question his assumption of consensual values and his view that deviance is an individual response.

A. COHEN sees deviant sub-cultures opposing middle class values.

MILLER sees them as part of mainstream working class culture.

CLOWARD and OHLIN combine sub-cultural theories with Merton to suggest that responses can be either individual or collective, depending on the perception by the deviant of the causes of his or her disadvantage.

D.J.WEST is an English criminologist who responded to S. Cohen's interactionist criticism of positivism by refining his research methods to study delinquents before they had been caught. WEST is a good critic to use when discussing labelling.

INTERACTIONIST THEORIES

BECKER asks why some people, and acts, are labelled deviant. He sees the consequences of the acts as important in this labelling process, rather than the acts themselves. In other words, social reaction to the acts and the characteristics of offenders and victims are important factors. He also asks 'who makes the rules?'

CICOUREL provides, perhaps, the best interactionist critique of crime statistics. He also introduces the ethnomethodologist's concept of *common sense assumptions* to explain the behaviour of law enforcers (see also Chapter 17).

LEMERT emphasises the importance of social reaction in transforming primary deviance to secondary deviance. (See Chapter 15 on *Health*.)

J. YOUNG gives an interactionist account of the role of the police in the amplification of deviance. He provides a useful account of crimewaves, which can be used to criticise crime statistics. In his more recent work, which has been described as 'left realist', he measures crime in a more positivist way through victim studies.

MARXIST THEORIES

S. HALL provides a link between interactionist and Marxist theory by explaining the interaction between the police, media and black youth in terms of the crisis of capitalism.

MARX himself saw the state, the law, agencies of social control and definitions of morality all as part of the superstructure of capitalist society. Criminals form part of the reserve army of labour and the threat of crime legitimises oppression.

ALTHUSSER sees deviance being defined and contained by both repressive and 'Ideological State Apparatus's'.

CHAMBLISS illustrates how specific laws and enforcement procedures can serve ruling class interests. He cites tax law in colonial East Africa and medieval vagrancy laws as examples. In his study of Seattle, he argues that those in power were part of organised crime.

PEARCE confirms this view, discussing corporate crime and other crimes of the powerful.

THE NEW CRIMINOLOGY of the 1970s combined interactionist and Marxist views. English interactionist writers, such as J. YOUNG, I. TAYLOR and WALTON, felt that labelling theories failed to relate police and other forms of social reaction to wider issues of power and inequality. As stated above, Young further refined his ideas, seeing these views as failing to give sufficient consideration to victims who, like offenders, usually come from the working class.

EXAMINATION QUESTIONS

1   How far has the work of labelling theorists and interactionists helped us to understand why some people become criminals and others do not?

(Cambridge 1989)

2   Assess the explanations sociologists have offered for the relatively low rate of convictions for white collar and corporate crime.

(AEB 1989)

3   Examine sociological contributions to our understanding of
EITHER a) soccer hooliganism
    OR b) deviancy amplification.

(AEB 1988)

4   Outline and assess Marxist explanations of crime and deviance.

(AEB 1988)

OUTLINE ANSWERS TO SELECTED QUESTIONS

Question 1

The key point is that becoming a criminal must be distinguished from actually offending.

Interactionists distinguish crime from rule-breaking. The criminal is someone who has been successfully labelled as a deviant. Interactionist theory deals with this process of being labelled.

Becker says this depends on:

i) The consequences of the act.
ii) Social reaction to the act.
iii) The characteristics of both offender and victim rather than on the act itself.

Lemert distinguishes primary deviance from secondary deviance which follows social reaction.

Cicourel concentrates on the role of law enforcement in creating crime and criminals.

Young describes the role of the police in amplifying deviance whereas S. Cohen emphasises the media.

(Half the answer could criticise interactionist theories).

Durkheimian theories argue:

i) It ignores the origins of actual crime.
ii) Deviants can be identified before they have been labelled (West).
iii) Becker's sympathy for the underdog lies with the offenders who commit trivial crime, not with the victims of serious crime.

Conflict theories argue:

i) It avoids the issue of the relationship between deviance and power. Who makes and enforces the rules and in whose interests?

ii) It accepts official definitions of crime.

iii) It ignores the active part that offenders may play. You might conclude by looking at S. Hall, who attempts an interactionist approach within a Marxist framework.

Question 2

Here you must consider **convictions** as well as, or instead of, the actual extent of crime. Define both white collar and corporate crime.

i) Durkheimian theories: these suggest reasons for a low rate of crime rather than just convictions. Merton's anomic theory would see ritualism as a middle class response but the other responses as characteristically working class.
   (Critics question the consensual basis of rules and the neutrality of law enforcement.)

ii) Interactionist theories: these see the explanation for differential conviction rates as lying in the reactions of police and the judicial procedures.
   (Critics say they take the law for granted and fail to explain offenders.)

iii) Conflict theories: here the law and its enforcement must be seen within the context of the class structure of society. Who makes the law and in whose interests is it administered? (Carson, Chamblis, Pearce and Gordon all offer Marxist studies.)

   An interesting conclusion might be based on Sutherland's pioneering pre-war studies. These begin by pointing out the low level of recorded white collar crime and seeing it as the result of low rates of reporting and detection and conviction. He then discredits conventional explanations of (low class) crime and offers the new theory of differential association.

Question 3a

This question requires evaluation of the various sociological approaches, not just a history of soccer hooliganism. The best answers will link the development of different approaches to changes in sociology in general.

A chronological account is just as appropriate as the more conventional list of approaches to deviance found elsewhere in this chapter.

i) Marsh *et al* wrote a psychological/ethological account, arguing that football hooliganism was not, in most cases, real violence but orderly rituals perceived as disorderly by outsiders.

   Williams thought that this was taken up by sociologists for political reasons as it appeared to blame the problem on social reaction and not on the alleged hooligans. Their study does neglect to consider structural influences on behaviour. The same emphasis on social reaction is found in S. Cohen's study of moral panics.

ii) The CCCS studies introduce a Marxist perspective to studies of youth in general. The rituals and symbols of youth are explained at a sub-cultural rather than an individual level and are seen as resistance to capitalism, e.g. skinhead style and behaviour was explained by looking at the changes in traditional working class communities. The acceptance of these theories, which tend to be assertions rather than based on empirical studies, was helped by the rising popularity of Marxist sociology in the 1970s.

iii) The Leicester work of Williams, Dunning and others attempts to trace a continuous, but changing, history of soccer hooliganism. They identify lower working class masculine aggressiveness as a continuing theme. Changes in the class structure, such as higher incomes permitting travel, and changes in race relations help to explain the changing extent and nature of the hooligan problem.

   The prolific nature of the Leicester work can be explained by the current perception of hooliganism as a social problem and by the existing tradition of sports research.

TUTOR'S ANSWER

Question 3b

Examine sociological contributions to our understanding of deviancy amplification.

Deviancy amplification can be approached from a range of sociological perspectives, though the concept is particularly associated with the interactionist view. Deviance amplification can mean one or more of the following:

 i) More deviant acts are being committed.
 ii) More serious acts are being committed.
 iii) There is an increased perception (true or false) and/or fear (justified or not) of crime.

A combination of these can produce a crime wave.

The various interactionist studies share a basic common assumption, that it is societal reaction which explains the increase in real or imagined crime rather than the biographies of deviants or social facts external to individuals. The foundations of the interactionist approach are found in Becker's view that labelling can encourage the development of a deviant career. Wilkinson addressed more specifically the notion of a deviancy amplification spiral, where a perceived increase in deviance produces increased social reaction from the public, media and police, which in turn produces more visible deviance and thus more reaction, and so on.

S. Cohen describes how 'Folk Devils' and 'Moral Panics' can be created and amplified by the media. Minor seaside disorder was described as a riot, worse was then predicted, and this led to the polarisation of 'mods' and 'rockers' who went to the resorts where the press had promised violence. More effective policing meant more arrests and therefore crime, which here depended on social reactions; for example, obstructing the police requires a police presence. Soccer violence and lager louts are more recent examples of moral panics. The violence may be real, but public perceptions and fears change irrespective of rises and falls in *actual* events.

Young looks at 'the role of the police as amplifiers of deviancy, negotiators of reality and translators of fantasy'. He describes in detail the special role of the police and courts in amplifying deviance associated with drug abuse. Law enforcement isolates drug users, puts drug sales in the hands of professional criminals and makes real the imagined distinction between corrupted innocents and wicked pushers. Typically, victimless crime rises in response to more active policing-importuning in public lavatories and insider trading are examples. The willingness of victims to report, say, rape or child abuse, has a similar effect on public perception of crime.

Moving to non-criminal deviance, Lemert argued that social reaction could be a cause (rather than an effect) of secondary deviance. He was able to apply this to stuttering and mental illness. Atkinson's early work on suicide showed how social reaction from media, academic research, and families, could not only influence the reported rate of suicide by affecting coroners verdicts but also the real rate of student suicide.

Conflict theorists have challenged the interactionist approach. S. Hall in 'Policing the Crisis', provides a Marxist context for the moral panic about mugging in the 1970s (see Victim studies, Chapter 17). He accepts the interactionist process described above but explains why it occurs by arguing that it legitimises the need for more repressive policing which is really required because of the coming crisis of capitalism. The panics about strikers and social security scroungers can be seen in a similar light.

Gouldner, specifically criticising Becker, argues that the interactionist view takes the nature of deviance for granted and sees the offenders as too passive.

Functionalist theory since Durkheim has also been able to offer an alternative and more structuralist approach to moral panics and deviancy amplification. Durkheim saw the function of social reaction against crime and criminals as reinforcing the collective conscience. This was taken up by Erikson, who saw the creation of crime waves by the authorities in puritan New England as an attempt to clarify and reinforce the existing religious moral standards. More recently M. Douglas cites the persecution of Jehovah's Witnesses in pre-war USA for not saluting the flag. This was initially perceived as a threat to national unity during a period of anomie, until Pearl Harbour served to reintegrate US society by finding a new enemy within and abroad. The integrating effect of the scapegoat echoes Hall's work on the racist undertones of the mugging scare.

STUDENT ANSWER WITH EXAMINER COMMENTS

Question 4

Outline and assess Marxist explanations of crime and deviance.

Theories of crime and deviance can be divided into three broad categories. The first of these is the functionalist theory investigated by the positivist approach of Durkheim, Merton and others. This assumes consensual rules for the good of society. Rule-makers and enforcers have legitimate power which is approved by all sections of the population. Deviance is rule-breaking and explanations are sought from within the structure of society.

The interpretive approach of a more individualist perspective is advanced by followers of Weber including Becker and Young. For them the deviant is the person who is caught and labelled deviant. There is an emphasis on the effects of social reaction and the role of the police as amplifiers of deviance.

The third view of crime and deviance is the conflict theory of Marx and others. Marx considered that the state agencies of social control, the law, judiciary and social definitions of deviance and morality are all part of the super-structure of society, produced by and reinforcing and supporting the economic sub-structure. Therefore social order is imposed by the powerful on the powerless and is not based on shared values. It serves the interests of the powerful and not the maintenance of social integration. Conformity too, rather than compliance with the rules is false consciousness and, according to Marx, even laws which appear to support working class interests like the legal entitlement to join a union are, in fact, only supporting false consciousness.

However, critics of this view claim that there does seem to be a genuine consensual view of some deviance. For example there is a general abhorrence of violence against children which does not appear to be false consciousness.

The functionalists see power as granted by populations to rulers to allow them to enforce consensual rules and not to support ruling class interests. However, if, as Marx claims, rules are not consensual but laws legitimise the power of the ruling class, then deviance (i.e. the breaking of rules) can be seen as a threat to the interests of the powerful. There is much evidence that enforcement of rules is applied differently to different groups who commit the same crime and working class crimes are policed more conscientiously than higher class crimes. Although other sociologists agree with these findings they do not share Marx's explanations and feel that they have not been demonstrated through research.

Marx claimed that crime supported the economic infrastructure. Criminals can be thought of as part of a reserve army of labour. Crime is a protection against poverty and theft is redistribution of income within the working class. The working class are generally both victims and criminals. During economic slumps there are more criminals and more police are needed to control the 'crime wave'.

This explanation of crime as a normal response to inequality may appear to glorify crime and can be criticised for failing to explain why the majority of people appear to keep the rules.

Crime is seen as being a threat to ruling class interests and because the ruling class feel their property to be under threat it legitimises their efforts to produce better means of protecting it. They acquire more locks, better security and larger police

Definitions and explanations of deviance, but not linked to question.

Should start here.

Good comparative points on order and integration.

Attitudes to violence against children are culturally and historically specific.

Differential enforcement also argued by interactionists.

This could link up with Hall in para 8.

> Not clearly argued. Crime prevention provides a legitimate reason for strengthening law enforcement which can be used against the working class.

> Gouldner.

> This explains paras 6 and 8.

> Last two paragraphs are not integrated into the answer but sensibly add relevant points to gain extra marks. It is often appropriate to consider gender or ethnicity.

force. This strengthens the power of the ruling class to control the working class as a whole and enables them to better deal with union activities or other threats to their domination.

One of the strengths of the Marxist theory compared with others is that it asks 'who makes the rules?' and looks for the answers within the economic and political structure of society. In contrast the interpretive approach restricts itself to individual encounters and might criticise Marxist theories for being deterministic and failing to consider individual interpretations of situations at all.

Another strength of Marxist theory is that whilst Becker's labelling theory criticises the police, social workers and other 'caretakers' it does not mention the 'master institutions' of the state and the ruling class who control the lower levels.

Marxists also question official definitions of deviance whilst others do not.

Marxist explanations do not conflict with the interactionist critique of 'crime waves' and Young's account of deviance amplification. These can be explained within the Marxist economic structural view. S. Hall claims the media representing the interests of capital, creates moral panics. If it is believed there is a crime wave, especially if it can be blamed on a section of the public such as black youth, it can be used as an excuse to increase the police force and perhaps add to their powers or change laws and thus legitimise a more repressive state more able to control the workers.

If the Marxist view of crime, as part of the superstructure is correct then countries with similar levels of economic development should have similar patterns of crime. In fact they do not. This suggests that causes of crime and deviance are more complex than Marxist theories imply.

Another important issue which Marxist theories do not explain is the very marked sex difference in criminality. The Marxists are not alone here as other theories of deviance also neglect this.

Overall comments

Overall a good B/A Grade answer with comparative and critical structure.

The opening could have been improved. You must address the question not reproduce arguments in the order that your notes or text book presents them. Given time and space actual Marxist studies could have been included e.g. Chambliss, Pearce, Gordon and the 'New Criminology'.

SUICIDE AND OFFICIAL STATISTICS

POSITIVISM

THEORETICAL AND EMPIRICAL STUDIES

STUDIES OF CRIME STATISTICS

GETTING STARTED

This chapter will deal with questions on official statistics, particularly crime statistics, as well as the various debates on suicide. It provides a link between various topics and with the more general issues of sociological approaches, methods and theories.

Suicide is a popular, but difficult, topic. Standards of answers tend to be high because it is covered so thoroughly by teachers and text books. The main problems appear to be in understanding some complex ideas and then applying them to the demands of specific questions. Far too often examiners see well prepared answers to questions that candidates were hoping would be set, rather than to the ones which were actually set.

The AEB syllabus says that students should 'consider the sociological issues raised by the study of suicide'. This means that you must debate methodological and theoretical issues, as well as the studies of suicide itself.

The main themes of questions set on this topic are:

1 **Explaining variations in suicide rates between different groups**.
2 **Evaluating Durkheim's functionalist explanations of suicide**.
3 **Explaining the social construction of suicide**.
4 **Evaluating the positivist approach to the study of suicide**.

In addition to questions which mention suicide specifically, you can use the arguments in this chapter to answer questions on:

- *Methods*: particularly the comparative method and the use of official statistics.
- *The nature of sociology*: for example, should it be the scientific study of 'social facts?'
- Evaluating *structuralist* and *action approaches*.
- The problems of defining and measuring *deviance, crime, religious belief, marital failure, strikes* and *health*, all of which can be seen as social constructions.

ESSENTIAL PRINCIPLES

POSITIVISM

DURKHEIM chose to study suicide in order to demonstrate that his 'rules of sociological method' could explain even this apparently most individual of acts. The debates over suicide involve a critical consideration of his positivist approach and the use of the comparative survey as the most suitable scientific method. Supporters question the specific variable which Durkheim identified as causes of suicide, but accept the existence of social facts which constrain individual behaviour.

The most difficult idea to grasp and explain is the argument that there is no real rate of suicide that can be discovered and objectively measured. Atkinson is not just accusing coroners of making mistakes (for A-level students to expose!) but is arguing that they themselves create the suicide statistics.

The contrasting views of positivists and their critics to official statistics such as suicide statistics, can be summarised as follows:

Positivist sociologists	use	official statistics	to study	objective social facts
Durkheim	used	suicide statistics	to study	the social causes of suicide rates
Anti-positivists	study	official statistics	as a form of	socially constructed reality
Atkinson	studied	suicide verdicts	to discover	coroners' commonsense assumptions

This distinction can be illustrated by the different ways in which we regard other kinds of description. We can compare the positivist use of statistics with the way a geographer uses an aerial photograph to study landscape or a botanist uses paintings of flowers to study their structures.

The interpretive approach to statistics can be compared with the study of photographs or paintings as constructions in their own right which, if they tell us anything, describe the techniques by which they were produced and perhaps tell us something about the producer.

THEORETICAL AND EMPIRICAL STUDIES

DURKHEIM

Durkheim found, following an exhaustive study of the suicide statistics of various countries, that despite variation between the suicide rates of different societies, any given society or group within that society had a stable suicide rate. This suggested that social causes rather than individual characteristics should be studied.

The social causes he discovered involved the degree of integration and moral regulation. This led him to distinguish four types of suicide. The first two were characteristic of simple societies or close-knit groups within a modern society. The second two were typical of industrialised society.

- *Altruistic suicide*, caused by too much integration.
- *Fatalistic suicide*, caused by overstrong moral regulation.
- *Egoistic suicide*, the most common type, was caused by under-integration.
- *Anomic suicide*, caused by too little moral regulation.

OTHER POSITIVISTS

These tend to support Durkheim's approach and his comparative analysis of statistics but have either offered alternative explanations (HENRY and SHORT) or tried to refine his methods (GIBBS and MARTIN).

SAINSBURY supports the integration hypothesis and reminds the critics below, that in the USA ethnic groups have distinct rates which resemble their countries of origin, rather than rates which vary with individual coroners in different states of the USA.

PSYCHOLOGICAL APPROACHES

Despite Durkheim's rejection of psychological causes, such as mental illness, modern studies continue to link suicide with individual disturbances. PRITCHARD estimates that 2/3 of all suicides in England are mentally ill. A study dealing with jumping in front of trains, claims that schizophrenics are 1 000 times the normal rate more likely to commit this act, and that this form of suicide clearly indicates the victims intentions.

STENGEL makes a valuable distinction between suicide and attempted suicide, based on the motivation of the victim rather than the outcome in terms of life or death. Thus failed suicide is distinguished from faked suicide.

INTERPRETIVE APPROACHES

The following critics are more concerned with challenging Durkheim's approach than with his specific explanations.

DOUGLAS rejects Durkheim's positivist approach and his view of social causes. Instead he argues for the need to search for the social meaning of suicide which varies between cultures and individuals. These variations in meaning in turn influence coroners decisions, which themselves produce the official suicide rate. He advocates the study of suicide notes as a useful source of data on meanings. His interactionist view of the statistics is that they are the product of the negotiation of reality by involved parties, particularly coroners.

ATKINSON has described the development of his sociological work through three phases. Firstly, as a positivist seeking to refine Durkheim's work. Secondly, as an interactionist supporter of Douglas when he became concerned with the labelling process. Thirdly, as an ethnomethodologist claiming that there was no possibility of discovering the 'true' rate of suicide. The focus of these studies ceases to be either suicide or even coroners, and concentrates on nothing more than the way in which humans make sense of themselves and each other. His actual research does give us some insight into the ways in which deaths become categorised as suicide. Firstly, he studied the social processes leading to student deaths being categorised as suicide; and secondly, he conducted an experiment where English and Danish coroners were given the same case notes, but found that the latter gave more suicide verdicts. Crucially, he denies the existence of a 'real' rate of suicide

SACKS also offers an ethnomethodological account of social life in general, using suicide as an example. He examined the transcripts of telephone conversations in a suicide prevention centre to see how suicides and staff make sense of the situation. His own interpretation is, of course, no better or worse than anyone else's.

NB Recent examination questions often require more thorough knowledge of Atkinson and Douglas at the expense of Durkheim.

STUDIES OF CRIME STATISTICS

Critical discussion revolves around two stages in the production and use of crime statistics.

1 The gathering of data. Have the figures been collected fully and accurately? Are they reliable or could the process be more accurate?
2 The interpretation of the data. Are the figures a valid measure of crime and criminals or are they a description of police and judicial processes.

Conventionally crime figures have been the official collections of crimes known to the police (CKP) and data about convicted criminals.

Following criticism from the interactionist school, both positivists and interactionists and even governments have become interested in alternative types of figures.

SELF-REPORT STUDIES

These have permitted a check on the reliability of CKP figures. HOOD and SPARKES, in a study in Utah, found 93% of a sample of young people had offended, yet hardly any of tens of thousands of offences had been detected and even fewer acted upon. D.J. WEST used *self-reporting* to overcome the criticism which labelling theorists had made of conventional studies linking delinquency to deprivation by identifying differences before the offenders had become known to the police.

VICTIM STUDIES

Victim studies, such as the British Crime Survey and YOUNG and LEA'S work in Islington and on Merseyside, have shown a greater extent of crime than the CKP figures suggested, and have also produced data on the fear of crime as well as on crime itself.

The reasons for unreported crime include:

1 Victims being afraid or ashamed, e.g. rape, domestic violence and incest. Illegal immigrants in California began to report crime when their resident status was no longer threatened.
2 Victims seeing reporting as a waste of time because the offence was trivial, or there was no realistic chance of detection or because property was uninsured, e.g. indecent exposure and petty theft. As insurance becomes more widespread, the amount of reported, though not actual, crime will rise.
3 Victims are unaware or unconcerned, e.g. theft from work.
4 'Victimless' crimes which require detection by the police, e.g. prostitution, drug abuse, bribery and importuning in public lavatories.

CICOUREL demonstrated the social construction of crime statistics by explaining the variation between two similar Californian cities in terms of policing policies and practices. A similar explanation has been given for dramatic rises in arrests for both importuning and for possessing obscene publications in Greater Manchester.

Finally, S.HALL'S study of the crime figures for 'mugging' in the early 1970s illustrates the way in which the debate can take technical, theoretical and ideological forms.

WADDINGTON claims that the figures Hall quotes actually show the increase in street crime which his study denies. Hall sees the moral panic developed through media reaction as evidence of the labelling process and of the importance of social reaction in defining deviance. Hall explains the moral panic in terms of racism and the need for the ruling class to 'Police the Crisis'. Whereas Waddington argues that, in the absence of any objective measure of what is a reasonable social reaction to crime, dismissing reaction as a moral panic is ideological.

EXAMINATION QUESTIONS

1 'What is defined as suicide is more a matter of what the coroner thinks, than what the dead person intended'. Discuss with reference to recent studies of suicide.

(AEB 1989)

2 What use are official statistics to sociologists trying to understand EITHER crime OR marital failure.

(Cambridge 1988)

3 Durkheim's study of suicide has been criticised on theoretical and methodological grounds. Outline Durkheim's study and examine these criticisms.

(AEB 1988)

4 'Statistical analysis always gets a bad press. The notion that you can 'make statistics prove anything you like' dies hard. But, ironically, a great deal of emphasis is placed on official statistics when recommendations are being made and new policies introduced. You are more likely to be allowed to build 10,000 new council houses if you can show that 20 per cent of a city's population is living in substandard housing than if you provide five or six detailed, but personal, accounts of living in damp and decaying conditions.

Official statistics drawn up by Government departments, trade unions, the census office and other organisations are obviously a useful source of information for sociologists, but they need to be used carefully'.

(Jane L. Thompson: *Examining Sociology*)

a) Give **two** sorts of official statistics 'drawn up by Government departments, trade unions, the census office and other organisations'. (2)
b) Explain why some sociologists use official statistics in their work. (8)
c) Some sociologists would argue that 'detailed but personal accounts' are more informative than official statistics. What advantages do such accounts have? (7)

(Total 17 marks)

(AEB 1987)

OUTLINE ANSWERS TO SELECTED QUESTIONS

Question 1

This is an unusual question. Instead of the usual debate using Durkheim, his work is scarcely relevant. You must contrast:

i) Those theories which deal with the work of coroners (Douglas and Atkinson).
ii) Those which focus on the intentions of the deceased (Taylor, Stengel and Giddens).

The coroners verdict is based on a complex set of commonsense assumptions which involve the media, families, police and sociologists' research. The suicide is defined **after** the event.

Theories which deal with intention are clearly more interested in what happens **before** death. Work with the Samaritans and suicide notes is helpful.

Durkheim can be made relevant if you emphasise his rejection of psychological explanations or use him as the springboard for Atkinsons and Douglas' criticism.

Question 2
NB 'either/or' so only do ONE.

crime

You should critically consider what sociologists can **use** official statistics for.

i) The positivist approach to crime uses official statistics as a more or less accurate and representative description of the real extent of crime. Historical and cross-cultural analysis can be carried out, as well as correlations made with the social characteristics of criminals.
ii) Technical objections to the uncritical use of official statistics by some positivists might question the methods used to gather and interpret data. The 'dark figure of crime', victim studies and white collar crime could be mentioned.
iii) The interpretive critique could form the major part of this answer. Official statistics are seen as a social construction telling us about police and judicial processes. Labelling theory and the work of Cicourel could be discussed.
iv) A brief reminder of Marxist criticism of the above and of the suggestion that official statistics are produced by agencies which are themselves part of the superstructure, using categories defined by the ruling class.

Marital failure

i) Statistics which may be used to describe the extent and effects of marital failure include: divorce figures, number of single-parent households, poverty statistics and figures for domestic violence and health, particularly mental illness.
ii) Positivist approaches might use divorce statistics to link marital failure with other variables, such as class, occupation, number of children, age at, and duration of, marriage.
iii) Functionalists, such as Davis, question whether rising divorce rates should be seen as evidence of a threat to the family as an institution. Instead they see them as indicating the higher expectations people have of marriage. Gibson sees serial monogamy as indicating discontent with partners, not with marriage itself.
iv) Interpretive sociologists would also question the meaning of the statistics and the process of producing them. The problematic nature of 'marital failure' could be discussed.

v) Practical criticism of divorce statistics as an index of marital failure might mention the effects of legal changes on the figures and the broken marriages which are never recorded as divorces or even legal separations. GOODE's discussion of family disorganisation is potentially useful.

TUTOR'S ANSWER

Question 4

a) Give **two** sorts of official statistics.

Crimes known to the police and unemployment figures.

b) Explain why some sociologists use official statistics in their work.

The decision to use official statistics either as a source of data or as a topic of study can be made on theoretical or practical grounds. In addition, if sociologists wish to influence social policy they may find it more effective to quantify a social problem and to support their arguments with official statistics.

Positivist sociologists use statistics as a more or less accurate description of an objective social reality, such as the extent of crime, the number of broken marriages, or the suicide rate. Durkheim's suicide remains the model for such studies. The statistics were used as data for a comparative survey which tested various hypotheses. Analysis of the statistics might also generate new hypotheses, such as those found in the Black report once class differences in health had been established.

The virtues of using statistics relate to the desire to be detached, to avoid contaminating subjects or being influenced by them, and to be scientific. The data is seen as reliable and available for others to test.

Practical points include the fact that such statistics may be the only source of data, such as the historical studies of Laslett and Anderson. The statistics also allow sociologists to study large numbers of subjects dispersed over a large geographical area quickly and cheaply. Studies based on divorce statistics by Gibson and Ross, and on strikes by Hartman illustrate this point.

Interpretive sociologists do not 'use' official statistics as much as regard them as a social phenomena worthy of study in their own right, for example, Cicourel's study of crime statistics and Atkinson's study of suicide figures. Rather than describing the objective social phenomena they claim to describe, the statistics are seen as revealing more about the processes by which they were produced.

c) Some sociologists would argue that 'detailed but personal accounts' are more informative than official statistics. What advantages do such accounts have?

The use of 'detailed but personal accounts' is advocated by interpretive sociologists who would wish to produce the accounts themselves, based on their own experiences, rather than use other people's as a form of secondary data.

The theoretical justification for participant observation, which is a major way of producing personal accounts, is illustrated by Weber's view that sociology should aim to provide 'interpretive understanding of social action'. It is seen as crucial that the sociologist identifies the meanings which individuals give to social interaction, the motives which individuals have for action, and the commonsense assumptions which individuals use to make sense of situations. Participant observation allowed Becker to understand the experiences of becoming a marijuana smoker and of working as a dance band musician. Conducting informal interviews, whilst joining in with students' everyday lives, allowed Aggleton to develop systematic as well as impressionistic data.

The theoretical arguments for participant observation and other methods which produce personal accounts are not restricted to anti-positivist sociology. Malinowski pioneered the use of participant observation by social anthropologists who shared his functionalist perspective. It enabled the researcher to see how apparently strange behaviour fitted the needs of simple social systems. He rejected the work of those who allowed missionaries and colonial officials to mediate between them and their subjects.

There are also practical arguments that detailed personal accounts might provide more valid data. In pre-literate societies which have not been previously studied there may be no

> **There are no inevitable links between theoretical assumptions and methods.**

secondary data available. Social groups which are secretive or indulge in illegal or shameful activities can only be studied from their point of view if the researcher gains their trust, or joins in and observes covertly.

Barker's study of the Moonies involved her in openly participating in their meetings. Humprey's study of casual homosexual encounters was based on covert participant observation, whereas Polsky advocates that the researcher be open when studying criminals.

It may be that the sociologist need not choose between the use of official statistics and methods producing more personal accounts, but instead can regard a variety of methods as complementary. Newby makes just this point in order to justify the use of a variety of methods in his study of farm workers.

STUDENT'S ANSWER WITH EXAMINER COMMENTS

Question 3

Durkheim's study of suicide has been criticised both on theoretical and methodological grounds. Outline Durkheim's study and examine these criticisms.

> Durkheim's positivist approach to sociology led him to believe that the subject matter of sociology is social facts and that individual behaviour was based on the culture of the society in which he exists.
>
> To prove this he decided to study suicide as this is the most individual and personal act and if his study was successful it could be used to examine other social behaviour.
>
> Using the official statistics he studied the suicide rates on a national basis. He found that they varied between communities and also between groups in different communities.
>
> He decided to dismiss certain social and health factors e.g. mental illness, race and smoking and non-smoking and assumed these variations must be based on integration.
>
> Based on his belief that integration was the independent variable he found that suicide could be put into four types:
>
>   i) Anomic — when social rules cease to exist e.g. Wall Street.
>   ii) Fatalistic — too much integration e.g. Eskimos.
> iii) Altruistic — too much integration.
>   iv) Egoistic — The most common and caused by too little integration e.g. single person households.

He then studied Jews and Protestants in Germany and found a higher suicide rate among protestants who were less religious and concluded that religion caused more integration. For example, family life and stability had a bearing on suicide statistics.

> Anti-positivists disagreed with the way Durkheim did sociology and his view of the nature of society. They thought that each individual determined the nature of his particular society and decided on his own social action and that there is no objective social reality. They disagreed with the way suicide statistics were produced and interpreted. They believed that suicide statistics should be the subject of a study. Douglas thought that it was the meaning of the act that was crucial. He studied suicide notes some of which were real and some of which were a cry for help.
>
> Coroner's reports were also criticised. The way they categorise suicide and the fact that they use commonsense assumptions based on information from doctors and families of suicides and also based on age sex and mental illness.

Examiner comments (margin):

" Should be between groups in the **same** society. The stability of rates should be mentioned. "

" Smokers? "

" Not an assumption but a hypothesis. "

" Examples are not helpful. "

" No reference to Catholics. The variable was Protestant or Catholic, as well as religious and non-religious. "

" Obscure. "

" No real rate of suicide. "

> They saw statistics as a social construction rather than as being inaccurate. They should be studied as a topic in their own right.

> Confused view of 'reliable', 'valid' and 'objective'.

Atkinson conducted a study on students that showed how shared definitions can influence suicide verdicts.

Although Durkheim rejected mental illness Pritchard's study of suicide showed 2/3 were mentally ill.

Atkinson thought that coroner's reports were unreliable because they were based on records and measurable.

Durkheim ignored the fact that because religious people were more integrated they were also more likely to hide suicides in the family because of shame.

Overall comments

Overall, a brave attempt which raises the major issues but often fails to develop them. Few candidates seem to be able to distinguish between the inaccuracy of suicide statistics because coroners make mistakes and the view that there is no real rate of suicide.

Atkinson deserves a more thorough treatment. His study of English and Danish coroners could be mentioned and his ideas on commonsense assumptions based on mode and circumstances of death used as illustration. Worth a D grade.

NB 'Theoretical' refers to his explanations based on integration and moral regulation. 'Methodological' refers to the debate over the value of a positivist approach to sociology.

CHAPTER 18

METHODS

REASONS FOR CHOOSING METHODS

THEORETICAL AND EMPIRICAL STUDIES

THE SURVEY

THE EXPERIMENT

CONVERSATIONAL ANALYSIS

CONTENT ANALYSIS

OBSERVATION

GETTING STARTED

All the syllabuses cover the use of sociological methods. Some of the examination papers have separate questions on methods, either in the form of critical essays or as part of structured stimulus questions. Where coursework is required, the ability to employ methods successfully and to critically evaluate their use is rewarded.

A critical understanding of the use of methods is helpful in understanding and criticising **any** topic on the syllabus.

The main themes of questions set on this topic are:

1 **Critical evaluation of a particular method or group of methods.**
2 **Comparison of the uses of particular methods or groups of methods.**
3 **Why do sociologists choose particular methods?.**
4 **What is the relationship between theoretical assumptions and methods?**
5 **The relationship between choice of method and the desire for a scientific and value-free sociology.**

Definitions

These terms are not used consistently by different writers.

- *Methodology* is the analytical study of the ways in which sociological research is conducted.
- *Methods* are systematic ways of collecting and analysing data, e.g. a survey.
- *Techniques of data collection* refer to the stage in research when information is gathered, e.g. an interview.

Specific methods and techniques are defined and explained below.

The use of secondary data, particularly official statistics, is discussed in the *Suicide* chapter. Other related areas are *theory* and *the nature of sociology*. *Methodological* issues arise when considering sociological research on any subject.

ESSENTIAL PRINCIPLES

This section will examine the reasons why sociologists choose particular methods and techniques. In particular we will discuss the assertion, made in many questions, that theoretical assumptions are the dominant influence on choice. The following discussion has been strongly influenced by BELL and NEWBY'S 'Doing Sociological Research' which asked contributors to describe how they **actually did** their research, instead of merely asking for a prescriptive list of how research **should be** done.

The factors influencing the choice of method in this list should not be seen as alternatives, as they are often inter-related. For example point 6 involves all the others.

REASONS FOR CHOOSING METHODS

The various reasons behind the choice of particular methods include the following:

1 Theoretical assumptions.
2 Practical restraints.
3 The topic to be studied.
4 Chance and inspiration.
5 Moral and ethical issues.
6 The sociology of sociologists.

THEORETICAL ASSUMPTIONS

The sociologist's perspective on society and approach to sociological problems can be a major influence on the method chosen.

Positivist sociologists prefer methods which can be employed scientifically. Research should be reliable, valid, generalisable and above all verifiable; e.g. Durkheim chose the comparative survey method using official statistics. This is also consistent with his functionalist perspective on society, as he sees the behaviour of individuals as being constrained by external structural influences.

Interpretive sociologists choose methods which provide insights into the social construction of reality by revealing the subjective experience of those studied. They are looking for the ways in which actors attribute meaning to their own, and others, behaviour, and at the commonsense assumptions which underly the way people define social situations; e.g. Becker chose participant observation to study deviants by sharing their experiences. Sacks chose to study conversation between potential suicides and staff at a suicide prevention centre.

There are exceptions to these generalisations. Both positivists and interpretivists use official statistics, albeit in different ways. Experiments are associated with positivist scientific research but have been employed by GARFINKEL, ATKINSON and ROSENTHAL and JACOBSON in non-positivist research. GOLDTHORPE and LOCKWOOD used the survey method in research influenced by social action theory. Participant observation was used by the functionalist, MALINOWSKI.

Many sociologists have used more than one method in a study in order to provide complementary forms of data. DANIEL'S study of racial discrimination used three methods. HUMPHREYS followed up his participant observation with interviews. NEWBY recommended the use of a variety of methods to gather different sorts of data in his 'Deferential Worker'.

PRACTICAL RESTRAINTS

The practical or technical advantages or disadvantages of particular methods are discussed below. They include the following points:

- Participant observation involves problems of access to powerful, exclusive, secretive or deviant groups.
- Sample surveys must compromise between cost and representativeness. The different sampling techniques have particular advantages and disadvantages.
- Postal questionnaires reach people cheaply if dispersed over a wide area, but have low response rates.
- Different types of interview can be compared on the basis of reliability and insight.

Use the studies below to illustrate these points.

THE TOPIC TO BE STUDIED

- Historical studies usually require the use of secondary data such as diaries, documents or official statistics; e.g. Anderson or Laslett's studies of the family.
- Large-scale studies often use secondary data (e.g. Murdock's cross-cultural study of the family in 250 societies), or sample surveys, such as studies of voting behaviour.
- The study of secretive and deviant groups often employs covert participant observation. HUMPHREYS,BARKER and WALLIS all followed up participant observation with interviews or questionnaires.
- The study of pre-literate societies often involves participant observation, because of the absence of written records and the need to learn new languages. MALINOWSKI and MEAD lived among simple societies. This is, of course, a constraint on those who wish to avoid long-term research.

CHANCE AND INSPIRATION

Most people know the stories of 'chance' scientific discoveries by ARCHIMEDES,NEWTON and FLEMING. There have been similar events in sociology. Malinowski was on his way to Australia when the Great War began. In order to avoid internment as an enemy alien he stopped in the Trobriand Islands and began a lengthy, participant observation study. DITTON was working as a bread salesman and happened to come across the institutionalisation of theft into the work role; he continued as a participant observer.

ETHICS AND MORALITY

Sociologists must make ethical decisions which may conflict with theoretical or practical demands. POLSKY has condemned Humphrey's advocacy of covert participant observation on ethical, as well as on practical, grounds.

Covert research involves both deception and invasion of privacy. Participant observation of deviants may involve joining in, or having knowledge of, crime, Polsky suggested that the researcher should make clear what kinds of activities he wishes to avoid.

Those who choose to conduct experiments must be prepared to interfere in their subjects' lives. This is seen as justifiable if, as in medical research, the subjects or the public benefit.

THE SOCIOLOGY OF SOCIOLOGISTS

There are sociological explanations of the behaviour of sociologists, just as there are for any other occupation. The previous five reasons could all be covered by this heading. The main issues identified by BELL and NEWBY are the problems of funding and 'institutional setting'.

ATKINSON explained his conversion to interactionist sociology as in part a result of getting an appointment at Essex University in the company of those pioneering this approach in England.

BURGESS pointed out the difficulty of writing a detailed research proposal to do participant observation and thus the difficulty of getting research funds. This problem can be overcome if the topic is seen as a social problem e.g. Williams' 'Hooligans abroad'.

GOULDNER criticised the domination of positivist research, which he saw proliferating because it gave insecure American sociologists the respectability they craved during the attacks on academic freedom in the 1950s. (See the discussion of value freedom in Chapter 20 on the *Nature of Sociology*).

THEORETICAL AND EMPIRICAL STUDIES

Critical evaluation of the various methods used in sociology should involve a consideration of theoretical, practical and ethical issues. There is no 'best' method. Sociologists are influenced by their theoretical assumptions but still have to balance often conflicting practical constraints.

Studies of large numbers of subjects tend to be more reliable and representative, but lack depth and insight. Minimising personal involvement reduces the problem of contamination, but limits the depth of possible understanding. High levels of control make research more reliable, but run the risk of making that research artificial.

THE SURVEY

The survey method involves both the collection and analysis of data. Many cases are studied, and data is quantified and analysed in a systematic way. The survey can be used to test hypotheses, for instance, seeking correlations between variables by using multi-variate analysis, as in Durkheim's comparative study of suicide.

Comparative surveys can be:

a) Longitudinal; e.g. the 1971 health longitudinal survey.
b) Cross-cultural; e.g. Durkheim's 'Suicide'.
c) Historical; e.g. Laslett's study of changes in household size.

Methods of data collection used in surveys include:

a) The use of secondary data; e.g. Durkheim.
b) (Postal) self-completed questionnaires; e.g. Wallis' study of Scientologists.
c) Interviews which can be more or less structured; e.g. Willmott and Young in Bethnal Green and Oakley's study of housework.

- *The sample survey* involves selecting and studying a small proportion of the population. This saves time and money. If the sample is *representative*, the results can be *generalised* to the whole population.
- *The population* is all those who could be included in the study and all those whom the study claims to describe.
- *The sampling frame* is a list of the population from which the sample is chosen. Daniel had no suitable list of ethnic minorities (see Chapter 4).
- *The sample* is those selected for study.

SAMPLING METHODS

Sampling methods are ways of choosing representative samples. They include the following.

a) QUOTA or STRATIFIED samples are chosen by dividing the population into strata with particular characteristics, and by selecting individuals from each strata in proportion to their numbers in the population. This method is cheap and quick, but the relevant strata must be known in advance.
b) RANDOM samples are chosen mathematically from the whole population so that each unit has an equal chance of selection. (Like playing 'Bingo'.)
c) STRATIFIED RANDOM samples are chosen randomly from predetermined strata, and not from the whole population. This ensures that relatively rare strata are represented even in a small sample.
d) PURPOSIVE samples are chosen so that specific subjects are included, and may sacrifice representativeness to achieve this. This may be the only solution if no sampling frame exists. Goldthorpe and Lockwood selected subjects from Luton to test the embourgeoisement thesis on the basis that if it had not occurred in such suitable conditions, it would not have occurred anywhere.
e) 'SNOWBALL' samples are chosen by allowing subjects to introduce the researcher to other suitable subjects. This is unlikely to be representative, but does permit access to secretive subjects.

INTERVIEWS

Interviews may provide structured data for surveys or take the form of unsystematic records of subject responses (see answer to Question 3, below). Surveys generally employ more structured and formal interviews, using standardised questions which can produce quantifiable and reliable data. The advantage of formal interviews over subject completed questionnaires is that the interviewer can explain and probe, e.g. Goldthorpe and Lockwood.

Less formal interviews are favoured by sociologists who wish to avoid imposing their views on their subjects, thereby limiting the validity of their responses. The advantage over other qualitative methods, such as participant observation, is speed; e.g. Oakley on housework.

Interviewer bias is the problem caused by interviewers affecting the responses of the subjects. The issue here is reliability. Different or even individual interviewers may act inconsistently. This problem can be minimised by training and by the standardisation of questions. Research has shown that the class (KATZ), gender (HYMAN), race (WILLIAMS), and political values (Rice) of interviewers can affect responses. LABOV argued that the interview situation itself might intimidate some subjects. BECKER however felt that the aggressive interviewing of teachers actually got them to reveal their true feelings.

QUESTIONNAIRES

Questionnaires are lists of pre-set questions used to measure attitudes, opinions and behaviour. They can be used to gather data from large numbers of perhaps widely dispersed subjects. If questions are standardised, such data can be easily quantified and analysed.

Postal questionnaires, as employed by WALLIS and HITE, risk low and unrepresentative response rates. The questions themselves can be criticised. Slight variations in wording can produce different responses. Pilot studies for the EEC referendum produced a 20% variation in results by using different wording to seek approval for continued membership. Opinion research on abortion, commissioned by interested pressure groups, has produced results actually supporting the opposing side's position.

A study by LA PIERE showed that answers may not indicate actual behaviour, as restaurants which had admitted a Chinese couple later answered a questionnaire saying they would not. When racial discrimination is not acceptable, the opposite response might be found (DANIEL).

THE EXPERIMENT

The experiment involves the manipulation of an independent variable (cause) and the observation of a dependent variable (effect), whilst controlling extraneous variables. Observation and surveys may be similar to experiments, that they look for naturally occurring differences rather than manipulate them; e.g. studies of the effects of unemployment on suicide. Experiments can take place in the laboratory (to maximise control) or the field (for naturalness).

In the natural sciences, the experiment is seen as the 'superior' method because of the possibility of control and reliability. We might expect that this method would be favoured by positivists but, in fact, it is rarely employed because of practical, theoretical and ethical reasons. DURKHEIM advocated the use of the comparative method as a substitute for experimentation. Positivist research using experiments is rare, unless we consider social psychological experiments which have sociological implications, such as MILGRAM'S 'Obedience to Authority' or ZIMBARDO'S study of the effects of allowing students to role-play prisoners and wardens. DANIEL used an experiment to test the extent of racial discrimination. MAYO began the Hawthorne studies with an experiment to test the effects of illumination on productivity and found that simply being in an experiment influenced the behaviour of subjects. This obviously has wide implications for research, as does Rosenthal and Jacobson's demonstration of the self-fulfilling prophecy.

Interpretive sociology has surprisingly shown a willingness to use the experiment. GARFINKEL used experiments to show that everyday behaviour is governed by 'common sense assumptions'. He created rule-breaking situations (e.g. responding to questions with random answers or getting students to act as lodgers in their parents' homes), and then observed how subjects made sense of these novel situations. ATKINSON had a similar intention of revealing the commonsense assumptions which coroners use to define suicide when he presented English and Danish coroners with identical case notes to see if they reached equivalent suicide verdicts or not.

CONVERSATIONAL ANALYSIS

This method is also employed in ethnomethodology to describe how people arrive at the meanings they give to social situations. Sacks used his own commonsense assumptions to study tape recordings of conversations between staff and callers at a suicide prevention centre. He noted that both parties saw the suicidal person as having 'no one to turn to', though that was precisely the role of the centre.

(*NB Refer back to the *Suicide* chapter and note that Sacks is not interested in suicide itself, only in the ways in which people make sense of the world).

CONTENT ANALYSIS

Content analysis involves the systematic analysis of written documents or broadcasts. It has been used in studies of the mass media to demonstrate bias in the selection and presentation of news by the GUMG and others.

Content analysis of school books has alleged that they reinforce racist stereotypes (Wright on geography text books) and sexist stereotypes (Loban on reading schemes).

OBSERVATION

As regards **observation**, SHIPMAN has argued that all research in the natural and social sciences depends on observation. He sees it as an active process where the researcher uses his mind to interpret what he sees and hears.

Examination questions tend to focus on participant observation, which is joining in the everyday lives of subjects. GOLD has distinguished four ideal types of observation, ranging from complete participation to complete detachment. The general aims of participant observation are to study subjects in natural situations, thereby avoiding some of the problems of involvement.

Since MALINOWSKI, functionalist social anthropologists have favoured participant observation to discover how apparently strange behaviour can be explained by looking at the way it 'fits' with other behaviour and contributes to social stability.

Interactionist sociologists have advocated participant observation as a means of sharing the experiences of subjects to discover the meanings they give to situations. BECKER and POLSKY have produced accounts of 'real' participation as a musician and poolroom player respectively. HARGREAVES was able to show that actual teaching was different from teachers talking about teaching. CICOUREL, in a study of juvenile delinquents, was able to describe the labelling process by joining in the routine activities of probation officers and sharing their conceptions of people and events.

Involvement, which is clearly the justification of participant observation, is also the source of most of the criticism directed against it, whether from a theoretical, practical or ethical viewpoint. WHYTE'S admission that he both influenced, and was influenced by, gang membership is often quoted. Interference can be reduced in different ways. KING found that being over six foot, remaining standing and avoiding eye-contact, allowed him to move among infant school children with minimal involvement. Polsky encouraged subjects to see him as a neutral observer, rather than as an official, thrill seeker or rival. He also stressed the importance of learning the language of subjects, in this case, the slang and non-verbal signals of pool hustlers. This is obvious when conducting anthropological studies of other societies, but is less so when studying deviant sub-cultures. DITTON noted the distinction between 'fiddling' (stealing from employers) and 'knocking-off' (from guest's hotel rooms); only the latter was condemned.

EXAMINATION QUESTIONS

1   Read the following extract written by a sociologist proposing to carry out research on a religious sect and answer the questions which follow.

I have always been sceptical of those who argue that sociology should model itself on the natural sciences. For me, studying people is not the same as studying natural objects such as chemicals or rocks; studying human actions presents its own particular problems and requires its own special techniques and approaches.   5

Although I accept that to some extent sociologists should maintain some detachment from their subjects. I think that we also have to get involved if we are to understand human behaviour. For this reason I have decided to carry out research on my chosen group by using ethnographic methods. For example, I intend to go along to a prayer meeting and pretend to be a potential convert   10
genuinely interested in their beliefs. I shall not reveal my true identity or

intentions, but use covert research methods. I believe that 'going underground' in this way will enable me to discover how the worshippers really behave as unaffected by my presence as possible. Although such methods do raise both practical and ethical or moral issues, I believe they can be justified because it's 15 the best way to study people by disturbing them as little as possible.

a) What term is used to describe sociologists who model sociology on the natural sciences (line 2)? (2)

b) What are the differences between studying people and studying natural objects
(lines 2–3)? (6)

c) What do you understand by the term 'ethnographic methods' (line 9) (3)

d) Using research studies from any areas of social life to illustrate your answer, outline the *practical* advantages *and* disadvantages of covert research (line 12). (8)

e) What do you think might be the 'ethical or moral issues' referred to in line 15 above? How could you criticise this sociologist's approach on ethical grounds? (6)

(Total 25 marks)
(JMB 1988)

2 The most common type of survey is the *cross-sectional* or snapshot survey. The researcher gets information from a cross-section of the group under study at one point in time. Thus the findings are gathered fairly quickly and cheaply to provide useful information . . . .

A less common and more expensive type of social survey is the *longitudinal* 5 survey. In this, a selected group is studied over a period of time. This enables the researcher to gain not only current information but also insights into the way people are changing their attitudes or behaviour over a much longer time-span.

Almost always used as part of a social survey is the questionnaire. This is 10 where the sociologist designs a set of questions about a particular subject to be answered by respondents (the people being surveyed). Questionnaires are difficult to write but are worth the effort because the sociologist can get a lot of information from respondents. However, some types of questions are easier to handle than others. 15
(Adapted from R. Power *et al: Discover Sociology*)

a) According to the passage, what advantage does the longitudinal survey have over the cross-sectional survey? (1)

b) Name **two** different types of question (line 14) which may be used in a questionnaire, and give an example of each. (4)

c) ' . . . .the people being surveyed' (line 12) are chosen by different types of sampling. Discuss the advantages and disadvantages of different sampling techniques. (8)

d) Examine the advantages and limitations of using questionnaires. (12)
(Total 25 marks)
(AEB 1988)

3 Examine critically the different ways in which interviews have been employed in sociological research. Illustrate your answer with examples.
(AEB 1986 and very similar specimen question for AEB 1991)

4 My aim is to provide an overview of the sorts of considerations that sociologists take into account when designing research and deciding which methods to use. These considerations can be thought of as falling into four groups. First, what is to be the researcher's *standpoint* in relation to the research? Is the researcher going to do the research, evaluate the research done by other people, or commission someone else to do the research? Second, what is the researcher's *approach*? Is the aim to produce positivist, interpretivist, ethnomethodological or structuralist explanations of whatever aspects of the social world are under study? Third, what *strategy* is the researcher adopting: a case study, a sample survey or an experiment? And fourth, what *techniques* is the researcher going to use to collect and analyse data? For example, will it be an

observation or an interview study? Will the data be quantified and statistically analysed or used raw in illustrative quotations?

(from Principles of Method – Peter Halfpenny)

a) Name **two techniques** used by researchers, other than those in the passage.

(2)

b) What does the author mean when he talks of data being 'used raw in illustrative quotations' in sociological research (line 12)? (5)

c) Explain what is meant by the term 'case study', and why sociologists might accept this strategy (line 9). (8)

d) Examine the relationship between a researcher's *approach* and her or his *technique*. (10)

(*Total 25 marks*)

(AEB 1985)

5 Compare quantitive and qualitative methods of collecting sociological data. Illustrate your answer with examples.

(AEB 1989)

OUTLINE ANSWERS TO SELECTED QUESTIONS 3, 4 AND 5

Question 3

(Questions may ask that examples be restricted to one area of sociology, e.g. conjugal roles.)

The question requires a knowledge of interview techniques, an awareness of the influence of theoretical assumptions on the way interviews are used, and criticism of the use of interviews.

The answer could use the debate between positivism and critics as a framework.

i) Positivists tend to use interviews as a technique for gathering survey data. They seek information which can be quantified and statistically analysed. Their preference is for formal and structured interviews using standardised closed questions, e.g. Blauner on alienation; Willmott and Young on conjugal roles.

ii) But informal unstructured interviews have been used by sociologists who do not reject the positivist approach but seek richer data which allows the subjects to speak with minimal interference, e.g. Bott; Oakley; both on conjugal roles.

iii) Criticism focuses on reliability, standardisation and interviewer bias. From a theoretical point of view validity is seen as threatened if the researcher imposes their views on subjects. Examples are found below.

iv) Interpretive sociologists use interviews to allow subjects to describe their own experiences. They emphasise non-interference, preferring unstructured informal interviews, e.g. Cohen and Taylor let prisoners describe their experiences with minimal interference.

v) But surveys have been employed by those who seek the subjects definition of the situation, e.g. Goldthorpe and Lockwood adopted a social action approach which emphasised the importance of the workers' instrumental attitude to work.

vi) Criticism from positivists focuses on the lack of reliability of informal interviews. Interpretive sociologists may see even unstructured interviews as involving too much interference from researchers.

vii) Some writers have employed interviews to complement other techniques; e.g. Daniels study of racial discrimination. Humphreys on homosexuality. Thus the researcher is not forced to make a choice between validity or reliability or between quantitative or qualitative data.

Question 4

Terms used in this passage (such as 'strategy' and 'technique') are not always defined in this way. However you should accept the author's usage.

a) Name **two** *techniques* used by researchers, other than those in the passage. Choose two from questionnaires, participant observation, content analysis, use of secondary data etc. (2)

b) What does the author mean when he talks of data being 'used raw in illustrative quotations' in sociological research (line 12)? (5)

You should discuss, with examples, the ways in which data can either be processed or alternatively presented to the reader in an unprocessed form so that the researcher's interpretation and analysis do not interfere with the subject's experience. Link this with anti-positivist approaches.

Examples could be drawn from:

■ Interactionist studies, such as Cohen and Taylor.
■ Ethnomethodology, such as Sacks on conversations with potential suicides.
■ Social anthropology studies where conversation is recorded.

c) Explain what is meant by the term 'case study' and why sociologists might accept this strategy (line 9). (8)

A case study involves studying a single example. This could be an individual or family if the research was medical, psychological or conducted by social workers. This is not, however, the way in which the term is used in sociology.

Case studies could be on a gang (Whyte), a school (Ball), a factory (Beynon), a hospital (Goffman), a community (Goffman on the Shetland Isles) or a society (most social anthropology studies, e.g. Malinowski).

The problem of case studies is the extent to which they are representative of other cases.

Uses include:

i) Testing a hypothesis by using an extreme case (Goldthorpe *et al* chose Luton as the most suitable environment for embourgeoisement).
ii) Choosing a representative case (Ford's study criticising comprehensive schools).
iii) Letting the study stand alone as a complete work or using it for comparison (Malinowski or Mead's anthropological studies).
iv) As (iii), but as an ethnographic study from an interpretive viewpoint (Keddie).

The case study is often, but not exclusively, favoured by non-positivist sociologists.

d) Examine the relationship between a researcher's *approach* and her or his *technique*.
(10)

i) Link structuralist and positivist sociology with quantitative, objective, large-scale techniques. Explain and illustrate.
ii) Give exceptional cases.
iii) Link interpretivist and micro-sociological approaches with qualitative, subjective, in-depth techniques. Explain and illustrate.
iv) Give exceptional cases.
v) Mention briefly other influences on choice of technique

Question 5

Here the term 'method' is used in the sense that 'technique' is employed in question 4.

In order to score high marks a variety of methods within each category must be considered in a critical fashion and comparisons made. Illustrations must help to explain a point and not just be listed. Crime and suicide provide useful examples to compare but should not exclude all others.

i) Link quantitative methods with positivist sociology. Explain and illustrate. Criticise by questioning the reliability, representativeness and validity.
ii) Give exceptional examples of positivist or structuralist sociology using qualitative methods.
iii) Link qualitative methods with interpretive and interactionist sociology. Explain and illustrate. Criticise as in i).
iv) Give exceptional examples of interpretive sociologists using quantitative methods.

TUTOR'S ANSWER

Question 1

a) What term is used to describe sociologists who model sociology on the natural sciences (line 2)?

Positivists advocate using the logic and methods of the natural sciences.

b) What are the differences between studying people and studying natural objects (lines 2–3)?

Natural objects have an objective existence; this means that they can be directly observed and measured. Like natural scientists, positivist sociologists and behaviourists in psychology restrict their subject matter to those phenomena which can be observed. Durkheim said that social facts should be treated like things.

People, unlike natural objects, have a consciousness and can reflect upon their own and others behaviour. Because the mind is not directly observable and people attach meanings to behaviour, many social scientists are critical of the scientific approach. Weber saw the aim of sociology as the 'interpretive understanding of social action'.

Interpretive sociologists do not see social phenomena as having an objective existence, like natural objects. Social reality is constructed by interaction between individuals and groups.

Social behaviour does not follow universal laws, like natural phenomena, although much useful sociology depends on the view that behaviour is still predictable. Establishing correlations between phenomena allows the statement of probabilistic laws, not unlike those found in mathematics and theoretical physics.

Some scientists and sociologists see ethical issues as arising in the study of people which do not apply to other natural objects. However, the defence of animal rights indicates that this is not an undisputed view.

c) What do you understand by the term 'ethnographic methods' (line 9)?

These are methods employed by ethnomethodologists to discover and describe the ways in which people make sense of social situations. Generally this involves participant observation or listening to conversations. The aim is to share the experience of subjects without interfering with their everyday behaviour.

d) Using research studies from any area of social life to illustrate your answer, outline the *practical* advantages *and* disadvantages of covert research (line 12).

The most common form of covert research is participant observation, although other undercover methods used include observation and experiments where subjects are either unaware of the real purpose of the research or unaware of being studied at all.

Covert methods allow access to groups who might exclude outsiders because their behaviour is illegal, shameful or secretive. Humpreys 'Tea room trade' illustrates this although Polsky's studies of criminals and Barker's study of the 'Moonies' shows that access is not always restricted to those undercover.

However the researcher may find himself restricted to studying groups where he (participant observation seems dominated by men) can pass as one of the subjects. Frequently young men have studied gangs, e.g. Williams on football hooligans. Pryce pointed out the necessity of being black for his study of Bristol, but Griffin was able to dye himself black for his research. Liebow made a virtue of his *difference* from his subjects, because, as an outsider, he was not seen as a threat.

The covert study of deviant groups may also entail a degree of danger. The researcher may risk discovery and reprisal during research or following publication. There is also the risk attached to joining-in or witnessing deviant or secret behaviour. Wallis is convinced that Scientologists tried to discredit him through anonymous accusations. Rosenhan found it difficult to get out of a psychiatric hospital.

Covert research limits the means the observer can use to gather and record data without revealing one's identity. Being 'underground' limits the opportunities for asking questions, although Aggleton in a study of college students was able to get answers to a memorised set of key questions from all his subjects through informal conversation.

Festinger used visits to the lavatory to make notes about an exclusive religious sect he had secretly joined.

Although there may be doubts about the reliability of covert participant observation, this criticism can be applied to all participant observation and other covert methods could be replicated. Zimbardo conducted an experiment which involved filming the vandalism of cars in various locations and Daniel's experiments to test for racial discrimination have been subsequently repeated.

Finally, the major advantage must be the ability to minimise contamination of the research by influencing the behaviour of subjects. This problem was demonstrated in the work of Mayo and later Rosenthal and Jacobson. Rosenthal and Jacobson not only demonstrated the problem of the self-fulfilling prophecy, they also suceeded in doing so in an experiment using deception.

e) What do you think might be the 'ethical or moral issues' referred to in line 15 above? How could you criticise this sociologist's approach on ethical grounds.

The researcher is invading the privacy of the group by observing them without their informed consent during what is likely to be an intensely personal activity. The presence of the observer in a non-religious capacity might be seen as offensive to their beliefs. Subsequent publication may cause embarrassment to individuals who could be identified (this can be overcome by disguising individuals, for example by scrambling different identities). The publication of research might expose the group to ridicule or threat.

Generally, covert participant observation involves the infiltration of relatively weak groups in terms of class or status and although Becker talks of providing the view of the 'under dog' it is frequently the exotic lives of weak outsiders which are exposed to scrutiny.

There are no generally agreed professional ethics for sociologists, as there are for doctors, priests or lawyers. Polsky and Humphreys have debated the morality of covert research and come to opposite conclusions. This author does feel that such deception can be justified although, if the study could be shown to be significant and useful the case would be more convincing. William's research into hooliganism produced recommendations to help control threatening behaviour.

STUDENT ANSWER WITH EXAMINER COMMENTS

Question 2

a) According to the passage, what advantage does the longitudinal survey have over the cross-sectional survey? *(1)*

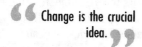
Change is the crucial idea.

> You can gain current information and insights into the way people change their attitudes and behaviour over a longer period of time.

b) Name **two** different types of question (line 14) which may be used in a questionnaire, and give an example of each. *(4)*

Yes.

> 1 Closed questions e.g. 'Did you vote Conservative?'
> 2 Open ended questions e.g. 'Why did you vote the way you did?'

c) '. . . .The people being surveyed' (line 12) are chosen by different types of sampling. Discuss the advantages and disadvantages of different sampling techniques.

Should define and explain 'population', 'representative' and 'generalise'.

> The different types of sampling are quota, random, stratified random, purposive and snowballing.
> A quota sample is chosen so that each unit is found in the same proportion that it is found in the population. This dispenses with

the need for a complete sampling frame and allows any person meeting pre-determined criteria to be chosen. In this technique you identify the relevant criteria i.e. you have to anticipate the result. You could miss an important category and therefore your generalisation would be wrong. Also there is the temptation to choose amenable subjects. Errors are not calculable.

> *Good points, but no examples!*

In a random sample every unit has an equal chance of being chosen. This requires a complete sampling frame and you must use the people selected. Errors are calculable. But if it is small then it may not be representative. The US presidential elections were wrongly predicted in 1936 and 1948 as the samples were mainly middle class.

> *How are random samples chosen?*

Stratified random samples are taken at random from sub-divided populations. This ensures, even with small samples, that all relevant categories are represented.

> *Yes, but no examples.*

Purposive sampling is not representative because a specific type of sample is required, e.g. Gavron's 'Captive Wife' used the national housewives register. Aggleton chose 'Spa Town' college because he knew the underachievers there. Goldthorpe and Lockwood chose Luton because it was 'ripe' for embourgeoisement.

> *Yes.*

Snowballing is when one person leads to another to create a sample, e.g. D. J. West chose self-reporting delinquents. Hite chose those who responded. Daniel had no sampling frame available. Both snowballing and purposive sampling sacrifice representativeness to achieve their aim.

> *Not explained. Examples inappropriate.*

d) Examine the advantages and limitations of using questionnaires. *(12)*

Questionnaires are a comparatively cheap, fast and efficient method for obtaining large amounts of quantifiable data. Responses may be open or closed depending on the type of questions asked. Open ended allow the respondent to compose their own answer and thus explain themselves fully whereas closed questions maybe an over-simplification. A problem with open questions is that the responses may be difficult to classify and quantify.

> *Relevant points.*
> *Unstructured interviews are unlikely to be used.*

Questionnaires may be administered in structured or unstructured interviews. Goldthorpe and Lockwood used structured interviews. This allowed any ambiguity to be clarified. But this type involves interviewer bias and is expensive. Standardised questions must be used to maintain consistency and reliability. Hyman showed the different results produced by using male and female interviewers.

Postal questionnaires are an inexpensive way of gathering data which is geographically dispersed. But the return rate is very low therefore it is unrepresentative. Hite had only a 3% return rate. Only the literate, interested or those with time return a questionnaire.

> *Relevant criticism.*

Questionnaires avoid or limit interviewer bias or contamination. But some respondents may not be able to understand a question. There is no need for trained interviewers. But there is already prejudice in the selection and wording of questions. This imposes reality on the subjects.

> *Good points.*

Wallis used postal questionnaires to study Scientologists. Questions should avoid prejudgement e.g. Oakley asked 'Do you feel dissatisfied with housework?' because she was looking for boredom. Variations in questions produce different answers. Kinsey rephrased 'How many times?' with 'Do you?' Sometimes respondents do not know the answers; Willmott and Young asked wives if their husbands had seen their families in the last 24 hours.

> *Wallis not used. Other examples better.*

66 Relevant point. 99

> Subjects may fear officials and therefore avoid answering questions or answer wrongly e.g. immigrants, criminals and religious sects.

Overall comments

Overall, a thorough answer with numerous good points. An equally good answer might make fewer points but develop and illustrate them more. The candidate does not examine theoretical issues but nevertheless an A grade.

CHAPTER

SOCIOLOGICAL THEORIES

FUNCTIONALIST THEORY

MARXIST THEORY

ACTION PERSPECTIVES

THEORETICAL AND EMPIRICAL STUDIES

GETTING STARTED

The study of sociological theory is, for many students and teachers, the most daunting part of A-level courses. However good, responses to questions on any topic require the ability to apply and evaluate one or more theoretical approaches.

A basic command of theory is essential at an early stage in order to provide the framework for answering questions. Most of the answers in this book are organised on the basis of distinguishing different sociological perspectives. A more sophisticated understanding is necessary for answering questions which are specifically about theories and for producing good answers to questions on substantive topics. For example, the ability to identify and apply a variety of Marxist or action approaches to topics such as deviance, education or power is likely to be expected by examiners for good answers.

The extent to which a detailed knowledge of theories is required depends on the syllabus. JMB asks more questions about theory than the other boards and requires a more detailed knowledge of the concepts used by the theories; this particularly applies to the different action theories.

The main themes of questions set on this topic are:

1 **Outline and critical evaluation of a specified theory.**
2 **Comparison of two particular theories.**
3 **Comparison of groups of theories such as structural and action theories or consensus and conflict theories.**
4 **Application of one or more theories to issues such as social change, social order or social control.**

Related material is found in the chapters on *Methods*, *Suicide* and *The Nature of Sociology*. Most chapters benefit from the application of theory to topics and provide useful examples for theoretical discussion.

FUNCTIONALIST THEORY

ESSENTIAL PRINCIPLES

Functionalism is not a single easily defined theory. It is more a common perspective shared by many sociologists which comprises a coherent though varied approach to sociological problems. Many sociologists mentioned in text books as functionalists, most notably Durkheim, did not describe themselves in this way and Radcliffe-Brown denied there was a functionalist school at all. Nevertheless, a common set of basic assumptions can be identified which are shared by most of the writers described as functionalists.

Functionalism is a structuralist perspective which emphasises the constraints imposed on individual behaviour by social forces. It is also a consensus perspective which explains social order in terms of shared values. The distinctive assumptions of functionalism include:

1 Society is seen as a system of interrelated parts. It is sometimes likened to a biological organism or a machine (see also the answer to Question 5, below).
2 The system has needs (functional prerequisites) which must be satisfied if it is to survive and remain stable e.g. integration.
3 The parts can only be studied and understood by considering the relationships between individual parts and the part and the whole system. These relationships are based on functions e.g. the relationship between education and the economy.
4 Functions are contributions that partial activities make to the working of the whole system. That is, the contribution the parts make to social stability by satisfying the needs of the system e.g. the functions of the family which include reproducing culture through socialisation of the young.
5 The system is integrated by shared values e.g. religious beliefs and interdependence e.g. based on the division of labour.
6 The precise form that social arrangements take depends on their functions. The whole system adapts so that the parts 'fit' e.g. the nuclear family developed to fit the needs of industrial society.
7 Inequality is seen as functional. Authority is given to those who can satisfy social needs and high rewards to those in functionally important positions.

CRITICISMS

These are general criticisms and may not apply to every functionalist writer or may apply to structuralist or consensus theories apart from functionalism.

1 Conflict theorists challenge the consensual view of human society. Harmony and integration are seen as over-emphasised. It is the content of values, not the fact that they are shared, which unites societies e.g. Western values of competitiveness and individualism can be seen as threats to integration. Conflict is seen as normal not pathological. Consensus theories idealise institutions like the family and legitimise inequality.
2 Action theorists claim that structuralist theories offer an over-socialised view of individuals. The deterministic nature of structuralism concentrates on external social causes and ignores the importance of individual subjective experience. Human behaviour is purposive not reactive. Individuals participate in the social construction of reality not simply respond to a given objective reality.
3 Specific criticism of functionalism suggests:
   ■ Functionalism is teleological. That is, it tries to explain the origins of phenomena by identifying their effects (on the social system). This may be because some functionalism confuses the view that functions can be seen as effects or consequences with the idea that functions are purposes. Social arrangements do not exist because they meet functional needs, as the needs could go unsatisfied or be satisfied by other arrangements; e.g. children can be socialised outside the family and roles can be allocated without inequality of rewards.
   ■ Functionalism does not produce testable hypotheses and is thus unscientific.
   ■ Functionalism does not adequately explain social change. It tends to justify the status quo. The role of individuals who change society through conscious activities is ignored.

MARXIST THEORY

The term 'Marxism' is used for a variety of ideas developed from the writings of Karl Marx and his collaborators, particularly Engels. Marx was both an academic and political writer and a political activist. His work combines an ambitious analysis of history and capitalist society with a revolutionary programme.

Marxism only began to influence sociology in a significant way during the 1960s, so for most of this century sociology has ignored Marxism and Marxism has dismissed sociology. However, more recently Marxism has become an important strand in sociological thought and an invaluable source of critical material for A-level sociologists.

What is Marxism?

1 It is a theory explaining how society works which emphasises the importance of social class.
2 It is a theory of social change.
3 It is a political philosophy and programme for political action.

In A-level sociology we are only concerned with the first two aspects but they are illuminated by an understanding of his revolutionary ideology and action.

Marxism is generally seen as a structuralist perspective which indicates how changes in society can change the consciousness and actions of individuals. However, it can also be seen as an action theory with individuals consciously pursuing goals and choosing the best means of achieving them. The constraints of the social (i.e. economic) structure restrict the rationality of the subject classes who are kept falsely conscious by the dominant ruling class ideology.

Marxism has become one of the dominant conflict theories in sociology and has influenced other conflict theories e.g. Weber's work and modern feminism. The basis of conflict is the class struggle.

The key to understanding Marxism is the relationship between economic production (which is the central human activity) and other social phenomena, both ideas and institutions.

Marxist analysis is based on an examination of the relationship between the economic substructure of society and the superstructure of society.

The *substructure* comprises:
1 The forces of production which is the term Marx gives to both the equipment and technological knowledge involved in producing goods.
2 The relations of production which are the economic roles shaped by the forces of production and crucially the relationships between these roles.

It is, thus, the relations of production which are the basis of social classes.

The *superstructure* comprises:
1 Social institutions such as the family, church, political system, education system etc.
2 Ideas, beliefs and values including definitions of health and deviance, religious beliefs and the school curriculum.

The substructure shapes the superstructure which in turn reproduces the substructure. Social change occurs when contradictions emerge in the economic substructure which prompt action by classes to challenge the domination of the ruling class. Thus feudalism fell when its ruling class could not meet the challenge presented by the rise of commerce and industry in towns. Marx similarly predicts the downfall of capitalism when contradictions will lead to the pauperisation of the proletariat who will become class conscious and revolutionary.

"" How to use Marxist theory. ""

The most usual application of Marxist theory to A-level sociology is to see various institutions as part of the superstructure of capitalist society and ask how they contribute to the preservation of ruling class interests.

CRITICISM

1 Consensus theorists maintain that conflict is abnormal and undesirable. They share Marxist views on the process of cultural reproduction (by institutions such as the family, school, church and media) but dispute its purpose and the content of that which is transmitted. They see consensual values being passed on by socialisation for the common good, rather than ruling class ideology being transmitted to maintain its hegemony.

Social problems are seen as related to industrialism rather than capitalism. Communism has been dismissed by Rostow (see Chapter on *Development*) as a disease of transition not a final goal of development.

2   Action theory since Weber has continually attacked the structuralism of Marxism particularly the alleged economic determinism. This is exemplified by Weber's explanation of the rise of capitalism which emphasises the role of ideas rather than technological development.

More modern interactionist theory puts increased emphasis on the consciousness of individuals. Rather than seeing this consciousness shaped by objective economic forces it is suggested that if social situations are defined as 'real' by actors they are real in their effects. Thus, there need be no objective social reality whether dominated by economic factors or not.

3   Conflict theories do not all accept Marxist analysis of phenomena such as the distribution of power (disputed by elite theorists) or family relationships (disputed by feminists). Above all, Marxist theories of class have been challenged, notably by Weber and subsequent followers.

ACTION PERSPECTIVES

These include:

1   Social action theories which have developed from Weber (and Marx).
2   Symbolic interactionism which has developed from Mead's social psychological approach.
3   Ethnomethodology which was developed by Garfinkel as a sociological activity (rather than a theory) from the phenomenological philosophy of Schutz. Schutz himself criticised Weber's view of social action.

Despite the differences between these various action perspectives there are some generally shared basic assumptions.

1   Individuals or small groups are studied not whole societies.
2   Roles are negotiated by individuals not imposed by society or the ruling class e.g. between doctors and patients or deviants and the police.
3   The social world exists in the minds of individuals it has no objective reality e.g. there is no real rate of suicide.
4   Social order emerges from shared meanings so 'if men define situations as real they are real in their consequences' (Thomas).
5   Weber suggests that sociology should seek the 'interpretive understanding of social action'. This involves examining the meaning actors give to their own behaviour and the behaviour of others rather than seeking the causes of behaviour.
6   The general approach is anti-positivist and anti-scientific. This influences the choice of research methods which should seek insight into the actor's experience of the world. Language is seen as very important. 'Talk' is both a method and a source of data.

Social action theory

Even within this perspective there are variations but the general model is one where 'actors' carry out actions to pursue goals. Their values and their perception of the situation influences their choice of goals and the selection of means to achieve them.

It is the meaning attributed to behaviour by the actor and others which distinguishes social action from biological behaviour.

Symbolic interactionism

The key concept is the 'self'. The self is how we see ourselves as objects in the social world. We can be self-conscious and act towards ourselves as well as others e.g. we can get angry with ourselves. We see ourselves as we think others see us. Cooley called this 'the looking glass self'.

Interaction, using symbols (particularly language), is possible because we can take the role of others. Others are either particular people, especially those who are important to us ('significant others' e.g. mothers, teachers and bosses), or 'generalised others' who represent the view that the wider society might have about us.

This ability to interact by taking the role of others is used by sociologists who use participant observation to step into the shoes of their subjects in order to see the social world as they do and share the meanings they give to symbols.

Deviant or abnormal individuals, groups or situations are often studied because the view deviants have of themselves is often different from the general or official view e.g. those labelled delinquent or insane may see themselves as ordinary.

Ethnomethodology

The aim of ethnomethodology is to describe how people make sense of social situations using 'commonsense knowledge'. Commonsense knowledge is the shared meanings given to everyday encounters and provides the basis of social order. Particular events are seen as examples (called 'documents') of a broader set of events so people know what is expected of them. The general set of events provides the context which makes sense of the individual acts e.g. coroners use their commonsense knowledge to reconstruct deaths to decide if they were suicides.

Garfinkel sees people as 'members' rather than 'actors' which is the term preferred by interactionists. Members assume the social world has an objective reality which is seen and experienced by everyone in the same way. Others are believed to share our commonsense knowledge and do so sufficiently to allow for orderly encounters. If they do not appear to share our commonsense knowledge then we assume there is something different about them e.g. they are mad, wicked, foreign or a child.

CRITICISM

1   Structuralist theories criticise action theories for their inability to explain or, in some cases, even recognise structural constraints on behaviour. Consensus based theories question the absence of consideration of the way individuals are socialised into a pre-existing culture.

Conflict theories are more specific in their insistence that neither conflict nor the unequal distribution of power are given adequate consideration. Structural restraints are imposed on individuals whether they like it or not. The failure to recognise such limitations is seen, by Marxists, as false consciousness. The famous saying of the interactionist Thomas 'if men define situations as real, they are real in their consequences' could be inverted by Marxists to say that if situations are real, they are real in their consequences however they are defined by individuals.

Symbolic interactionism could be alleged to explain nothing as it suggests little more than that social situations are the product of action and that action is governed by the actors perception of the situation.

2   There are internal debates within the action perspective. These may take the form of arguing that a theory goes too far in emphasising individual choice and the subjective nature of social reality. Or conversely, not far enough by still accepting the existence of an objective reality with which subjective meanings can be compared.

TOURAINE argues it is necessary to recognise structural constraints and distinguishes 'action' which is creative or innovative behaviour from 'conduct' which is conforming to established norms.

Ethnomethodology, unlike other action theories, does not see the sociologist as a detached observer capable of finding the right answer and explaining behaviour with theories. Sociology is just another form of commonsense shared by sociologists. This is why ethnomethodology often studies other sociology and sociologists e.g. the suicide debate. However, sociology can differ from other forms of understanding if it is done in a 'self-conscious reflexive way' and is not based on unacknowledged commonsense assumptions.

CONCLUSION: MAKING SENSE OF THEORIES

The paragraph above suggests why ethnomethodology is seen by some as a waste of time. The possibility of sociologists studying sociologists studying sociologists and so on, is not an enthralling prospect. Ethnomethologists recognise this and choose not to do it. They have still been criticised for studying trivial issues and ignoring major social problems.

However, the action perspectives have made a significant impact on most sociology which can no longer ignore the issues of meaning and the consciousness of actors.

The accounts of the various theories have naturally over-simplified them and tended to exaggerate the differences between them. The enduring problem for sociology is to find a way of locating individual action in the context of social structure. The founding fathers were aware of the problem even if they may not have resolved it.

DURKHEIM saw society as moral order which would contain the actions of individuals whether they were aware of it or not.

WEBER saw social structure as based on the shared meanings given to social action but generally deals with action and structure separately.

MARX saw society as based on economic relations which influence the individual's consciousness and action.

THEORETICAL AND EMPIRICAL STUDIES

This section covers some of the variations within the perspectives.

FUNCTIONALIST THEORIES

Durkheim

Although functionalism could be traced back before Durkheim he can be seen as the major influence in establishing sociology as a distinct discipline studying social facts in a scientific manner. Certainly the influence of Comte's positivism and 'social engineering' and Spencer's biological analogy can be seen in his work. For Durkheim functional analysis involved finding both the causes and functions of social facts i.e. how they maintain social order.

Durkheim saw society as a system based on a moral consensus. He distinguished simple societies, characterised by mechanical solidarity, from modern societies, characterised by organic solidarity. Integration in the former was based on common values, roles and practices. This solidarity was threatened by the division of labour which accompanied industrialisation but re-established through the interdependence of the differentiated parts.

Malinowski and Radcliffe-Brown

Malinowski used functional analysis to examine simple societies thus bringing a sociological perspective to anthropology. He saw societies as social systems of interrelated parts which develop to meet common human needs.

Radcliffe-Brown was also a social anthropologist and shared Durkheim's concern with social solidarity and confirmed his views on the integrating effects of religion.

Functionalism helped modern social anthropology reject evolutionary views which dismissed unusual practices as primitive by identifying their current functions.

Parsons

Parsons produced the most complete modern version of functionalism and made it the dominant paradigm in post-war American sociology. His structural-functional analysis identified four functional prerequisites of social systems. These were:

1 *Adaptation* to the environment through economic activity.
2 *Goal attainment* which is achieved through the allocation of resources by those given authority.
3 *Integration* which is the need for social solidarity emphasised by Durkheim and Malinowski.
4 *Pattern maintenance* which is the need to motivate members of society to play necessary roles and to conform to rules.

The first two are concerned with the demands made on the system from outside and the latter two are problems generated inside the social system. Social structure consists of the institutions which persist through time to satisfy these needs. The form they take depends on the value system of the society.

Merton

Merton developed a critique of functionalism and attempted to amend it to make it more appropriate for the analysis of modern industrial societies. He introduced new concepts which challenged the view of functions as universal, indispensable and positive.

Dysfunctions were the negative effects phenomena had on some people e.g. Vogel and Bell's description of scapegoating the emotionally disturbed child to integrate the family.

Functional equivalents were alternative solutions to social needs. Thus we could question Davis and Moore's view that either social inequality or religion are 'necessary' if another social arrangement could be shown to have the same consequences for society.

MARXIST THEORIES

The Marxist contribution to modern sociology, primarily as a critique of consensus theories can be found in most topics sociologists study. Rather than repeat accounts of research found above, e.g. the debates over the role of the state and the nature of schooling, it might be more useful to try and identify distinctive schools in Marxist sociology.

The Frankfurt school

There are common themes in the work of the founders (MARCUSE, ADORNO and HORKHEIMER) and followers (HABERMAS) of the Frankfurt school. They emphasise the obligation for sociologists to get involved in the critical analysis of capitalist society. This would reveal exploitation and constraints on freedom and then the potential for action to change the world. They are aiming at challenging false consciousness and encouraging class consciousness.

MARCUSE became notorious in the 1960s for suggesting that students could be a 'detonator' of a revolutionary movement among, not the proletariat, but deprived groups such as ethnic minorities. He saw the relatively rich working class in the USA as enslaved by 'chains of gold' working to satisfy 'false needs'.

Althusserian structuralism

Althusser's attack on consensus based positivist sociology is not based on a humanistic disapproval of alienation or the desire to encourage individual consciousness and action. He does reject crude economic determinism but still insists on structural explanations of behaviour (see also the Marxist approaches to education, Chapter 9). He argues that ideology and the institutions of the superstructure are largely independent of the economy (although ultimately the substructure is dominant). The superstructure supports the substructure through ideological and repressive state apparatuses (ISAs and RSAs). The need to ideologically control the working class is reminiscent of Gramsci's account of hegemony.

Marxist-Feminism

There are a range of feminist theories which have borrowed more or less from Marxism. Some have used Marxist concepts but in a feminist context e.g. the argument that women who do not see their exploitation are falsely conscious. Women's labour is seen as expropriated by men rather than the ruling class. DELPHY'S work exemplifies this approach.

Others see the explanation of women's exploitation and subordination as lying in the capitalist system and insist women are part of the working class. Sexism is seen as part of the superstructure of capitalism. MITCHELL'S pioneering writing on women's position in society follows this view.

ACTION THEORIES

Weber

Weber introduced the idea that sociology should study social action rather than social facts. He thus presented a challenge to the positivism of Durkheim and the alleged economic determinism of Marx.

He distinguished four ideal types of social action on the basis of their 'modes of orientation' i.e. the extent to which they were rational. He saw an action as rational if it involved the assumption that goals could be achieved by the use of particular means. The extreme types were:

1 Affective social action which is spontaneous and stems from impulse and emotion.
2 Instrumental rationality where the actor assesses the costs and benefits of pursuing a particular goal in a certain way.

Goffman

Goffman developed Mead's concept of the self, describing the presentation of self as like a dramatic production. He used the insights of symbolic interaction to describe the 'mortification of self' inflicted on psychiatric patients by the institution. He does not see the patient as a passive victim, however, and also describes various strategies they use to fight back. He has employed participant observation to describe the meanings subjects give to behaviour and situations.

Becker

Becker has become familiar to A-level students because of his work on he labelling of deviants. This is consistent with the interactionist viewpoint. In addition we could mention earlier work which describes, like Goffman, the way in which roles are not just imposed on children through socialisation but actively and consciously acquired by adults. In a study of medical students he describes how they abandon the aim of learning to be doctors for the short-term role of being a successful student.

Cicourel

Cicourel is also a significant figure in the sociology of deviance particularly in his criticism of crime statistics. His ethnomethodological account of the way police and probation officials define delinquency and delinquents using commonsense assumptions is a reminder that not all ethnomethodology can be dismissed as trivial, as he is obviously prepared to look at the 'tacit understandings' of the powerful and how they can be imposed on the weak. This is similar to the later work of Atkinson on suicide where the commonsense assumptions of coroners play a major part in the definition of suicide.

EXAMINATION QUESTIONS

1 Comment on the assertion that there is not a unified interactionist perspective but several distinct intellectual strands.

(Question adapted by author)

2 Examine the similarities and differences between consensus and conflict perspectives in sociology.

(AEB 1986)

3 Assess the contribution of different sociological perspectives to an understanding of social change.

(AEB 1989)

4 Sociologists have often distinguished between theories of social structure and theories of social action. Outline and assess these two approaches to sociological theory.

(AEB 1989)

5 Outline and assess the usefulness of the analogy between society and a biological organism.

(AEB 1988)

OUTLINE ANSWERS TO SELECTED QUESTIONS

Question 3

A good answer to this question will go beyond simply outlining the relevant arguments from Durkheim, Marx and Weber. Although this would provide a suitable framework for an answer.

Perspectives must be critically assessed. Credit will be given for suitable illustrations. An awareness of variety within a perspective is always rewarded.

i) Functionalism presents an evolutionary model of change where social institutions adapt to 'fit' the changing needs of the social system.

   a) Comte saw 'dynamics' (the scientific laws which explain social change) as one of the two main branches of sociology.

   b) Durkheim on the effects of division of labour on social solidarity.

   c) Parsons on the difference between traditional and modern society and the modernisation theory of development.

ii) Critics point out the tautological nature of such theories and the overemphasis on consensus.

iii) Marxism offers a revolutionary model of change which results from class conflict. Contradictions between the means and relations of production e.g. competition between employers forcing down wages and concentration of capital encourage the development of class consciousness and revolution.

   One internal debate is on the extent of economic determinism or the influence of social action e.g. the importance of Marxist ideas and revolutionary parties. The development chapter distinguishes between Marxist views which emphasise national development and those which are global theories.

iv) Critics have identified alternative causes of change e.g. Weber and also reject the alleged universalism or economic determinism of some Marxists. Mosca's explanation of the changes in ruling elites could be used.

v) Weber's 'Protestant Ethic and the Spirit of Capitalism' emphasises the rejection of economic determinism and the significance of ideas in the development of Capitalism.

vi) Criticism should come from those who reject not just Weber's specific concern with the protestant ethic but from those Marxists who reject his ideas on the relationship between ideas and materialism.

Question 2

Examine the similarities and differences between consensus and conflict perspectives in sociology.

Good answers must deal adequately with both similarities and differences, though more emphasis on differences is acceptable and likely. Relevant illustration will aid comparison. As usual, diversity within the perspectives should be noted.

i) Similarities:

   a) Both structural perspectives.

   b) Both study objective social phenomena.

   c) Both usually adopt a positivist approach and related methods.

   d) Note non-structural Marxism, and Parsons' views on social action.

ii) Differences; contrasting explanations of:

   a) Social order, social control and deviance.

   b) Social change.

   c) Ideas and ideology (refer to education, religion and media).

   d) The nature and distribution of power.

   e) Roles.

Question 5

Rather than just outline various versions of the biological analogy this question (and most similar ones) asks for a critical assessment of its usefulness to sociologists.

i) Explain that analogies are models not theories. They do not explain how society works, but compare it to a biological organism in order to simplify a complex abstract concept by portraying it in a simpler, more familiar and concrete form.

ii) Identify the main principles of the biological analogy and show how they can be used as models of human society.

   a) Structure: biological organisms are systems made up of interrelated parts. The structure is the relationship between the parts. Human society has structures which survive individuals and govern their behaviour.

   b) Functions: biological organs perform activities that have functions i.e. are related to the working of the system. Social arrangements have functions which contribute to the fulfilling of social needs.

c) Growth: biological organisms develop through a life cycle and evolve into more complex forms. Societies evolve into more complex forms (Durkheim), and the arrangements become more specialised (Parsons).

d) Equilibrium: Canon's concept of homoeostasis suggests that organisms are self-regulating. That is, they balance internal working with environmental conditions e.g. sweating cools the body on hot days. This could be likened to Parsons' notion of 'fit' where social arrangements adapt to changing conditions.

e) Normality and pathology: just as biological organisms have a normal balanced state so, too, do societies. Social order is seen as normal and deviance as pathological.

iii) Critics:

a) Functionalists, including Spencer, who argued for the appropriateness of the analogy have pointed out discrepancies in the comparison e.g. biological organisms have a specific form societies do not.

b) Marxists and other conflict theories point out the absence of consideration of power, the overemphasis on integration and the mistaken view of social order being based on equilibrium and normality.

c) Interpretive sociology criticises the biological analogy for presenting an over-socialised view of man who appears enslaved by social structures. Instead, they see order as socially constructed through interaction.

TUTOR'S ANSWER

Question 4

Sociologists have often distinguished between theories of the social structure and theories of social action. Outline and assess these two approaches to sociological theory.
(**NB** There is a great deal of material which could be included here and there is, therefore, the risk of producing an unbalanced or badly organised account. Good answers must include critical assessment.)

Structuralist theories are holistic and concerned with the influence of society on individuals as well as the relationships between different parts of society. They emphasise the ways in which individuals conform to social order. Functionalists see order as based on the acceptance of consensual values whereas Marxists see order imposed by the powerful. Individuals are seen as being born into particular social structures and learning the beliefs and values of their societies. Functionalists see this process as socialisation whereas Marxists and feminists see it as indoctrination.

Structuralist theories are conventionally divided into consensus and conflict perspectives. The dominant theories in the two perspectives are functionalism and Marxism. There are, however, not only divisions within each perspective (e.g. non-Marxist and anti-Marxists conflict theories such as radical feminism and elite theories) but also disputes and differences of emphasis between those sharing similar theoretical assumptions. There are both varieties of functionalism and Marxism. Some Marxists would not want their work categorised as exclusively structuralist (see Willis below).

Functionalists see society as a system of interrelated parts. These parts are linked by their functions i.e. the contribution that institutions make to satisfying the needs of the system, thus encouraging survival and stability. The emphasis on equilibrium has led critics to claim that functionalism is conservative and fails to explain change. This has led some anthropologists to turn their backs on Malinowski in favour of the structuralism of Levi-Strauss or Marxist historical materialism. Where change is recognised it is seen as evolutionary as institutions adapt to 'fit' the needs of the system.

Marxism emphasises revolutionary rather than evolutionary change. It is a dynamic theory which stresses the importance of one aspect of social structure, the economy, over all others. The methods and relations of production explain the development of other institutions and ideas which are seen as the superstructure which is produced by and in turn reproduces the existing economic substructure. In a pre-communist society conflict not stability is seen as normal.

Structuralist theories are frequently associated with a positivist approach to research and the use of the logic and procedures of the natural sciences. This is not inevitable but is encouraged by the view that individual behaviour is explicable in terms of external constraints. These external constraints are seen like biological facts as having an objective existence. Durkheim identified the causes of variations in suicide rates as being different degrees of integration or moral regulation. Marx saw both ideas and behaviour as explained by the group's relationship to production. Thus structuralist theories look for the causes of human behaviour in the structure of societies.

Those theories which stress social action rather than structure tend to adopt anti-positivist methods. The interpretive critics of Durkheim's 'Suicide' do not just reject his functionalist explanations but also his methodological approach. They deny the existence of social facts which exist independently of individuals. Instead they concentrate on trying to describe either the social meaning of suicide (Douglas) or the process by which such meanings arise (Sacks).

The assumptions of those non-structuralist theories which emphasise the importance of social action vary according to their origins and development. The two main strands of thought are symbolic interactionism and ethnomethodology. Both reject the view that individual behaviour can be explained by identifying objective social causes external to individuals.

Symbolic interactionism studies the ways in which individuals interact by responding to symbols, particularly language. (Talk also assumes great importance for ethnomethodologists both as a method and a topic of research.) The individual is seen as having more freedom of action than is implied by structuralism. Individuals attribute meaning to the behaviour of self and others. The self is seen as developing from the actual or anticipated reaction of others (either significant or generalised others) to ourselves. Social reality is negotiated between active actors (teachers and pupils, police and 'offenders') not imposed by outside forces.

Ethnomethodology is concerned with how individuals make sense of the world. Studies describe the 'commonsense assumptions', 'background expectancies' and 'tacit understandings' which are at the heart of social order. They reject the structuralist view that order can be imposed on individuals and instead see order as more fragile, constantly being created and recreated by everyday routine encounters. Whereas interactionists favour participant observation to share the experiences of subjects ethnomethodology also uses experiments to identify how everyday routines develop (Garfinkel) or analyse conversation to identify commonsense assumptions (Sacks).

Those who support the individualist approaches stress the way they do not reduce people to the status of mindless puppets nor take social reality for granted. Critics dismiss their findings as either trivial or incomplete as they ignore the influence of power on individual behaviour.

So far this answer has suggested a crude juxtaposition between theories of structure and social action. However, this is not necessarily the case. Weber combined both in his work. He criticised Marxist economic determinism and the failure of Durkheim to consider social action as well as social facts. He advocates what he refers to as *verstehen* as the way to explain social meanings (like interactionists) but also sees social action as providing the basis of social structure. This view is echoed by the work of Parsons as well as those more obviously influenced by Weber such as Rex.

Marx himself discussed social action and modern Marxists like Willis have used interactionist methods to examine the ways individuals can actively construct reality within the constraints of capitalism.

Perhaps the most influential recent attempt to unify the two apparently conflicting paradigms has come from Giddens. He has synthesised action and structural approaches. Like interactionists he sees men constructing their own social reality but not in isolation from the external influences resulting from the structures produced by the interaction of others.

STUDENT ANSWER WITH EXAMINER COMMENTS

Question 1

Comment on the assertion that there is not a unified interactionist perspective but several distinct intellectual strands.

> **❝Interactionists criticise those who see society as a system. ❞**

```
Interactionism is also known as interpretive sociology and it is
concerned with the dynamics of individuals and how they experience
the world around them. Interactionists see society as being a
```

> Should define, explain, and perhaps illustrate, social action.

> Language is the most important symbol.

> First sentence good, but needs developing.

> Should be linked to symbolic interactionism and explained.

> Sound conclusion pointing out unifying factors. Should point out differences.

system and man as being a product of that system. He both creates and is created by the system. It would be true to say that there are several intellectual strands in the interactionist school of thought, however, it must be noted that there are several factors which unify them.

Max Weber in an attempt to analyse social action developed 'ideal types' to which all action could be compared. These included emotional types, rational types, and traditional types. All of these types govern social action.

Symbolic interactionism is a major type of interpretive sociology. Its founding father was George Herbert Mead who was influenced by the writings and concepts of Cooley. Mead developed the concept of the self which is built up by an individual through continuous interaction with others through shared values and symbols. An individual goes through various stages in the building of the self concept. Beginning with the play stage where roles of important others are taken on, through the game stage where there are 'generalised others' and then to a point where roles are internalised and interaction means that individuals have to analyse the roles of others and react accordingly. Symbolic interactionists have used a 'dramaturgical' analogy to describe how individuals take on roles to play to real or imagined 'audiences' or a narcissistic self. Herbert Blumer suggested that social reality therefore only exists so far as the individuals themselves perceive it.

Ethnomethodology is the study of the methods individuals employ to explain their interactions and experiences. Harold Garfinkel developed the stage critic analogy where an individual stands back in a detached way and observes social action in the world around him.

In his book 'Stigma' Goffman showed how individuals, through social interaction, 'label' others in order to understand them. People still try to play a role in spite of these labels.

All interactionists are non-positivists and criticise deterministic sociology such as functionalism and Marxism for failing to give credit to man as a controller of his own action. They also tend to use observation and participant observation in their research in order to see the world from the point of view of the actors. Interactionist theories are micro theories which are concerned with individuals rather than social systems.

Overall comments

Overall, just a C grade answer which shows promise without sufficient development. The candidate does demonstrate an understanding of the main types of interactionist theory but should offer further explanation and illustration with research studies.

The differences, not just the similarities, within the overall perspective need bringing out explicitly.

THE NATURE OF SOCIOLOGY

SOCIOLOGY AS A SCIENCE

SOCIOLOGY AND VALUES

THEORETICAL AND EMPIRICAL STUDIES

GETTING STARTED

This chapter attempts to answer the question 'What is sociology?'. It might appear to have been more logical to have begun the book here, but the examination questions which are answered below are possibly the most difficult to be found on the various syllabuses.

Under consideration are a collection of issues which are all concerned with the nature of sociology as a form of enquiry. The unifying theme of the chapter is the idea that there is a 'sociology of sociology and sociologists'. This means that there are sociological explanations of:

1 Relationships between sociologists and other people, particularly their employers and colleagues.
2 The way that people choose to do sociology.
3 Sociology as a form of knowledge produced by sociologists.

The main themes of questions set on this topic are:

1 **Assessing whether the logic and procedures of the natural sciences are appropriate for sociology.**
2 **The sociology of science.**
3 **Whether sociology can or should be value free.**
4 **The relationship between sociology and social policy.**
5 **Comparing sociology with other academic disciplines of non-academic forms of description.**

Definitions

The problematic nature of most of these definitions is often a central issue in examination questions.

- *Sociology* is the study of human social behaviour. However it is the distinctiveness of sociological approaches and methods, rather than the subject matter, which make it different from other behavioural and social sciences.
- *Natural science* can also be defined in terms of its methods, although critics see it as more socially defined.
- *Value freedom* implies detachment and impartiality at all possible stages of sociological research.
- *Social problems* are issues of public concern.
- *Sociological problems* are phenomena which await sociological explanations.
- *Social policy* is the ideology which underlies the management of social, political and economic institutions in order to achieve a particular kind of society. Usually it is described in terms of areas of public policy, such as health, education and welfare.

Related topics include *sociological theory and methods, positivism* and the *suicide* debate.

ESSENTIAL PRINCIPLES

SOCIOLOGY AS A SCIENCE

The main issues in the discussion of the relationship between sociology and the natural sciences are:

1 Is it possible to do sociological research following the methods of natural sciences?
2 Is it desirable to do sociology scientifically?
3 What are the problems and difficulties of applying the logic and procedures of the natural sciences to sociology?
4 What is science?

The main positions in the debates over these issues can be summarised as follows:

a) If the definition of science is uncritically taken for granted (i.e. as following particular procedures advocated by Medaware and Popper) then positivist sociologists argue that sociology could and should be scientific. This would produce the best data which would be logical, generalisable and testable.
b) Whilst still accepting this conventional view of the superiority of scientific methods for the study of natural phenomena there are those who question the reliability and validity of employing the same methods to do sociology.
   Practical, theoretical and ideological criticisms have been levelled against positivism in sociology. These are found below and in the chapters on *Methods* and *Suicide*.
c) The conventional definition of science has been questioned by sociologists, philosophers and scientists themselves. Instead of accepting an objective definition, which sees science as involving particular procedures, some writers suggest that 'science' is socially defined and is thus culturally and historically specific.

If science is neither a special activity nor produces superior knowledge then the issue of its application to sociology seems far less important. It is, however, necessary when answering questions to assess the implications for sociology of the various conceptions of science.

SOCIOLOGY AND VALUES

The main issues in this discussion are:

1 Can or should sociology be value free?
2 Is sociology inevitably ideological?
3 What are the sociological causes of bias in sociological research?
4 What are the effects of bias on sociology itself and the wider society?

The case for objectivity has been made by positivists who, following Comte and Durkheim, see a scientific approach helping to find the truth which in turn will be beneficial to society. The sociologist should aim to be detached rather than involved with his subjects and morally neutral rather than committed to particular values. This freedom from social influence of context will produce objective and value-free sociology.

The case that sociology cannot be value free is frequently made by interpretive sociologists who see the very subject matter of sociology as socially constructed rather than having an objective existence. Gomm argues that the very idea of sociology, which is a social activity, being value free is unsociological.

The Marxist view that sociology is inevitably ideological and an apology for the existing system is not shared by lay critics of sociology in this country who ses sociology as biased in favour of the left. Marsland, a professor of sociology, made the national papers in a report which accused sociology at O- and A-level of 'Bias against Business'. His research was based on content analysis of text books and examinations.

THE CAUSES OF BIAS IN SOCIOLOGY

Coercion

Bell and Newby mention libel laws, the Official Secrets Acts and intimidation by disgruntled subjects. Non-conforming academics have been denied employment or even imprisoned in many countries. (See 'Reasons for choosing methods', Chapter 18.)

Finance

Research requires money. Financial support tends to come from government or business either directly or indirectly. This can influence the topic of research chosen as well as the methods employed and ultimate publication of findings.

The profession

Sociologists belong to an academic community who can influence research. They work in institutions with career structures, ideologies and, as is increasingly recognised, markets for their work. This need not be seen as sinister as the effect may be no more than the development of a distinctive school of sociology where particular topics are chosen and studied from a particular perspective using a particular set of methods. The influence of Chicago University and the London School of Economics could be used to illustrate this point.

Involvement

Sociologists have a variety of characteristics e.g. gender, class, age, and ethnicity. These will influence the way they interact with subjects. These characteristics and the influences listed above are at the centre of sociological research. This leads us to the next section.

THE EFFECTS OF BIAS

Effects on sociological research

" Refer to chapter on Methods. "

We can identify effects on the choice of topic (Who is paying? What is seen as a social problem?) as well as on approach and methods which can be influenced by the institution.

Bias in findings to conform to the sociologists perspective has often been alleged. Marxists, functionalists and feminists seem to produce predictable findings. On a less political level we could note the problem of the self-fulfilling prophecy.

Effects on the wider society

It has been alleged that sociology can be used to control people in political, military and industrial contexts. Sociologists are employed to improve industrial relations and organisational effectiveness. Sociological research is used to explain and control social problems and to create and evaluate social policy.

Sociology can also be seen as a form of ideology used to legitimate the existing order. For example, by blaming poverty on the poor or educational failure on families. Of course we could select examples with opposite effects.

THEORETICAL AND EMPIRICAL STUDIES

SOCIOLOGY AS A SCIENCE

MERTON has written a sociological account of science as a profession. He saw scientists as both emotionally and rationally committed to certain ethics which ensured the purity of science and protected it from criticism. Science was described as universal, rational, public, detached, and sceptical. No wonder sociologists wished to emulate this impressive way of doing research!

POPPER claimed the defining characteristic of a scientific theory is that it can be falsified. This means it states explicitly what evidence would be necessary to refute the relationship it asserts. Evidence can of course support a theory but Popper sees all verification and thus all scientific theories as provisional. They are never finally proved and need constant re-examination. Thus, Popper defined science in terms of its logic as well as its procedures. He sees the controlled experiment as one of the most powerful tools available but it can only test a pre-existing hypothesis. The data gained depends on the initial purpose of the research. Hypotheses depend on pre-conceived theories. Thus, in a way he agrees with Kuhn who sees experimentation as doing little more than support theories and not leading to discoveries. Popper is noted as a critic of Marxist theory on the grounds that it is irrefutable. Good theory is logical, general and can be refuted. Many sociologists, particularly positivists, approve of Popper's model and see it producing the best rational knowledge.

KUHN denies the claim that scientists are open minded. During periods of 'normal science' they operate within existing paradigms. These paradigms are sets of basic assumptions which are taken for granted. They set limits on the questions which are asked, the subject matter of the discipline and research methods. Evidence which is gathered and does not fit into the existing paradigm is either ignored or distorted or increasingly complex explanations are sought. When the evidence against the paradigm is overwhelming then a scientific revolution occurs until the new paradigm is generally accepted.

DARWIN established a new paradigm which dominated biology to such an extent that even his own reservations, about the possibility of the eye or cerebral cortex evolving by random mutation, were long ignored. The pioneers of the new paradigm in biology resulting from the identification of DNA have expressed their doubts about Darwin's model of evolution. The implication for sociology is that in the absence of generally accepted truths it remains pre-scientific.

ZIMAN is a physicist who emphasises the social dimension of scientific knowledge by insisting it must be public knowledge. This means that scientists cannot work in isolation but must have their work tried and tested by others. After considering and rejecting conventional definitions of science, which reduce it to a particular procedure, he defines science as:

a) An activity done by 'scientists' i.e. those accepted by the scientific community. (Nazi Germany excluded Jewish scientists and those who followed Einstein.)
b) A body of knowledge tested and agreed by scientists i.e. a consensus of rational opinion.

Sociologists could be seen as comprising an academic community who examine each others' work.

KAPLAN distinguished 'logics-in-use' from 're-constructed logics'. The former describes how research is actually done and what scientists actually think. (According to Watson's biography which describes the discovery of DNA, scientists are sometimes jealous, narrow minded and they cheat.) The latter describes the published version of research which suggests that an open-minded and logical procedure was followed when, in fact, they were looking to confirm predetermined answers. Bell and Newby and also Hammond have described a similar discrepancy between published accounts of sociological research and what actually took place.

BROAD and WADE show how deciding on the result before research has led some scientists to dispense with the research altogether and fake it. They describe Newton and Mendel as 'good cheats' and Burt as a bad one.

SKLAIR has described the development of 'big science' which, rather than being open minded, serves the interests of business and government. If the sources of finance for sociology were investigated similar claims could be made. The professionalisation of science and its later domination by government bureaucracy could be seen as challenging the idealised view of the open minded individual and supporting Sklair's view.

SOCIOLOGY AND VALUES

COMTE in advocating a positivist scientific approach to sociology might be seen as a champion of value freedom. However he did argue that the point of sociology was to change society for the better which is not the spirit of detachment we find in contemporary positivism. Comte felt that the revelation of sociological laws would lead to the developing of the best possible society.

WEBER reminds us that knowledge is socially constructed and the sociologist employs his, or his society's values when deciding what to study. He does recommend that when evaluating results the sociologist should be non-judgemental.

GOULDNER described how American sociology drifted from a position of social criticism and reform to the professed neutrality of post-war positivism. The value-free collectors of facts enhanced their professional status and escaped criticism from a conservative establishment. Gouldner denies that this self interest and ignoring of controversial social issues can be seen as value freedom as the sociologists could be used by those in power.

Following Gouldner's criticism the more open academic climate of the 1960s and 1970s saw the adopting of more critical positions by interactionists like BECKER who advocate 'sympathising with the underdog' as the point of view of the 'overdog' (those with power) was already well known. Gouldner remained dissatisfied and claimed that Becker studied the underdog as a passive subject not from the radical position of resisting those in power.

SHAW supported Gouldner's demand for commitment from a Marxist perspective. He analysed the history of sociology as both knowledge and activity produced by the economic substructure. He dismissed social criticism as a substitute for revolutionary action by those in safe professional employment.

BOHANNAN offered a much more personal justification for abandoning value freedom in an anthropological study. She defends human involvement rather than scientific detachment on two grounds. Firstly, she had to challenge existing gender roles to gain access to the men's world of magic, religion and politics. Secondly, despite protests which were due to the tribe having no faith in modern medicine, she tried to get her sick friend to the modern hospital, suggesting that sociologists should not abandon their humanity to achieve value freedom by refusing to get involved.

EXAMINATION QUESTIONS

1 'Whether we consider sociology to be scientific or not depends on which definition of science we choose'. Explain and discuss.

(AEB 1988)

2 Examine the view that sociology can and should be value free.

(AEB 1988)

3 'The social sciences all aim to give us an understanding of the individual and society but they use different methods and concepts and study different topics.'

Using evidence from any substantive area(s) (e.g. family, crime, economy, politics, child-rearing) and with reference to sociology and at least one other social science discipline, assess this point of view.

(JMB 1988)

4 Examine the relationship between sociology and social policy. Illustrate your answer with examples.

(AEB 1987)

5 'Value judgements influence research both in the social sciences and the natural sciences.' Discuss.

(AEB 1986)

OUTLINE ANSWERS TO SELECTED QUESTIONS

Question 3

The problem with this question is imposing a simple framework in order to produce a coherent and balanced account within the limited time available. It is permissible to compare the approach of sociology and just one other discipline to a single substantive area.

Possibilities include comparisons with:

- Anthropology on family or religion.
- Psychology on race, gender or educational achievement.
- Political science on the state or power.

Economics on the division of labour or immigration.

If you are not sufficiently familiar with one discipline a more general account can be written. A possible plan is:

i) Explain the different methods favoured by disciplines e.g. discuss controlled laboratory experiments in psychology and sociology.

ii) Explain the use of similar methods e.g. participant observation in anthropology and surveys in political science.

iii) Describe distinctive concepts e.g. intelligence, memory and personality in psychology.

iv) Describe shared concepts e.g. bureaucracy, division of labour, socialisation, role self, alienation, power etc. You might indicate how similar concepts are employed differently.

v) Identify distinctive topics. (This may be difficult as sociology covers in some way most areas of social life e.g. biological bases of behaviour in psychology or mathematical models of the economy).

vi) Identify shared topics and the different approaches to them.

vii) Point out the internal diversity within sociology and other disciplines you are familiar with. You might remark on the similarity between social psychology and interactionist sociology and compare the positivist approach found not only in structural sociology but also psychology which emphasises the influence of biology.

Question 4

Answers must emphasise that there is no one simple relationship between sociology and social policy. Relevant material can be found in the debate on value freedom and reference made to the relationship between natural science and public policy. Examples of policy issues could include health, education, welfare, race relations, equal gender opportunities and crime.

i) The positivist view. Comte and Durkheim saw the potential of a scientific sociology explaining society and thus permitting prediction and control to improve it.

The modern view where the role of the sociologist is seen as providing reliable data for social policy. Compare with medical research which is scientific in procedure but committed to finding cures.

ii) Gouldner's critique of the claimed neutrality of post-war positivism.

iii) The role of sociology in defining social policy issues:

a) Pointing out that private problems have a social dimension e.g. homelessness and feminist criticism of the family.

b) Making latent (hidden) problems manifest (public), e.g. the social and economic costs of educational inequality of opportunity or racism and sexism.

c) Identifying who has the power to define social problems and influence policy, e.g. Marxist or interactionist views on professionals. Becker on who defines social problems.

d) Encouraging reform, e.g. the influence of sociological research on educational reform and race relations policy.

iv) Point out that sociology can be divorced from social policy. Sociology can be concerned with the normal and acceptable as well as social pathology, e.g. the concern of ethnomethodology with everyday events or studies of ordinary, rather than deviant, youth.

Question 5

This question involves a consideration of some of the issues raised in questions 1 and 2. Good answers will show an awareness of debates about the influence of political, moral and academic beliefs on research in both the natural and social sciences.

i) Explain the positivist claim for the neutrality of the natural sciences and the justification of the application to sociology of the scientific method (Comte and Durkheim. Popper's view of science).

ii) Criticise the claim that either natural or social scientists are open minded (Kuhn and Kaplan).

iii) The ethnomethodological critique of scientific and positivist sociological research as no more than 'commonsense'.

iv) Causes of bias in both sociology and natural sciences:
  a) Coercion.
  b) Finance.
  c) The academic institution and the professions.
v) Effects of bias in both on:
  a) Research itself.
  b) The wider society.

TUTOR'S ANSWER

Question 1

'Whether we consider sociology to be scientific or not depends on which definition of science we choose'. Explain and discuss.

The definition of science is problematic. If a conventional definition of science is adopted then arguably some sociology is scientific. However, if science is seen as socially not objectively defined, then some sociology may have similar characteristics to natural science but the attempts to emulate the scientific model seem less important.

Medaware claimed that science could be defined in terms of its method. He saw science as following a particular logic and procedure rather than being defined by its subject matter.

Popper refined and developed this view of science. He saw science as logical, useful and above all refutable. Scientific knowledge is built up by a continuing process of conjecture and refutation. It is not the final truth but the best provisional explanation. Popper criticised Marxism for being unscientific because it could not be falsified. (Popper means Marxism has not been expressed in a way which is capable of being disproved, not that it has been shown to be false.)

If we accept this definition of science then some sociology does indeed aspire to be scientific. The positivist tradition in sociology, pioneered by Comte and Durkheim, did try to emulate scientific methods because they were seen as superior ways of producing and testing knowledge. Durkheim advocated the use of the comparative method as an appropriate substitute for the experiment which is the favoured scientific method because of the possibility of control and its reliability.

Assuming the superiority of the scientific approach positivists nevertheless encounter considerable difficulties in applying it to sociology. Involvement with subjects must be avoided because of the effects on their behaviour. This is illustrated by the Hawthorne studies and the self-fulfilling prophecy described by Rosenthal and Jacobson. Natural scientists encounter similar problems. The fact that the sociologist is part of the phenomena he studies may however exacerbate the problem.

Even if scientific knowledge is refuted and becomes obsolete scientists still assume that the phenomena they study follow universal and invariable natural laws. This is clearly not the case in sociology as patterns of social behaviour are culturally and historically specific. Indeed sociological research itself may lead to changing patterns of behaviour, for example, teachers during training are made aware of sociological research which may influence subsequent behaviour.

Even if the idealised conception of natural science was accepted by anti-positivist sociologists they would not consider it a suitable model for studying social behaviour. In fact ethnomethodologists have dismissed science as being no different from other forms of commonsense with the scientific observer relying on subjective experience and interpreting his observations within a particular social context.

The main objection of interpretive sociologists to a scientific approach lies in their different view of the subject matter of sociology. They dismiss the existence of objective social facts and see social reality as socially constructed. Searle has argued that social scientists need explanations not of social facts but 'intentionality and its effects'. He is emphasising the purposive nature of human behaviour and the meaning we attach to it. Winch has suggested that sociology should seek 'reasons for' not 'causes of' behaviour. This critique of positivism is exemplified by the debate over Durkheim's 'Suicide'.

There is a wealth of material which can be used to criticise the idealised conventional definition of science. There is a sociology of science and scientists as well as a philosophical debate about the nature of science. Most of the following writers share the general assumption that science is socially rather than objectively defined. The implications for the scientific nature of sociology depend on the particular study.

Ziman follows Popper to the extent that he claims science must be tested and agreed knowledge. Like Merton he sees the scientific community as openly testing ideas. He describes science as 'public knowledge'. The consensus of rational opinion he sees developing from this process is similar to Kuhn's notion of a paradigm.

However Kuhn sees the scientist not as open minded and rational but operating within limits which influence the questions asked, the subject matter and the research methods employed. Paradigms are the generally accepted foundations upon which subsequent theory is built. This applies during a period of normal science. Evidence which does not fit the paradigm is distorted or ignored. When the evidence against the existing paradigm is overwhelming then a scientific revolution occurs and a new paradigm emerges.

The implication of this view for sociology is that sociology, lacking the rational consensus described, is pre-paradigmic and therefore not (yet) a science. Although sociologists do work within academic communities and publish their research for criticism conforming to the views of Merton and Ziman

Kaplan has distinguished 'logics-in-use' (what scientists really do) from 'reconstructed logics' (the way in which their findings are presented in scientific papers). The presentation of research in conventional form suggests open-minded and rigorous procedures and legitimises science in the public's mind. Bell and Newby have described a similar distinction between the way sociological research is actually done (influenced by libel laws, institutional and financial pressures) from the way it appears in formal publications.

The approving view of the open minded scientist is also questioned by Sklair who looks at the way 'big science' is dominated by government and business interests. This, he claims, influences choice of subject matter and interpretation of findings. Broad and Wade have shown how this can lead to cheating by scientists e.g. American scientists are alleged to have falsely claimed simultaneous and independent identification of the HIV as the cause of AIDS with French scientists.

Sociologists, as shown by Bell and Newby, also conform to outside pressures. This could be illustrated by the bias towards employer interests in some industrial sociology. Most social research in the UK is directly or indirectly government sponsored. Gouldner sees the commitment to science itself, by sociologists, as an evasion of their responsibilities as it allows them to be used by government and business.

STUDENT ANSWER WITH EXAMINER COMMENTS

Question 2

Examine the view that sociology can and should be value free.

Sounds like a 'science' essay.

Comte also talked about control which could be linked to value freedom.

Links positivism with value freedom.

Comte believed that the application of the methods and assumptions of the natural sciences would produce a positive science of society. Sociology would show society followed invariable laws and enable predictions to be made.

Supporters of this view were known as positivists. The most important was Durkheim who agreed that scientific methods should be used and advocated the comparative method. One important aspect of this method was the concept of value freedom. Durkheim believed that by using the comparative method social facts could be studied as things. He believed that these social facts were external to the sociologist and therefore it was possible to study them objectively.

However, since sociologists are usually members of the society they study, they will have already a set of values which could overtly or inadvertently influence their study by introducing value judgements. Also if we knew before we were to study a topic that the research was done by a functionalist, Marxist or feminist

Yes, but examples would help.

Consciousness rather than life distinguish people from other subjects.

Yes, but de-humanise is an inappropriate term. Neutral is better.

Should include Gouldner's attack on positivism.

Becker gives other reasons for giving the underdog's view.

Good. Could be illustrated.

Avoid 'only natural'. This is the sociology of sociologists.

Example not explained.

Reasonable summary of Popper on science.

Good application of Kuhn to value freedom, but conclusion is unclear.

Not helpful. Talking about science not sociology.

we would ask ourselves whether preconceived ideas had influenced the study.

It is argued that value freedom is not a problem in the natural sciences since they are concerned with the objective study of usually inanimate objects. Sociology usually involves the subjective study of people and their actions and can not be a scientific process.

Weber, who advocated social action theory, argued that sociologist's values did enter into their subject choice but that after that the sociologist could be de-humanised by keeping their values separate from their analysis of the social world.

However this point has been criticised by Gouldner in 'Anti-minotaur the myth of a value-free sociology'. He argues that the separation of facts and values is as impossible as the separation of the man from the beast in the mythological creature the minotaur. Gouldner argues they are integral parts of the same entity.

Becker also agrees that values will enter sociological research and that objectivity can only be achieved by making clear ones values so they can easily be separated from the study. In 'Whose side are we on?' he argues for a compassionate sociology sympathising with the underdog. He believes that since values are inevitable the sociologist will also be accused of bias.

Marxists share the view that any science of society would be ideologically biased according to its class position. Shaw explained changes in sociology as part of the superstructure deriving from and supporting class relationships. To gain objectivity Marxists believe that false consciousness must be overcome.

Therefore we can see the possibility of sociology being value free is virtually an impossibility. Sociologists themselves are human and it is only natural that they could be influenced by money, coercion or their employers. Bohannan justifies involvement at the expense of detachment as otherwise she would not have been able to gain such insight as she did into a tribal society.

However, the problem of value freedom can also lead us to question the nature of the natural sciences. Many have criticised the natural science model from which Comte and Durkheim developed positivism. The general view of science is that hypotheses could either be verified or refuted by experimentation and that objectivity is possible by constantly trying to disprove previous theories.

However, Kuhn has argued that science is governed by paradigms which are accepted assumptions that all scientists have when entering a field of study. Thus natural scientists are not open minded since they share prevailing assumptions about a topic. An enormous amount of evidence must be available for these assumptions to be replaced by new paradigms. Looking at sociology from this perspective the question of value freedom would not arise as there is no generally acceptable paradigm in sociology and is not then a science.

Also, the question of whether natural science is and should be value free is questionable. Many believe that scientists are detached from their area of study because studying chemicals for example is conceptually different from studying human behaviour. Winch believes social science is concerned with reasons for actions not their causes. However, can scientists be detached from their findings or the use to which research is put? For example, Einstein said he would rather have been a watchmaker had he known in advance the consequences of his theories.

> This is more an ethical debate yet it proves that scientists have values which affect their studies. Therefore, the question of whether sociology should be value free is almost irrelevant owing to the many questions hanging over natural science.

" Unhelpful. Science again. "

Overall comments

Overall, a sound C grade answer which suffers from overemphasis on the science issue. It does address both parts of the question, i.e. 'can and should'. The answer would be improved by considering the sociology of sociologists and how values influence sociological research.

ADDITIONAL READING

INTRODUCTION

The reading I have suggested includes books, extracts from books and articles. It is neither an essential nor an exhaustive list but one based on material found useful by my students over a period of time. None of them read all or even most of the list.

Ask your teacher to guide you through this and any reading list recommended by examining boards, as the degree of difficulty varies considerably. At the beginning of your course you might find it useful to refer to text books written primarily for GCSE students. They will contain useful references to studies even if the overall approach is different to A-level.

Chapter 1

The syllabus, examination papers, examiner reports from your Board.

Chapter 2

M. Morrison and J. Pey	*Writing Sociology Essays*	Longman, 1987
N. Jorgensen	*The Sociology Manual*	Framework Press 1987
Social Studies Review (SSR)	Has various articles on examination technique	
R. Burgess	*Doing School Ethnography*	SSR Vol.3 No.5, 1988
R. Gill	*Altered Images: Women in the Media*	SSR Vol.4 No.1, 1988

Burgess and Gill might give you some ideas on doing your own research. Also see the references for Chapter 18.

Chapter 3

E. Cuff and G. Payne	*Perspectives in Sociology*	Unwin Hyman, 1984.
B. Jessop	*Varieties of Marxism*	Teaching paper in Sociology, Longman
J. Hughes	*The Concept of Class*	Teaching paper in Sociology, Longman
J. Westergaard and H. Resler	*Class in a Capitalist Society: A Study of Contemporary Britain*	Heinemann Gowen, 1975
M. Banton	*The Davis and Moore Theory of Inequality*	Social Studies Review Vol.3 No.2, 1987

Chapter 4

A. Pilkington	*Race Relations in Britain*	Unwin Hyman, 1984
J. Richardson and Lambert	*The Sociology of Race*	Causeway, 1985
R. Miles	*Racism and Migrant Labour*	RKP, 1982
in P. Trowler	*Active Sociology*	Bell and Hyman, 1987
K. Pryce	*Endless Pressure*	Penguin, 1979
in P. Trowler	*Active Sociology*	Bell and Hyman, 1987
in M. O'Donnell ed.	*New Introductory Reader in Sociology*	Nelson, 1985

Chapter 5

M. Maynard	*Current Trends in Feminist Theory*	SSR Vol.2 No.3, 1987
C. Buswell	*Gender and Sociology*	SSR Vol.4 No.5, 1985
S. Lees	*How Boys Slag Off Girls*	New Society, 13.10.83
A. Oakley	*The Woman's Place*	New Society, 6.3.87
P. Mayes	*Gender*	Longman, 1986
E. Clarke and T. Lawson	*Gender*	UTP, 1984

Chapter 6

P. Saunders	*The Sociology of the State*	SSR preview, 1985
I. Crewe	*Can Labour Rise Again?*	SSR Vol.1 No.1, 1985
J. Scott	*Does Britain Still Have a Ruling Class?*	SSR Vol.2 No.1, 1986
J. Beynon	*A Prolonged Conservative Ascendancy in a Divided Britain*	SSR Vol.3 No.1, 1987
M. Riley	*Theories of voting*	SSR Vol.5 No.1, 1989
H. Himmelweit *et al*	*How voters decide*	Academic Press, 1985
in M. O'Donnell ed.	New Introductory Reader in Sociology	Nelson, 1985
I. Crewe	Various post-election analyses in the *Guardian*	13.6.83
in P. Trowler	*Active Sociology*	15.6.87, 16.6.87.

Chapter 7

A. Foster-Carter	*The Sociology of Development*	Causeway, 1985
A. Webster	*Introduction to the Sociology of Development*	Macmillan, 1984
M. Slattery	*Urban Sociology*	Causeway, 1985
D. Smith	*Exploring the City*	SSR Vol.4 No.4, 1989

Chapter 8

J. Hood-Williams	*The Family: Demographic Trends*	The Social Science Teacher Vol.14 No.1, 1984 and Vol.14 No.2, 1984
Research round-up	*In Search of the New Man*	SSR Vol.3 No.4, 1988
M. Anderson	*How Much Has The Family Changed?*	New Society, 27.10.83
K. Chester	*The Rise of the Neo-conventional Family*	New Society, 9.5.85
Data base	*The Family*	New Society, 6.3.87
N. Timmins	*Article on General Household Survey*	The *Independent*, 6.12.89
A. Wilson	*Family*	Tavistock, 1985

Chapter 9

S. Ball	*Education*	Longman, 1986
S. Ball	*Beachside Comprehensive*	Cambridge University Press, 1981
in Trowler	*Active Sociology*	Bell and Hyman, 1984
P. Willis	*Learning to Labour*	Saxon House, 1978
in M. O'Donnell	*New Introductory Reader in Sociology*	Nelson, 1985
A. Pilkington	*Race Relations in Britain*	Unwin Hyman, 1984

Chapter 10

D. Ashton	*Unemployment; why pick on youth?*	SSR Vol.1 No.1, 1985
M. McCullagh	*Teaching the Sociology of Unemployment*	SST Vol.15 No.1, 1985
R. Hyman	*Strikes*	Fontana, 1984
in Trowler	*Active Sociology*	Bell and Hyman, 1984
L. Taylor and P. Walton	*Industrial Sabotage: Motives and meanings*	
in S. Cohen ed.	*Images of Deviance*	Penguin, 1971
S. Parker	*The Sociology of Industry*	George Allen and Unwin, 1972
S. McIntosh	*Leisure Studies*, in A. Tomlinson ed. *Leisure and Social Control*	Brighton Polytechnic, 1981
Both Parker and McIntosh in M. O'Donnell	*New Introductory Reader in Sociology*	Nelson, 1985

Chapter 11

G. Salaman	*Class and the Corporation*	Fontana, 1981
in M. O'Donnell	*New Introductory Reader in Sociology*	Nelson, 1985
E. Goffman	*Asylums*	Penguin, 1970

Chapter 12

| T. Johnson | *Professions and Power* | Macmillan, 1972 |
| Chapter by same author in G. Hurd ed. | *Human Societies* | RKP |

Chapter 13

R. Wallis	*The Sociology of the New Religions*	SSR Vol.1 No.1, 1985
B. Wilson	*Secularisation and its Discontents*	The *Times*, 10.11.73 and 13.10.73
C. Glock and R. Stark	*Religion and Society in Tension*	Rand McNally, 1965
in K. Thompson and J. Tunstall	*Sociological Perspectives*	Penguin, 1971

Chapter 14

Research round-up	GUMG	SSR Vol.2 No.1, 1986
Research round-up	CCCS	SSR Vol.2 No.4, 1987
GUMG	*War and Peace News*	Open University Press, 1985
in P. Trowler	*Active Sociology*	Bell and Hyman, 1987
S. Cohen and J. Young	*The Manufacture of News*	Constable, 1981
G. Palmer and C. Littler	*The Invisible Heroes*	New Society, 14.5.79

Chapter 15

H. Graham	*Women Health and Illness*	SSR Vol.3 No.1, 1987
I. Waddington	*Inequalities in Health*	SSR Vol.4 No.3, 1989
R. Gomm; Howlett and Ashley in R. Meighan, I. Shelton and T. Marks eds.	*Perspectives on Society*	Nelson, 1979
R. Gomm	*Teaching the Sociology of Health and Underdevelopment*	The Social Science Teacher SST Vol.14 No.3, 1985
R. Gomm	*Unemployment and Health*	SST Vol.12 No.1, 1982
W. Fahey	*The Social Aspects of Mental Illness*	SST Vol.15 No.1, 1985

Chapter 16

J. Muncie	*Much Ado About Nothing? The Sociology of Moral Panics*	SSR Vol.3 No.2, 1987
H. S. Becker	*Key Thinkers*	SSR Vol.3 No.2, 1987
J. Williams	*England's Barmy Army*	SSR Vol.4 No.1, 1988
J. Williams	*Football Hooliganism*	SST Vol.15 No.3, 1986
H. Becker in M.O'Donnell	*Outsiders* *New Introductory Reader in Sociology*	Collier Macmillan 1966 Nelson, 1985
P. Trowler	*Active Sociology*	Bell and Hyman, 1987
P. Aggleton	*Deviance*	Tavistock, 1987

Chapter 17

P. Jones	*Theory and Methods in Sociology*	Unwin Hyman, 1985
J. M. Atkinson in C. Bell and H. Newby eds.	*Doing Sociological Research*	Allen and Unwin, 1977
J. M. Atkinson in S. Cohen ed.	*Societal Reactions to Suicide* *Images of Deviance*	Penguin, 1971
S. Taylor	*Suicide*	Longman, 1988
M. Slattery	*Official Statistics*	Tavistock, 1986

Chapter 18

P. Jones	*Theory and Methods in Sociology*	Unwin Hyman, 1985
R. Meighan, I. Shelton and T. Marks eds.	*Perspectives on Society*	Nelson, 1979
K. Pryce in M. O'Donnell in P. Trowler	*Endless Pressure* *New Introductory Reader in Sociology* *Active Sociology*	Nelson, 1985 Bell and Hyman, 1987
M. Morrison	*Methods in Sociology*	Longman, 1986
P. McNeill	*Research Methods*	Tavistock, 1985
M. Shipman	*The Limitations of Social Research*	Longman, 1981

Chapter 19

P. Jones	*Theory and Methods in Sociology*	
C. Brown	*Understanding Society*	John Murray, 1979
D. Berry	*Central Ideas in Sociology*	Constable, 1979
I. Craig	*Structure and Action in Modern Social Theory*	SSR Vol.4 No.5, 1989

Chapter 20

R. Gomm	*Neutrality and Commitment in Sociology*	
F. Reeves	*Sociology: A World of Scarecrows and Supermen*	
Both Gomm and Reeves in R. Meighan, I. Shelton and T. Marks eds.	*Perspectives on Society*	Nelson, 1979
M. Coulson and C. Riddell	*Approaching Sociology*	Routledge, 1980
P. Trowler (material on science in Chapter on *Knowledge*	*Further Topics in Sociology*	UTP, 1985
D. Glover and S. Strawbridge	*The Sociology of Knowledge*	Causeway, 1985
D. Berry	*Central Ideas in Sociology*	Constable, 1979
H. Burrage	*The Sociology of Science and the Science of Society*	SSR Vol.4 No.2, 1988